THE NATIONALISATION OF MULTINATIONALS IN PERIPHERAL ECONOMIES

THE NATIONALISATION OF MULTINATIONALS IN PERIPHERAL ECONOMIES

Edited by

Julio Faundez and
Sol Picciotto

First published 1978 by
THE MACMILLAN PRESS LTD
London and Basingstoke
Associated companies in Delhi
Dublin Hong Kong Johannesburg Lagos
Melbourne New York Singapore Tokyo

Printed in Hong Kong

British Library Cataloguing in Publication Data

The nationalisation of multinationals in
   peripheral economies
   1. Underdeveloped areas – International business
   enterprises   2. Underdeveloped areas – Government
   ownership
   I. Title   II. Faundez, Julio   III. Picciotto, Sol
   338.8'8'091724   HD2755.5

   ISBN 0-333-23341-7

Contents

Notes on Contributors
and their Papers

Reginald H. Green was Economic Adviser to the Ministry of Finance of the Government of Tanzania, and as such took a major part in the implementation of that Government's nationalisation programme, including negotiations with the companies and the initial reorganisation of the public sector. He is also the co-author of a well-known paperback, *Africa—Unity or Poverty*, and of numerous articles and monographs. He is at present Fellow of the Institute of Development Studies, University of Sussex.

His contribution is a systematic treatment of the main issues that arise in implementing a nationalisation decision, in particular the negotiation of compensation. The issues are treated in a realistic way, and in very great depth, with a wealth of practical example and illustration, in a manner never before attempted in any published work. His contribution is directly relevant to the general political and academic discussion of the principles involved in nationalisation, and can prove useful to civil servants or consultants called upon to advise in such situations.

Victor Rabinowitz is a partner in the US law firm of Rabinowitz, Boudin & Standard, and acted as lawyer for the Governments of Cuba and Chile in litigation following their nationalisations.

He provides a detailed account of a sequence of very important cases written from a ringside seat, which is at the same time an analysis of the attempts to develop a legal response (in the Congress and the academic legal establishment as well as the courts) to these nationalisations by Cuba's most powerful and nearest neighbour.

Carlos Fortin was in charge of the marketing of Chilean copper in London during the Allende administration. He was formerly Professor of Political Science at FLACSO (Latin American Faculty of Social Studies), and is at present Fellow at the Institute of Development Studies, University of Sussex.

His chapter begins by complementing the previous one, in discussing the litigation in European courts by which the copper companies attempted to hinder the marketing of nationalised Chilean copper, and evaluating the effects of the legal processes and the companies' embargo. The legal procedures are then considered within the overall context of diplomatic and international economic pressures on Chile, by the

companies and by the US government. The paper attempts to evaluate
the importance of the copper nationalisation in the events that led to the
overthrow of the Allende government, and discusses the terms of the
settlement agreed by the military junta.

Julio Faundez B., formerly Senior Research Fellow, University of Chile,
completed his doctorate on international law at Harvard in 1972, and is
at present Lecturer in Law, University of Warwick.

The deduction for 'excess profits' inserted into the Chilean copper
nationalisation law had a widespread impact. Mr Faundez provides a
detailed analysis of this provision and of its origins in the political
conjuncture in Chile at the time and within the parliamentary process.
His controversial account shows how the Allende government's commitment to parliamentarism led to the unexpected consequence of the
opposition parties' forcing upon the executive branch more responsibility for the compensation issue than it might have wished, thus
undermining the very legitimacy which the government sought. This
study provides an essential complement to the paper by Green, by
illuminating the often complex political context within which apparently technical economic decisions are taken.

Petter Nore is a Norwegian journalist and editor, a graduate of the
London School of Economics, at present teaching at Thames Poly-
technic and completing a Ph.D. on Norwegian petroleum policy. He is
the co-editor of *Economics: An Anti-Text*.

While focusing on Norwegian petroleum policy, his chapter considers the various forms taken in the relationships between oil-producing
states and the oil companies, contrasting Norway on the one hand with
the OPEC states and on the other with Britain. He explores the reasons
for the changes in these relations in the seventies, and the extent and
limits of state control over the oil industry, in the context of its role in
national economic development.

Sol Picciotto, a graduate of Oxford and Chicago, and formerly lecturer at
the then University of East Africa in Dar es Salaam, is at present
Lecturer in Law, University of Warwick. He has recently co-edited *The
State and Capital: A Marxist Debate*.

His paper provides a historical and theoretical perspective on the
changing relations between states and private business firms. This shows
that the idealised view of competitive business operating in a laissez-
faire environment is an impossible and historically unexampled ideal. It
traces the changing nature of private business firms, from the chartered
trading companies, through the family industrial company to the
multinational corporation, and the related changes in the forms of state
and of state intervention in the economy. At the same time these changes
involve also the international state system, most crucially the changing
nature of international inequality and the problem of underdevelopment of the periphery. It is in the context of the failure of private

business to contribute to the development of the periphery, or indeed its contribution to underdevelopment, that the nationalisation of foreign-owned firms must be viewed. Yet what is important is not so much the nominal ownership by the state of business companies, but rather the domestic and international political context and the use made of the assertion of political control to transform economic relations.

1 Introduction

JULIO FAUNDEZ and SOL PICCIOTTO

The multinational enterprise is emerging as the dominant form of productive unit in the contemporary world capitalist system. Orthodox economic indicators provide some familiar evidence about the importance of this new form of private enterprise.[1] But this evidence, though impressive, does not by itself reveal the qualitative change involved in the emergence of multinational enterprise. This new form of organisation, based upon a flexible internal structure and on the capacity to mobilise vast resources towards the development of new technology, can effectively integrate and orchestrate world-wide operations, thus acquiring a monopolistic control over key sectors of production. Multinational enterprise marks a new stage in the process of concentration and centralisation of capital on a world scale.

Although the stage of absolute predominance of the multinational enterprise has not yet been reached, there is a growing awareness that the world economy is undergoing a major restructuring in order to accommodate the political and cultural instances to the development of the forces of production. This awareness has been expressed in the publication of innumerable studies on multinationals and in the establishment of several 'think-tanks' and 'policy-science' institutions, which are diagnosing and recommending policy alternatives for the pattern of development towards the year 2000. There are also a plethora of activities at a more immediate level. For instance, the OECD has issued a detailed Code of Conduct for multinationals, the EEC is busy trying to formulate a comprehensive European Company Statute, and the United Nations has recently set up a Centre on Transnational Corporations.[2]

In different ways most of the efforts to understand the role of multinationals in the world today tend to concentrate almost exclusively on the conflict of interests existing between the nation-state and the multinational. That it is possible and desirable to harmonise these interests flows almost logically from this perspective. But from the standpoint of an interpretation which seeks an explanation about the historical development of contemporary capitalism, an excessive concentration on isolated nation-state/multinational conflicts is not very fruitful. This narrow focus often distorts the analysis to such an extent that the problem tends to be defined in terms of an adversary situation with either winners or losers or in terms of a happy resolution to the conflict. The currently popular phrase 'north-south confrontation' with its corresponding ideal-types of 'Northerners' and 'Southerners'—apart from mystifying the issue—constitutes an extreme manifestation of this same problem.[3]

Very few people would be prepared to suggest seriously that a single nation-state is capable of disrupting the structure of a large multinational enterprise. On this point one would expect almost no controversy. But consider the proposal which suggests that nation-states should join forces and set up multi-state ventures in order to compete with and to act as a countervailing power against multinationals.[4] Here there is plenty of room for argument and for informed academic opinion. Yet the second proposal, to the extent that it posits the existence of a conflict between political and economic power and to the extent that it assumes that the juxtaposition of political interests (i.e. those of the aggregate of nation-states) can yield an economic force qualitatively different from that of private enterprise, bears an interesting relation to the initial suggestion which we had dismissed.

A serious consideration of this controversial proposal would require a detailed examination of some fundamental questions concerning the historical relation between economic and political power and the nature of the evolving forms of social control to be found in the world today. Such an inquiry would require the seemingly conflicting nation-state/ multinational interests to be subjected to an historical and critical appraisal. In the absence of such an inquiry, this proposal would involve no more than the reproduction, on a global scale, of some familiar institutional forms of particular nation-states.

The purpose of Sol Picciotto's article in this book (Chapter 7) is to consider the nature of the relationship between the state and the individual economic unit, the firm, in an historical and theoretical perspective. He rejects the superficial analysis that characterises capitalism as an aggregation of firms related through the market, from which the state is deduced to be the necessary extra-economic instance. Instead, he begins from the basic class relation of capital to labour, which is characterised by the separation of the worker from the means of production and on which is based the classic Marxist analysis of surplus-value. It is from this starting-point that the separation of the economic from the political and the autonomisation of the state as an apparently neutral power standing above society can be traced. From this theoretical standpoint the notion of the state as non-capitalist, standing over and against the individual firms, is exposed as a myth. Rather, the autonomised state and its 'interventions' in the economy are seen as an essential moment in the reproduction of the social relations of capital. Picciotto also goes on to stress the need to trace the historical emergence and development not only of 'the state', but of the international state system in relation to the growing dominance and continual development of capitalism.

An adequate explanation of the development of capitalism and its relation to the international state system requires the adoption of a global perspective. The national and international expansion of capital involves the simultaneous occurrence of the process of accumulation of industrial capital and the process of primitive accumulation of capital in the periphery. This double process—itself an expression of the law of uneven and combined development—reveals the essential unity of the development of capitalism on a world scale. While the relationship between these two processes of accumulation has, at different stages, undergone changes its function as a mechanism of exploitation of the periphery by the centre has remained the same. Whether the mechanism of exploitation has been based on the appropriation of surplus profits or on the exchange of unequal quantities of labour its effect has been to act as a brake on the process of industrialisation in the periphery. From this perspective, the predominant position of multinational enterprises provides further evidence of the limits of peripheral capitalism and of the global vocation of capital as a whole.

The nationalisation of parts of the operations of multinational enterprises in peripheral economies has been generally circumscribed to the primary products sector. Several factors account for the continuous importance of this sector. From the point of view of the trade structure of peripheral economies well over 80 per cent of their export is composed of primary products.[5] There is also evidence to suggest that demand for primary products by developed countries will continue to expand. In this context, the decision to nationalise companies operating in this sector can be a component of a national economic policy seeking either to establish the basis for an 'independent' development process, or to initiate a transition to socialism. These factors, combined with the nature of the technology involved in the primary products industry, account for the frequent occurrence of nationalisations in this sector of the peripheral economies.[6]

Although the global perspective of the development of the world capitalist system remains essential to an adequate understanding of multinationals, at an immediate level, nation-states appear entangled in an endless spiral of bilateral conflicts. The existence of these conflicts would appear to vindicate the view that the nation-state/multinational perspective constitutes the best framework for the study of multinationals.

Although the articles in this book generally take the nation-state/multinational relationship as a starting-point for their analyses, they avoid the theoretical limitations which might result. The articles therefore deal with situations broadly described as nationalisations.[7] They deal specifically either with the nationalisation of one industry in a specific country, or with a comprehensive programme of nationalisations undertaken by a

single nation-state. None of the articles attempts to develop a comprehensive theory of nationalisations. Instead, they concentrate on a
particular aspect of the conflict, providing an in-depth study of its relation
to the more general features of the system of relations involving the nation-
states and the multinationals. They also focus on technical issues related to
the process of nationalisation and call attention to their political
implications. Thus, the articles push the nation-state/multinational
perspective to its limits and raise questions concerning the validity of the
widely accepted technical-political dichotomy.

The nationalisation of affiliates of multinationals constitutes one form
among several which the nation-state/multinational relationship may
assume. The range of options open to nation-states—generally classified
under the rubric 'attitudes to foreign investment'—include a combination
of fiscal mechanisms in the form of taxation and subsidies designed to
regulate the income of the state in the operations of the foreign investor and
to channel investment to a specific sector of the economy or to a particular
geographical region in the country. The regulation of royalty payments
and some attempts to change the structure of ownership (joint ventures,
management contracts, etc.) are often used in the manufacturing sector.

Multinationals can generally respond quite effectively and flexibly to
these state policies, partly due to the fact that they are never the captives of
any single national market and partly due to the nature of their
organisational structure. Thus, in order to respond to unwanted state
policies, multinationals may resort to financial strategies such as transfer
pricing and dividend remittance; marketing strategies, such as control of
channels of distribution abroad; or production strategies based on the type
of technology they employ. Often multinationals also resort to 'direct
action'—in the form of bribes and other corrupt practices—thus adding
efficiency to their innate flexibility.

Nationalisation as an instrument of state policy constitutes the one
option which goes beyond the realm of what is regarded as acceptable
international behaviour. Indeed, most politicians, journalists, and academics working at the centre of the capitalist world are generally quick to
react and condemn nationalisation attempts by governments in the
periphery. These condemnations are often combined with appeals to the
nationalising government's self-interest and to the demands of global
interdependence. This helpful advice is sometimes complemented with less
friendly descriptions of the particular nationalisation policy as an action of
a government suffering from the infantile disorder of nationalism, and
manipulated either by clever Marxists 'who always know what they want'
or by local monopolists 'who obviously want to perpetuate their privi-
leges'. Thus, the defence of multinationals against the threat of nationalisations is surreptitiously transformed into the defence of political freedom
and economic efficiency. While there may be an element of truth in such
arguments they are so distorted as to amount to mere propaganda.

But beyond the ideological debate and against the background of a broader interpretation of the place of peripheral economies in the world economy, each instance of nationalisation—defined in terms of a nation-state/multinational conflict—calls for immediate political action. Contrary to the assertions made by the academic defenders of multinationals, the event of a nationalisation does not represent an abrupt collapse of a particular investment relationship. Indeed, the formal act of nationalisation sets in motion a complex set of processes involving political negotiations, legal proceedings, accounting riddles, and managerial problems. These processes surrounding the formal act of nationalisation are generally regarded as having two components: a political component—handled by the Party or the individual political leader; and a technical component—handled by the professionals, i.e.: accountants, lawyers, economists, and civil servants. This two-fold division, generally accepted as a datum, has implications which run deep into the very nature of the dominant tendencies in social theory. Surely the professionals involved in the process are occasionally aware of the political significance of their technical tasks, but the intricacies of the technical factor ultimately frustrates any possibility of integrating systematically these political insights with the immediate technical problem. The analysts who later undertake a general economic and political evaluation of the process of nationalisation are inclined to dismiss or to underestimate the political relevance of the technical problems. Thus the arbitrary division between the political and the technical spheres is reaffirmed.

These observations raise a fundamental question which is neither novel nor easy to answer. Can a systematic study of the political relevance of the technical problems surrounding nationalisation processes yield a better understanding of the process as a whole? Our contributors deal with this question, although they do so from different angles and perspectives. R. H. Green (Chapter 2) treats the question of the relationship of the technical to the political in connection with the actual process of negotiations which opens up after the decision to nationalise has been taken, while J. Faundez (Chapter 3) focuses on the domestic political debate which precedes the formal act of nationalisation.

Green examines the negotiation of settlements with the ex-owners of nationalised firms; however, he does not see it as the culmination, but rather as the starting-point of a process. He emphasises the fact that the valuation of assets and negotiation of compensation must not be taken to be the aim of nationalisation—it is, rather, one step towards the basic goal of restructuring the economy under state control. Green's stance is that of the negotiator on the side of the nationalising state, concerned to limit the compensation to the minimum while remaining consistent with the views of 'fairness' held by the persons and groups involved in domestic and international political processes. The strength of his article lies in not simply providing guidelines about compensation at a general level, but in carrying his analysis through a detailed account of the criteria and processes for valuation of assets.

His starting-point for valuation is discounted net cash flow, which is the basic economic criterion underlying the ideological formulation normally used—'prompt, adequate, and effective'. He then examines the arguments which, from the nationalising state's viewpoint, may justify variations up or down. These variations hinge largely on the relationship between past and projected future earnings, which is in effect the essential question from which the assessment of value on purely economic criteria abstracts. The assumption that the state must pay the value of the income stream that the capital might generate in the future completely disregards the fact that what is taking place is a restructuring of capital by means of state intervention and not simply an ordinary purchase.

Throughout his paper Green analyses the professional techniques firmly within the political and diplomatic context. Above all, he is concerned to ensure that the acquisition is effective and that there should be an acceptable transition to state operation. Thus, to take an example, note how he treats the question of the method of payment. He states that the payment must be made, naturally, in the country where the foreign investor is and in its currency. But this is subject to two important provisos: the payment is denominated in the currency of the paying state; and is treated as an ordinary contract, so that instalments are subject to foreign-exchange controls. In this way the actual compensation negotiations are not hindered unnecessarily by conflicts of principle.

Green argues from a position which at first glance seems simply that of a hard-headed pragmatic technocrat faced with a negotiating situation. This attitude appears to be justified by his view that the individual negotiation or acquisition is not the proper context to explore the possibilities for accelerating the desirable changes taking place in the general principles governing nationalisation of foreign-owned property. As he correctly emphasises, it is much easier to push individual negotiations through to a definite conclusion, if they are conducted in technical terms and not in terms of more general political and economic issues. However, as he also indicates, it is the accretion of these specific and individual cases that builds up to the establishment of general principle. Furthermore, even if the arguments in a specific negotiation are not articulated in terms of general principle, the implications of specific proposals are likely to be weighed by the parties in relation also to other cases and general principle. This is particularly true for the large multinational firm which is likely to be more concerned with the overall implications of a particular negotiation—for its corporate image and its global-investment position—than with the specific terms, which certainly in the case of Tanzania would amount to relatively little in financial terms. This is even more so for capital-exporting states or international agencies which are essentially interested in the general diplomatic, legal, and economic issues, since experience has shown that they are willing to sacrifice the interests of individual investors in order to achieve an amicable settlement which may in their view secure the long-term trade and investment climate. Why, then, does Green insist that nationalising governments should, while refusing to compromise principle, negotiate on the valuation by applying solely technical criteria?

Essentially, Green's emphasis is on the need to accept the material circumstances of the situation. For the foreign investor this may mean that there is no political alternative but to accept the acquisition of its local assets by the nationalising state, while the latter must realistically evaluate its needs and possibilities for the uninterrupted operation of those assets. Green repeatedly returns to the essential parameters which determine the freedom of movement available to the nationalising state: the ability to withstand (politically and economically) an interruption in production; the extent of reliance on the ex-owner or related foreign sources for the material inputs or know-how or for access to markets; the availability of adequate replacement for these assets, at home or abroad. It is in relation to these crucial factors that the general issue of value and fairness does indeed appear largely irrelevant.

The implication of this is that a large part of the international legal framework which purports to regulate the nationalisation situation is of marginal relevance only. This can be seen most clearly in relation to the issue of compensation, as Green's approach shows. The property rights protected by the claims of fair and effective compensation are essentially ownership rights over fixed assets. Green shows that the real issue is control over an income stream. This is not merely a matter of difference in conceptualisation. The point is that the local fixed assets of a firm that is a subsidiary of a multinational, or even of one that is closely tied to multinational capital through contractual arrangements (joint ventures), do not embody the essence of that capital's profit-producing operation. Acquisition of those fixed assets is as likely to give control over the whole organism as chopping off the tip of one tentacle from an octopus.

Faundez's paper concentrates on the domestic political process leading to the nationalisation of copper in Chile. His paper focuses specifically on the excess profits clause, a controversial mechanism introduced by Chile, which had a decisive impact on the computation of the compensation due to the nationalised companies. This feature of Chile's copper national-isation led to serious international complications for the government, which are explored in detail in C. Fortin's paper (Chapter 5).

Faundez argues that the government had initially put forward a very cautious proposal for nationalisation which envisaged that compensation would have been paid to the U.S. companies. This cautious policy was, according to Faundez, consistent with Allende's non-contentious foreign policy. He then goes on to argue that the changes introduced by Congress, which at first appeared to be very favourable to the government—as they involved a substantial delegation of power—brought about a disruption of Allende's copper and foreign policies. Faundez does not argue that Chile's failure to pay compensation may explain the downfall of Allende. He does, however, raise some general problems which concern the link between political goals and their actual implementation. According to his interpretation Allende originally had intended to draw into the nationalisation process several other branches of the State apparatus, such as Congress, the Judiciary, and the state bureaucracy, in order to neutralise the expected allegations that a minority government led by Marxists had confiscated property belonging to U.S. corporations. Faundez also argues that the government tried to present the excess profits deduction as a purely technical decision by entrusting its implementation to a high-level bureaucrat. But the Chilean Congress did not accept sharing political responsibility with the leftist government of Allende and transferred the power to deduct excess profits to the President, thus reasserting the essentially political character of the deduction.

This controversial interpretation raises several questions which concern the viability of Allende's peaceful road to socialism. But this paper also revolves around the political/technical dichotomy. To what extent were Allende's efforts to neutralise international public opinion politically sound? Does it matter whether or not the procedures established to determine compensation are carefully worked out? If Allende had chosen to pay some compensation, would this have amounted to an unacceptable compromise of his revolutionary goals? To what extent can Allende's decision be interpreted as an error of judgement brought about by a misplaced notion of the 'imperialist enemy'? And finally, to what extent could this supposed error of judgement about the identity of the 'enemy' be attributed to the immediate perception of the problem in terms of the narrow nation-state/multinational perspective?

The preceding comments would seem to suggest that in the process surrounding nationalisations International Law plays a very limited role. If, as Green suggests, questions about adequacy of compensation are at best marginal; and if, according to Faundez, the decision to pay compensation may be governed by purely tactical considerations, what then is the function of International Law?

The general outline of the legal controversy over nationalisations has not changed since the time of the Mexican nationalisations of oil and land in the late thirties. On that occasion the United States and the United Kingdom, representing the interests of former owners, maintained that the sovereign right to expropriate was conditioned by the obligation to pay prompt, adequate, and effective compensation and by the observance of the principle of equality of treatment. Mexico replied that it recognised no rule of International Law which made payment of compensation obligatory, although it did acknowledge the principle of compensation as provided in its own domestic legislation. But Mexico also put forward an argument which until today describes the nature of the contradiction between foreign capital and the states in the periphery. In a note to the United States Government the Mexican Ambassador stated[8]:

> The future of the nation could not be halted by the impossibility of paying immediately the value of property belonging to a small number of foreigners who seek only a lucrative end.

The legal-ideological definition of the conflict of interests involved in the process of nationalisation has not changed. The United Nations has adopted several resolutions which do not provide clear guidelines to resolve nationalisation disputes but underline the nature of the conflict.[9] The ambiguity of these resolutions reveals that the problem is related to the contradictory task of establishing a stable framework to reconcile the global economic strategies of multinationals with national economic policies of particular peripheral states. From the perspective of each peripheral state the issue is defined in terms of its capacity to control economic decisions within its territory.

The unstable compromise on the allocation of spheres of economic activities between multinationals and the variety of states in the periphery is reproduced in the complex network of legal forms governing nationalisations. These forms, fully developed by the United States government, and more recently adopted by the governments of other capital-exporting countries, are generally grouped under the rubric 'protection of foreign investment'. Some of these legal forms are: bilateral treaties of friendship and commerce which obligate each contracting state not to expropriate property belonging to citizens and companies of the other contracting state without payment of full compensation[10]; government insurance against the risk of expropriation, administered in the United States by the Overseas Private Investment Corporation (OPIC)[11]; and political pressure exerted through international financial institutions which assess the credit-worthiness of a particular country in terms of its ability and willingness to pay compensation for nationalised property.[12] These mechanisms are complemented by domestic law provisions, most notably, the Hickenlooper Amendment which provides that the President shall suspend assistance to countries that nationalise without paying equitable compensation.

Some lawyers regard this network of legal forms as an unequivocal expression of the rules of International Law governing nationalisations.[13] Regardless of whether one agrees with this appraisal, there is ample evidence that these mechanisms are promptly activated by capital-exporting countries in order to deter, disrupt, or regulate nationalisations in the periphery. In this respect these legal mechanisms constitute an essential component of the structure of political power at the international level.

Yet the response of legal institutions to economic changes is generally slow, often indirect, and never fully satisfactory. This is particularly true in the regulation of international affairs. Victor Rabinowitz's paper (Chapter 4) provides a detailed analysis of the way in which traditional legal doctrine responds to the demands imposed by the restructuring of the world economy.

Rabinowitz has been counsel for several nationalising governments, including Cuba and Chile at the time of Allende. In this capacity he has represented these governments in the sequel of law suits which former owners of nationalised companies or private individuals have brought against the nationalising states in the Courts of the United States. The setting usually involves former owners of a nationalised company seeking to collect the proceeds of a sale connected with the nationalised assets, or seeking to attach property belonging to the nationalising state, which may be found in the jurisdiction of the United States. Although the legal proceedings in these cases are ostensibly designed as a means to obtain legal redress for the lack of compensation, they do in fact often act as effective instruments of political and economic pressure.

Rabinowitz tells us the inside story of one such set of litigations: those involving Cuba and a variety of companies, banks, and individuals affected by Cuba's nationalisation decrees. He concentrates on the act-of-state doctrine in American law and traces the attitudes of the United States Courts, the State Department, and Congress to this particular legal doctrine.

The act-of-state doctrine governs the relations between domestic courts and foreign governments. Under the act-of-state doctrine Courts refuse to inquire into the validity of certain acts of foreign states. For example a private company, nationalised in Cuba and seeking a legal remedy in New York, will argue that Cuba's nationalisation decrees are invalid in New York, either because they violate United States legislation or because they violate the public policy of the forum, and that Cuba therefore cannot validly transfer title of the nationalised assets or their produce to third parties. Applying the act-of-states doctrine the Courts will refuse to examine the validity of the Cuban decrees and will dismiss the ex-owner's action.

The situation is complicated if the plaintiff argues that because the nationalisation decrees violate International Law, the act-of-state doctrine cannot be applied. In this situation the Court would be called upon to decide whether the foreign government violated International Law. In the famous Sabbatino case, discussed by Rabinowitz, the lower Courts found that Cuba had violated International Law because the nationalisation decrees did not provide for adequate compensation, and because they were discriminatory and unrelated to a public purpose. In other words the legality of Cuba's nationalisation was subjected to judicial review by a national state Court. The case reached the Supreme Court which, reversing the decisions of the lower courts, held that the act-of-state doctrine precluded the judiciary from examining the domestic or international legality of Cuba's legislation.

The Court's decision came as a surprise. Congress reacted by enacting a law, the Sabbatino Amendment, also known as the Second Hickenlooper Amendment, designed to change retroactively the law as announced by the Sabbatino decision. Rabinowitz discusses the role of the anti-Sabbatino lobby in Washington and explains the position adopted by the State Department. His paper contains a wealth of information on the way the doctrine of separation of powers operates in the field of foreign affairs.

It is interesting to note that the Sabbatino Amendment involved a retroactive change of the Supreme Court's decision. When retroactive decisions are taken by governments in the periphery, e.g. Allende's excess profits decision, academic lawyers and journalists do not hesitate to describe such actions as constituting violations of the fundamental legal principles shared by most civilised nations. But when such retroactive decisions occur at the centre of the capitalist world the civilising function of legal doctrine is seldom mentioned.

The academic writings on the Sabbatino episode have concentrated mainly on the technical legal aspects of the problem; e.g. to what extent did Congress really overrule the Sabbatino decision.[14] Rabinowitz takes the reader one step further. His paper provides not only a very useful description of the legal developments after Sabbatino, but also poses the more fundamental political question which underlies this particular case. In a very important sense, as Rabinowitz explains, the act-of-state doctrine constitutes a healthy traditional legal solution to the regulation of relations among states. The act-of-state doctrine in fact acknowledges the division of the world into a large number of territorial units known as nation-states. This doctrine recognises therefore that there is a sphere of domestic affairs where local rulers can act freely and independently of outside pressure or interference. To the sceptic this formal acknowledgement of each state's sovereignty will appear as mere legal ideology. This may be so, yet the doctrine does provide for a uniform and predictable legal solution to ordinary controversies. Diplomatic and military procedures will always be activated when a solution of a more fundamental character is required.

But in the contemporary world economy, with nation-states actively involved in economic affairs and companies pursuing global strategies, the traditional act-of-state doctrine no longer performs a useful function. The 'Tobacco' cases discussed by Rabinowitz illustrate this point. Yet if the act-of-state doctrine was abandoned, what would replace it?

If the act-of-state doctrine were completely abandoned, municipal courts in the United States would be called upon to decide on the legal validity of innumerable decisions taken by foreign governments or their instrumentalities. For example, a Court may be called upon to decide whether a particular decision on exchange controls taken by the Central

Bank of a given country violates International Law. In order to decide such cases the Courts would have to resort to their own normative standards which they would euphemistically describe as the minimum international legal standard of civilised nations. These judicial decisions would in fact tend to make the world more homogeneous from the legal point of view, albeit a homogeneity in terms dictated by the courts of the dominant states. Thus, underlying these technicalities, there is this fundamental political question which the Courts of the United States are hesitant to resolve.

Chile confronted problems similar to those presented by Cuba in the Courts of the United States. In the case of Chile, however, the legal confrontation spread to the Courts in Europe. Carlos Fortin, who at the time was in charge of Chile's copper agency in London, describes and analyses the nature of the legal problems involved in this series of law suits. In some European countries Courts were called upon to decide whether Chile's nationalisation of property owned by American companies violated the public policy of the forum. The notion that a lower Court judge of a country not directly involved in the dispute should be called upon to decide whether the legislature of a country several thousand miles away has violated the public policy of his jurisdiction is bound to sound absurd to readers not familiar with the subtleties of legal reasoning. Fortin's paper offers a very useful explanation and analysis of these specific incidents which constituted an important part of the world-wide strategy employed by the nationalised companies against the government of Allende.

But Fortin's paper brings us back once again to the question concerning the nation-state/multinational perspective. Fortin isolates two aspects of the conflict: the conflict between Chile and the multinational companies on the one hand; and the conflict between Chile and the U.S. government on the other. Essentially Fortin argues that the companies failed in their efforts to disrupt the production and marketing of Chilean copper, and equally the United States' government blockade against Chile did not represent an insurmountable problem for the Allende government. In his view, however, the activities of the CIA combined with Chile's internal political conflict account for the downfall of Allende.

Certainly Fortin's analytical distinction between the two types of conflicts corresponds to the actual policy of the Chilean government at the time. The Allende government did indeed try unsuccessfully to argue that the conflict with the multinational copper companies based in the United States should not be allowed to interfere with the friendly relations between the Chilean and United States governments. The efforts to introduce this distinction are obviously part of the diplomatic game. Yet it may be doubted whether either the individual parts of the conflict (compensation, copper-marketing, CIA intervention) can be meaningfully isolated from the overall problem which the presence of Allende represented to the hegemony of the United States in Latin America and to the global interests of the multinational companies in that part of the world.

In Chapter 6 Petter Nore provides a study of oil nationalisation which counterpoints the specific experiences of Norway with the momentous changes in the world oil industry. The initial concentration on Norway in his article reminds us once again that it is impossible to draw general conclusions from the analysis of pure economic trends, but it is necessary to situate them historically and trace their development in a particular country. Norway provides a perhaps surprisingly appropriate focus for the study of the oil industry, since it gives a contrasting perspective that sets into relief the OPEC countries, which due to their domination of oil production tend to be treated as an undifferentiated monolithic bloc. The consideration of North Sea oil also highlights the particular characteristics of oil as a global industry, dominated by vertically integrated giant companies controlling sources of supply with costs of production varying as widely as does the North Sea from the Middle East. It is these features, Nore argues, that give rise to a rent—a return in excess of average industrial profits. He traces in detail how the changes in Norwegian oil policies have affected the division of this rent between the state and the multinational oil companies. His general conclusion is that neither fiscal devices nor nationalisations based on the mere transfer of legal ownership to the state can fundamentally affect the state's role. The crucial factor is the formation of a state oil company, directly involved in production and marketing.

However, while this fact may be decisive with regard to the state's financial revenues, such a development still leaves open a further question about the nature of the state's intervention. Even though the oil majors' share of oil rent has been sharply reduced, the drastic change in the price structure since 1973 has left them in absolute terms much better off financially. This reinforcement of their commanding position, which had been undermined by the 'cheap oil' boom in the sixties, leaves the multinational oil companies well placed to dominate the transition to new energy sources. In this pattern we see the importance of state intervention as a catalyst for the global restructuring, not only of oil but of the entire world economy. This pattern also emphasises the importance of analysing state intervention on an international basis, involving the International Energy Agreement (IEA) as well as OPEC, and taking into account the importance of the links between the United States and Saudi Arabia and the role of the oil companies in this special relationship.

The possibility that this form of state intervention may be deflected by popular political movements is again well illustrated by the Norwegian case. Nore's analysis points to volume control and the ecology question as the key issues which will test whether the state oil corporation responds to the pressures for capital accumulation or for social responsibility. Although national factors are important here Nore again emphasises the relevance of the international conjuncture, notably Norway's position in NATO and the IEA and her relations with the United States.

The articles in this book explore the nation-state/multinational relationship in the context of one of the forms which it may assume:— nationalisations in peripheral economies. By focusing the analysis on this issue it is possible to identify and explain some of the mechanisms which govern the spread of multinationals in peripheral economies. The detailed case studies which provide the starting-point for each of the articles underline the inseparable connection existing between the technical and political aspects in the process of nationalisation in particular, and in the relation between multinationals and nation-states in general. The study of the link between the technical and the political spheres merits further consideration, particularly in view of the current efforts to enact Codes of Conduct for multinationals and to help peripheral States in their bargaining with multinationals. There is a real danger that in the process of drafting these international codes and developing bargaining devices the technical imperative may reassert itself, only because it is mistakenly regarded as performing a neutral function and thus diverting the attention away from divisive political issues. Experience has shown, however, that on purely technical grounds the political problems of economic under-development will remain unsolved.

Indeed, what emerges generally from these essays is the need to situate the immediate technical issues and political goals in the context of the integration of peripheral economies into the world economy. Nationalisations are political decisions having implications which spread beyond the framework of any single nation-state. Nationalisations also represent a form of state intervention which may lead either to a mere restructuring of the relations of production within the same capitalist framework, or which may represent a step towards the assertion of popular control over the immense productive forces controlled by multinationals. The ultimate direction which the process of nationalisation may take constitutes a vital issue which is essentially political. Thus, behind the apparently technical minutiae dealt with in this book—amendments moved in parliamentary committees, claims and counter-claims, writs of attachment, profit multiples, and discounted cash flow—lies this fundamental and decisive political issue.

NOTES

1 See generally: U.S. Department of Commerce, *The Multinational Corporation* (Washington: U.S. Government Printing Office, Vol. 1, 1972, Vol. II, 1973); U.N. Department of Economic and Social Affairs, *The Impact of Multinational Corporations on Development and International Relations*, Doc.E-5500/Rev-1, ST-

ESA-6 (New York: 1974); G.L. Reuber *et al*, *Private Foreign Investment in Development* (Oxford: Clarendon Press, 1973). A representative selection of the abundant literature on multinationals should include: John H. Dunning, *The Multinational Enterprise* (London: George Allen and Unwin, 1971); Hugo Radice (ed.), *International Firms and Modern Imperialism* (London: Penguin Books, 1975); Raymond Vernon, *Sovereignty at Bay* (London: Penguin Books, 1973).

2 For a recent survey of developments in this area see: Seymour J. Rubin, 'Harmonization of Rules: A Perspective on The U.N. Commission on Transnational Corporations,' 8 *Law and Policy in International Business*, 875 (1976).

3 See, e.g. John W. Sewell and the staff of the Overseas Development Council, *The United States and World Development Agenda 1977*, (London: Praeger Publishers, 1977). See in particular the way the authors of this book deal with the issue of human rights (at p. 74).

4 See e.g. *Reshaping the International Order A Report to the Club of Rome*, Jan Tinbergen (coordinator), (London: Hutchinson, 1977).

5 United Nations, *Monthly Bulletin of Statistics*, xxx, No. 8, (August 1976), Special Table C.

6 A recent analysis of data on expropriation compiled by the Harvard Business School's ongoing Multinational Enterprise Study and by the State Department shows that manufacturing companies are relatively immune to expropriations in the Thirld World. The data used in this same analysis shows that only thirty plants of United States manufacturing companies in the Third World have been expropriated in the period 1960–74. This figure represents only 1·2 per cent of the United States manufacturing companies in the Third World. By strange coincidence, as the author of this report notes, the governments of Sukarno in Indonesia and Allende in Chile were responsible for 80 per cent of these manufacturing seizures. See David G. Bradley, 'Managing Against Expropriation', *Harvard Business Review*, July-August 1977 at p. 75.

7 The term nationalisation is usually employed to describe situations where the state attempts to exercise full control over economic activities—generally in the primary products sector—controlled by foreign capital. In this book the term is used in a somewhat broader sense to include other forms of state interference, such as requisition and intervention of industries and re-negotiations of contracts which may lead to joint ventures or management contracts. Some international lawyers accept the distinction between nationalisation and the classical expropriation situation which involves the taking of a single item of property for a specific public purpose, such as building a public road. See, Ian Brownlie, *Principles of Public International Law*, 522 (Oxford: Oxford University Press, 1973). Other international lawyers reject this distinction on the grounds that there is no difference between these two forms of state action and that therefore 'the term "nationalisation" is not one of art'. D.P. O'Connell, *International Law for Students*, 307 (London: Stevens and Sons, 1971).

8 The quotation from the Mexican Ambassador's note is taken from Frank G. Dawson and Burns H. Weston, 'Prompt, Adequate and Effective, A Universal Standard of Compensation?' 30 *Fordham Law Review* 727 (1962). This article also provides a very useful discussion of the issue of compensation. More detailed studies on the Mexican nationalisations can be found in J. Kunz, 'The

Mexican Expropriations,' 17 *New York University Law Quarterly* 327 (1940). An adequate overview of the Mexican background can be found in Moises Gonzalez Navarro; 'Mexico the Lop-sided Revolution' in C. Veliz (ed.), *Obstacles to Change in Latin America*, 206 (Oxford: Oxford University Press, 1965). The political economy of compensation is discussed by Norman Girvan in 'The Question of Compensation: A Third World Perspective,' 5 *Vanderbilt Journal of Transnational Law*, 340 (1972).

9 Paragraph 4 of U.N. Resolution 1803 on Permanent Sovereignty over Natural Resources provides:

> Nationalization, expropriation or requisitioning shall be based on grounds or reasons of public utility, security or the national interest which are recognized as overriding purely individual or private interests, both domestic and foreign. In such cases the owner shall be paid appropriate compensation, in accordance with the rules in force in the State taking such measure in the exercise of its sovereignty and in accordance with international law . . .

17 U.N. GAOR Supp (no. 17) 42, U.N. Doc.A/5217 (1962). See also, Resolution 2158 (**XXI**) adopted on 25 November 1966 (*6 International Legal Materials*, 147 (1967)); Resolution 3171 (**XXVIII**) adopted on 17 December 1973 (13 *International Legal Materials*, 238 (1974)); Resolution 3201 (S-VI) On the Establishment of a New Economic Order, adopted on 1 May, 1974 (13 *International Legal Materials*, 715 (1974)); and Resolution 3281 (**XXIX**), Charter of Economic Rights and Duties of States, adopted on 12 December, 1974 (14 *International Legal Materials*, 251 (1975)).

10 See e.g. Treaty between the United States and Pakistan 1959, 12U.S.T. 111, T.I.A.S. 4683. See generally, *The Protection of Private Property Invested Abroad*, (American Bar Association 1963).

11 See, R. Lillich, *The Protection of Foreign Investment*, 147 (New York: Syracuse University Press, 1965); William P. Macht, 'Financing Developing Countries Enterprises Through the Overseas Private Investment Corporation (OPIC)', 3 *Law and Policy in International Business*, 469 (1971).

12 International Bank for Reconstruction and Development, *Policies and Operation: The World Bank, I.D.A. and I.F.C.*, 31 (Washington: June 1971); U.S. Library of Congress, Foreign Affairs Division, Committee on Foreign Affairs 93d Congress 2d Session, *The United States and the Multilateral Development Banks*, 50–1 and 120–2, 165 (1974).

13 See e.g. D.P.O'Connell, 2 *International Law*, 776 ff. (London: Stevens and Son, 1970); B.A. Wortley, *Expropriation in Public International Law*, (Cambridge: University Press, 1959) p. 115–35.

14 There are some exceptions, for example, see Stanley D. Metzger, 'The Act of State Doctrine and Foreign Relations,' 23 *University of Pittsburgh Law Review*, 881 (1962); Richard Falk, 'Toward a Theory of the Participation of Domestic Courts in the International Legal Order: A Critique of Banco Nacional de Cuba v. Sabbatino', 16 *Rutgers Law Review*, 1 (1961).

2 A Guide to Acquisition and Initial Operation: *Reflections from Tanzanian Experience 1967–74*

REGINALD H. GREEN

On a cloth untrue
With a twisted cue
And elliptical billiard balls

Gilbert and Sullivan

I have a little list. . . .
They never would be missed

Lord High Executioner in *Gilbert and Sullivan's Mikado*

The neo-colonial situation in which the working classes and their allies struggle simultaneously against the imperialist (foreign) bourgeoisie and the (local capitalist) class is not resolved by a nationalist solution; it demands the destruction of the capitalist structure implanted in the national territory by imperialism, and correctly postulates a socialist solution.

Amilcar Cabral

The question is not between change and no change; the choice for Africa is between changing or being changed.

Mwalimu Julius Nyerere

1. INTRODUCTION

Nationalisation has become a widely used policy instrument among third-world governments. Its use leads almost inevitably to a series of issues in respect of acquisition, compensation, and initial operation. While in one sense technical and, perhaps, general these are in another integrally related to broader political economic issues and to specific objective and goal contexts.

This study centres on these issues as they arose, were debated, were acted upon, and appear on reflection in relation to the United Republic of Tanzania between 1967–74[1]. The data are drawn largely from first-hand involvement in the process and from discussion with other participants.[2]

Tanzania's nationalisations began in February 1967 following the Arusha Declaration's restatement in more precise form of the commitment to a transition to socialism of the sole party—TANU.[3] Public ownership of directly productive assets well beyond the public utility range has a longer tradition in Tanzania, but a somewhat haphazard one during the late colonial period[4] and based on a standard Lewisian modification of the British gap filling and private sector supporting model in the early years of independence from December 1961 through to January 1967.[5]

The initial nationalisations were within a three sector model: public, public-private, private. However, that model never really operated as such. While the 1967 nationalisations were consistent with seeking a dominant public sector role and no more, by both specific accretions and policy shifts, the 1974 position was clearly toward a phasing out of all large-scale, majority private economic activity.

In February 1967 100 per cent nationalisation was applied to commercial banking, insurance,[6] large and medium-scale grain-milling (and as a consequence medium-scale tinning) and general large and medium-scale importing and wholesaling (and as a consequence some general exporting). Partial nationalisations included cement, beer, tins, pyrethrum extract, shoes, and cigarettes, with petroleum refining added *de facto* soon after.[7]

Later in 1967 the majority of the sisal industry (and consequentially a substantial minority of sisal-processing and of estate tea) was acquired partly to avert a collapse of the sector. Most of the acquisitions were initially of 60 per cent but were soon transformed to 100 per cent. In 1970 the second largest sugar estate was *de facto* nationalised (technically a negotiated purchase from the investors led by the IFC, CDC, NOFC) under somewhat similar circumstances.

Large and medium-sized rented buildings were nationalised in 1971. These were the first group of nationalised units dominantly citizen-owned (albeit significant minorities of sisal and grain-milling were in citizen, not foreign, ownership prior to nationalisation). In 1973 the largest metal products firm (Aluminium Africa) was nationalised and in 1973–4 a variety of estates including almost all foreign-owned acreage in northern Tanzania except for one sugar estate plus a number of citizen sisal and coffee estates.

Parallel to these major legislated or quasi-legislated nationalisations were four other strands. Firstly a number of 'negotiated' takeovers—the largest being 50 per cent of the Shell-BP and AGIP petroleum distribution companies, 100 per cent of the Dar bus company, 75 per cent odd of the two largest private textile firms which were merged and 50 per cent of the third largest—were concluded. In the Tanzanian context both the state and the firms saw these as *de facto* nationalisations which both sides felt would be better handled without an actual recourse to legislation. Secondly a number of 50-50 or public majority ventures were changed to 100 per cent (or public dominant majority) status. These included some pre-Arusha cases, e.g. Tanganyika Packers (a joint venture with Brooke Bond-Liebig), and the CDC stake in the precursor to the Tanzania Housing Bank, but also phasing out of some post-Arusha foreign partners and managers, e.g. Tanganyika Portland Cement, BAT Tanzania (renamed Tanzania Cigarette Company). Thirdly a number of economically minor statutory nationalisations were made, usually of abandoned firms or ones in which a total breakdown of worker-owner relations had developed. Several local government units restricted certain lines of business to local (district or regional) public sector enterprises, sometimes acquiring certain assets. The most widespread example was petrol stations and the largest single case Dar es Salaam butcher shops.

By the end of 1974 the totally private large-scale enterprises had declined to one sugar estate, two radio and phonograph factories (one also producing dry cells), a glass factory, two sweet factories, two or three soft drink bottlers, two tea plantations, a soap factory, four lorry sale and vehicle repair firms, two petroleum distribution firms and two to four specialised import and service firms. About 80–85 per cent of large and medium-scale economic activity was in the public sector (including Tanzania-Zambia joint ventures and the then East African corporations together with 100 per cent majority and 50-50 Tanzanian parastatal firms).[8]

The Tanzanian experience—apart from its interest in itself, in any broad study of nationalisation or in relation to analyses of Tanzania—is potentially of direct relevance to a significant number of peripheral polities. How much relevance it will have depends in part on how closely their situations correspond to Tanzania's in respect of purpose, political context, need to operate, and capacity constraints.

PURPOSE

Nationalisation was seen as a means and, in many cases, a necessary precondition for the exercise of positive national economic sovereignty. The role of the public directly productive sector was seen as a major and continuing one. While part of Tanzania's experience relates directly to its ruling party's commitment to achieve a transition to socialism, Tanzania's experience could be relevant in situations where such a commitment is not clearly established. For one reason, in 1967 (the first, post-Arusha Declaration nationalisations) the statements of TANU establishing commitment to a control of commanding heights were not self-evidently a commitment to full phasing out of large and medium-scale private economic activity in the foreseeable future, although it became so by the early 1970s.

POLITICAL CONTEXT

Nationalisation must be at least consistent with maintaining the dominant decision-taking group's political base. In the Tanzanian case it was critical to reinforcing it. Externally Tanzania was not perceived as either economically or geopolitically critical, either by any major power or any major transnational corporation. If it had been, the quantity, range, and quality of pressures brought to bear would probably have been significantly different.

NEED TO OPERATE

Continued operation (not necessarily without transitional problems but without long gaps in production) was of concern for most of the units nationalised. Tanzania's was therefore unlike the Libyan case in which reserves would have covered three year's non-oil-related imports, so that a year's halt of petroleum production would have been sustainable at bearable economic, social, and political costs. Serious capacity to relate broad sociopolitical and political economic goals to detailed policies in relation to the directly productive sector existed, and the enhancement of that capacity was a priority goal of government decision-takers.

CAPACITY CONSTRAINTS

A significant capacity to manage and to control a limited number of productive enterprises already existed in Tanzania in 1967. However, a need for significant inputs (material, knowledge and/or personnel) in relation to a number of nationalised units and for establishing new public sector enterprises was perceived as a constraint on compensation and initial operation decisions. Similarly, Tanzania's national political and economic base was strong enough to withstand some pressures, but not to make sustained confrontation with all or almost all major capitalist industrial states and the international institutions controlled by them appear practicable.

Variations in degree need not radically limit the relevance of Tanzania's experience, but major divergences will do so. For example, Cuba clearly could not have followed a Tanzanian approach to, and implementation of, nationalisation. One reading is that it sought to do so and was forced by U.S. intransigence to a more direct confrontation. A special situation arises in states which have won independence by armed struggle or a government which has both overthrown its predecessor and is in some broad sense revolutionary. Algeria and Mozambique faced different parameters, especially in respect of French and Portuguese property than did Tanzania; TANU after fifteen years of rule cannot afford (for internal and self-interest as well as external and foreign-reaction reasons) to take the same inherently sceptical view of past state contracts and commitments as can the Derg in Ethiopia. The Tanzanian experience is also not very relevant to the cases either of export-oriented minerals or component manufacturing. Both have quite special possibilities and limitations in respect of nationalisation.

2. IN THE PUBLIC INTEREST

The public interest[9] in practice means either what the dominant decision-taking group considers it to be or what some 'outside' observer considers it to be. In neither case is it likely to be a simple sum of component interests, much less a monolithic whole. One need not be an orthodox Marxist to see that class, national and group interests conflict (if they did not national-isation would be a somewhat whimsical policy) and that how to favour, balance, compromise, synthesise or reject them is a critical part of the decision-taker's role. In a national decision-taking group there is usually no unanimity as to those for whom the decision-takers are spokesmen or representatives. In 1967 TANU was largely agreed on nationalising some foreign firms; but there was much less agreement on the need for a clearly dominant public sector and on the limiting of public sector roles to non-capitalists which the nationalisations were a means to imple-menting.[10]

If there is no consistent and coherent policy—because the decision-taking group is very disparate and unstable—then in one sense no revealed public interest as perceived by decision-takers emerges and by definition no civil servant or manager can seek to implement it. Equally if the decision-takers literally reduce the public interest to their own direct pecuniary interest it requires only a very limited willingness to pass normative judgements to say that purported revealed public interest is a fraudulent cover for private privilege. Such situations are not unknown. Until President Leopold Sedar Senghor's elimination of the decision-takers associated with the then Mali President, Modeiba Keita, and with the then Premier, Mamadou Dia, Senegal may have exemplified the first situation, and by 1964–5 pre-coup Nigeria was very nearly a perfect example of the second. However, they are inherently rather unstable; the first for evident reasons, the second because the support base becomes too narrow. Neither pertained to Tanzania before, during, or after the relevant period.

An 'outside' observer's judgement of the public interest may be based on an illusion that a uniform, undifferentiated, maximum-utility function exists. Otherwise it is based on a selection of which interests he perceives as worthy of support, limitation, suppression, and to what degree; i.e. it is similar to a decision-taker's except that the observer is free from the need to be able to articulate how to act on it and—especially!—from the consequences of acting on it.[11]

The Tanzanian experience has been presented as relevant to a range of decision-taking coalitions but not to all, partly because of differences in revealed public interest definitions. Some parts of Tanzania's experience would be relevant to the Ivory Coast, but not most, because of different revealed public interest definitions of the dominant national decision-taking group. In the case of Algeria the basic revealed preferences are relatively more similar, but the nature of the liberation struggle and the special factors surrounding the petroleum industry limit cross relevance in many (not all) respects.

WHY NATIONALISE?

Why nationalise? Ultimately this is a question for the decision-takers and precedent to the issues of implementation discussed here. However, it affects civil servants (including negotiators) and managers—and for that matter analysts—in two ways:

(a) to the extent that they are involved in advising on the extent of nationalisation—e.g. by sector, by company, by share of ownership taken (100 per cent or less)—they cannot advise sensibly, even in the narrowest technical sense, without knowing the basic ends sought;
(b) in implementing a nationalisation—including details of acquisition as well as initial operation and compensation—understanding what is sought and what therefore is critical (or secondary) is equally essential to informed action on technocratic, bureaucratic, managerial, and negotiating fronts.

It is relatively easy to say that reasons for nationalisation fall into four basic categories:

(a) acquiring a larger share of resources flows (e.g. profits, foreign exchange);
(b) achieving a greater degree of control over ongoing decisions (e.g.

output and investment levels, pricing, citizenisation of posts, purchase of local inputs, expansion into export markets);

(c) maintaining or enhancing the decision-taking group's political base (e.g. mobilising peasant—or elite—support by taking over and allocating foreign plantations, acceptance of egalitarian wages/salaries structure by citizen managers through enhancing their promotion prospects);

(d) facilitating a basic shift in political economic ideology (e.g. transition to socialism, to state capitalism, to domestic capitalist ownership of a broader share of productive units.)

This categorisation is useful in identifying, grouping, and prioritising goals. It is a first step toward formulating means to implementation likely to further, not limit or thwart, them. However, as even the few examples given illustrate, the facets of these basic goals appearing in respect of any particular nationalisation are varied, and must be identified case by case or at least in terms of small similar groups of cases before actual implementation can proceed effectively let alone efficiently.

POLITICAL GOALS – TECHNICAL REQUIREMENTS

Identifying the dominant goals in respect of particular nationalisations may be especially critical to identifying what elements are critical in respect of their initial operation. For example, the main reasons in Tanzania included:

(a) banks—control over the mobilisation and allocation of savings (including but not limited to bank profits);

(b) grain-milling—improving control over provision, pricing, and location policy of an industry closely identified with basic urban (and to a lesser extent rural) needs;

(c) shoes—increasing national production and input use;

(d) all three—raising the size of the public productive sector relative to the private (and especially the foreign private) to increase the positive weight and scope for initiatives of government political economic policy; reducing dependence on external personnel and suppliers; implementing national wages and salaries policies; and generating significant surpluses towards financing both public services (via taxation) and public sector investment (not necessarily in the same firm).

Implications include:

(a) Inappropriateness of continued foreign minority ownership or broad managerial role in banks, plus an urgent priority for consolidating and restructuring them, probably with particularly close working liaison links with the Treasury and Central Bank;

(b) somewhat similar but perhaps less acute issues in respect of milling;

(c) more room for joint venture or broad foreign managerial role (by the ex-owner or others) in the shoe firm, if institutional and manpower constraints prevent effective public sector direct management of all the acquired ventures in the initial period;

(d) careful identification of specific foreign inputs: human; knowledge; materials; capital goods, for each unit and possible sources, e.g. foreign transaction expertise/correspondent banks, training for master millers/ technical assistance, shoe machinery spares/a manufacturer unrelated to ex-owner;

(e) a structure running from management through board of directors through parent sectoral ministry and coordinating ministries (e.g. Treasury, Planning) to political decision-takers (presumptively Cabinet or equivalent and/or Party Executive or equivalent) should be created for all acquired enterprises. The structure should provide for two-way flows of information, proposals, discussion, and coordination subject to clear identification of responsibilities (including joint ones) and lines of ultimate control;

(f) special bodies, e.g. in respect of public sector (government and public enterprise) wage, salary, fringe benefit, training, promotion, recruitment, and allocation of manpower may be needed or exisiting ones may need significant refocusing and restructuring;

(g) special concessional tax rates (for public enterprises in general and partially nationalised joint ventures in particular) should be avoided;

(h) surplus as well as production targets should be set in an iterative process involving at least the firm and the directly responsible ministries, and the results should be reviewed against the targets;

(i) the need to operate control frameworks for public enterprises (whose individual institutional interests will not be identical to the public interest, and who are in any case in no position to assess or decide on the general public interest) should be recognised and acted on so as to minimise intra-public sector conflicts and actions at cross purposes.

Equally specific goals and their priorities will determine attitudes to exogenous events or those only selectively and partially within government control. For example:

(a) in the case of banks continued operation for normal business is highly desirable and more than a very brief closure likely to be seriously damaging. (Thus if key foreign personnel are about to be withdrawn by ex-owners, adequate citizen or new foreign replacements must be found before, or parallel to, the withdrawal);

(b) a prolonged closure of grain-milling is equally unacceptable, but—

depending on stock levels and import availability—a brief one may not
be serious;

(c) for shoes a near or total closedown of some weeks or even months
while reorganising and replacing withdrawn ex-owner inputs will create
some surplus and foreign exchange losses but normally no unhandleable
macroeconomic or sociopolitical costs.

COMPENSATION CONSIDERATIONS

It may appear odd that compensation plays such a limited role in the goal
articulation and modalities process. The reason is quite simple—payment
of compensation is not a goal of nationalisation. Compensation—or rather
looking ahead to limiting it—may play a role in modalities, e.g. by
avoiding formulas likely to raise it and/or tie government hands more
effectively than those of ex-owners. However, compensation really turns
on:

(a) concepts of fairness—either of the decision-taking groups or of
external bodies it cannot afford to ignore;

(b) questions of practicality usually directly or indirectly related to
continued need for foreign markets, supplies, knowledge, personnel,
and/or finance from groups directly or indirectly concerned enough
about compensation for it to be relevant to their decisions and terms.

These two areas largely inform the difference between nationalisation of
domestic and foreign-owned assets. Foreign bodies rarely concern themselves much with whether a state compensates its own nationals, but
national decision-takers may be more concerned with some standard of
fairness, or hardship-averting, either for citizens in general or for particular
groups of them. Foreign ex-owners and those associated with them have
absolutely greater power than citizen ex-owners, but in most cases are less
likely to exercise it to the full. Domestic capitalists may unite and seek to
forge a political countercoalition if they see a limited number of
nationalisations as the thin end of a wedge leading either to state capitalism
or socialism; albeit in Tanzania they did not in practice have the power or
organisational structures to do so to any real effect.[12]

Any discussion of means underlines the fact that nationalisation (rather
like formal political independence) is a point of departure or a milestone
not an arrival. This is important, for as the Chinese proverb points out:
'Even the longest journey starts with the first step'. Being sure that it is in
the right direction and placed on relatively firm ground is critical. It is
unwise to emulate the Greek colonel who is said to have declaimed: 'We
stood on the verge of a precipice. Now we have taken a great stride
forward'.

PURPOSES, PROCEDURES, AND LIMITATIONS

Three quotations may help summarise the issues of purpose, procedure, and limitations. The first from President J. K. Nyerere indicates why nationalisation is likely to be used widely and why Tanzania's experience is likely to be relevant to more than those decision-takers sharing in full TANU's particular political economic, and sociopolitical commitments. The second from Finance and Planning Minister A. H. Jamal underlines that a large-scale nationalisation if accompanied by inadequate consideration of initial operation may have very high macroeconomic and therefore social and political costs. The third from the then National Bank of Commerce Chairman and Managing Director Amon Nsekela warns of the limitations of nationalisation and consequential public ownership if left in isolation rather than systematically built upon.

> Ideological differences between countries affect the method, not necessarily the fact, of securing national control. The real ideological choice is between controlling the economy through domestic private enterprise, or doing so through some state or other collective mechanism. But . . . it is extremely doubtful whether it is a practical choice for an African nationalist. The pragmatist in Africa . . . will find that the choice is between private foreign ownership on the one hand and local collective ownership on the other . . . A capitalistic economy means a foreign dominated economy . . . The only way in which national control of the economy can be achieved is through the economic institutions of socialism. (Mwalimu Nyerere)

> The efficiency of the parastatal institutions will have to be given the highest priority attention. Every shilling of potential investible surplus needlessly lost by a parastatal is a shilling more on taxes and price increases. Where the substance of economic management is vested in the state's and the people's institutions, our future sources of investible funds are those institutions and activities. (Minister Jamal)

> The point I am making is a simple one. We must avoid drawing the conclusion that the activities of public corporations in Africa can or do significantly and automatically alter the basic mechanism of our economies and, likewise, that the creation of each and every new industrial plant under the auspices of such corporations necessarily means 'Development' in any meaningful sense. . . . Ownership of the means of production has therefore given the state, through its public corporations, the ability to pursue policies in furtherance of socialist development, but the problem now is to design economic strategies and management systems which turn this possibility into a

reality . . . depends very largely upon the broader economic, political and social situation in which they are created and in which they have to perform. (Chairman Nsekela)

The opening quotations illustrate three facets of acquisition, compensation, and initial operation. First it is difficult to assess what is desirable (sociopolitically and political economically) at any given point in time and even more so to value it. Second real questions of equity primarily to taxpayers and consumers but also to ex-owners arise. Third the difficulties must be overcome, because the political commitment to a transition to greater productive sector control and toward economic independence absolutely requires continued erosion of the foreign private sector as well as expansion of the domestic public. In the case of a transition to socialism the same holds true in respect of the domestic private sector. The issues on selection, timing, and tactics in Tanzania were ones of what, when, and how; not whether. Failure to accept this fact would not halt or slow nationalisation; it could merely prevent analysis and advice which could increase its efficiency being prepared, given, or taken.

For example in 1967 in Tanzania discussion on which grain mills and sisal estates to acquire was open, because the immediate goal was a dominant position in both industries plus insuring the future stability of sisal. Control without ownership in sisal (for which elaborate proposals were made by quite radical technocrats and politicians) was not an open alternative. Similarly, the only question of bank nationalisation coverage was whether to exempt the Co-operative Bank on the grounds that it was already in the public sector. Because it was held (correctly) that, to be an effective socialist transitional planning tool, commercial and investment banking must be 100 per cent public sector; no question of majority participation (as opposed to 100 per cent takeover) or exempting one or two private sector banks (to provide 'competition') was valid.

In many respects a nationalisation situation is analogous to a 'takeover bid' by an outsider intending to take control of a firm or a body of assets and use them to serve his ends; ends which will usually vary in greater or lesser degree from those of the previous owners. Thus the fact that Tanzania acquires to effect a transition to socialism or Nigeria to strengthen the share of domestic ownership is not an essential difference, but does affect some aspects of valuation and initial operation. As in any takeover bid situation the standard top limit is what the assets are worth to the new owner and the bottom is what the old owner will accept. The latter limit is somewhat special since he cannot refuse to sell nor seek alternative buyers.

Because it is the area giving rise to the greatest debate, the most work for the Treasury or other coordinating body and the most profound confusions, valuation will be considered first. Secondly, albeit logically preceding valuation, will be an examination of how to proceed with the nationalisation process: first in cases in which sector, firm, or asset identification is dominantly political level pre-decided and only interpretation and follow-through involves analytical/managerial level responsibilities; and second in cases in which analytical/managerial advice and proposals precede the political decision to acquire. Finally the very critical issue of initial operating arrangements—including as one option associated contracts with ex-owners as part of the settlement package—will be discussed.

3 FAIRNESS

Fairness in respect to compensation is a very relative concept and one used in very different ways. At least five can usefully be noted:

(a) fairness of private ownership of productive assets and therefore of payment for them when expropriated by the state;
(b) historical context of overall foreign penetration of the territory and therefore of the overall national claim against foreign states and their nationals in respect of past exploitation;
(c) national decision-taker's attitudes in respect of what is fair to specific classes, formations, groups—attitudes usually partly related to what support or cooperation is sought from these groups;
(d) the broad guidelines of international legal and commercial opinion on what is fair as they influence government, international agency (e.g. World Bank), and business actions in respect to the acquiring state;
(e) the particular views of the ex-owners (foreign or domestic) insofar as the acquiring state needs something from them (e.g. inputs, markets, personnel, knowledge) and their provision of that something will be affected by how fairly they believe they have been treated.

The first concept of fairness is quite beyond the scope of this chapter or the realities of negotiated settlements in general. The second is relevant only in special cases in which it has a foothold of acceptance in the framework of international legal and commercial opinion. These cases include:

(a) enemy property seized during a war (e.g. former French or American property seized by the present Vietnamese and Cambodian governments);
(b) colonial property seized after a liberation struggle pursued largely by military means (a less clear cut case of general acceptance exists here, but Algeria is a partial example and the concept is relevant to Mozambique, Guinea-Bissau, Angola, and Bangladesh);
(c) property acquired by a government perceived as revolutionary (the

classic example in the USSR in the 1920s, but the principle is relevant to Cuba and Ethiopia).

In the second two of the foregoing cases compensation is less clearly seen as fairly expected, because the new state really does not inherit the obligations of the old. Such repudiation—if intended—should be done relatively speedily if it is to gain acceptance and in the knowledge that general acceptance will take time. It is a once-for-all consideration because the new state's own obligations cannot be repudiated on the same basis; e.g. Cuba cannot advance the same case for repudiating 1970 Euro-currency borrowing as for pre-1960 external debt issues. Further unless the repudiation is clearly once for all, and followed by strict acceptance of liability of new contracts and obligations, serious problems of credit and contract-worthiness will arise. Cuba is seen as credit and contract-worthy because it honours the contracts and debts incurred by the present state—if it had repudiated these then both capitalist and European socialist business units would decline to enter into normal contracts with Cuban parallels not on grounds of morality but of total uncertainty as to probability of payment and contract fulfilment.

Domestic decision-taker's concepts of fairness are also largely beyond the scope of this study. They vary widely depending on objective facts as to support groups and need to maintain some type of cooperation by target (ex-owner) groups as well as to ideological and goal commitments. In the Tanzanian case there was a generalised view that reducing an individual to poverty was not a fair result of nationalisation and that, by and large, ex-owners should receive about the book value of their net assets, unless they had engaged in gross exploitation (in the colloquial not the Marxian sense). Landlords with high (over $4000 net) incomes were seen as *de facto* guilty of gross exploitation. Small-scale landlords (whose ratio of rents collected to assets employed was much higher but whose incomes were typically about $300 – 1000 net) were not similarly viewed, perhaps luckily as the acquisition and operation of their buildings would have posed nearly insuperable technical problems.

The domestic decision-taker's concept of fairness is very relevant to the valuation of acquired assets and to compensation negotiations, because it sets certain targets and limits for public sector officials, analysts, managers, and negotiators. However, once it is identified the main problems and constraints turn on international and ex-owner concepts of fairness. These will be discussed in detail, not because of their moral superiority or intellectual power, but because in the context of actual compensation exercises they pose the greatest number of practical problems.

This approach does not imply that International Law is a body of immutable principles. It is changing away from a rigid defence of the sanctity of private property and performance of contracts, whatever the history and context of the property or contracts. That change is in part the result of nationalisations and 'inadequate but agreed' compensations and of broadening direct intervention by states into commercial contracts. These changes need to be studied, analysed, and promoted by the peripheral polities engaging in foreign asset acquisition, but the context for doing so is rarely the individual negotiation or acquisition *per se*.

In respect of general international commercial and of ex-owner acceptance of 'fairness' there are certain concrete steps an acquiring state can take to minimise negative actions:

(a) demonstrate that it is willing (and able) to accept costs (e.g. two British banks' blocking of the London balances of their former branches in Tanzania) and to mobilise domestic support to do so;

(b) locate, announce, and make use of alternative sources of whatever was provided by the ex-owners (e.g. external clearing facilities and personnel in the Tanzanian bank case);

(c) secure speedy settlements with selected significant ex-owners (preferably chosen in such a way as not to set high payment precedents) to demonstrate that fair settlements are being sought (e.g. one semi-major bank case was settled within a few weeks of nationalisation in Tanzania);

(d) ensure that innocent bystanders (e.g. creditors of acquired firms) are not injured and that contracts and debts other than those with or to nationalised units are honoured. Such a course of action reduces general uncertainty and increases the attractiveness to businesses (not excluding ex-owners) of avoiding a breach of commercial relations;

(e) indicate and act on a general willingness to negotiate with all ex-owners on applications and computations resulting from compensation principles (not on the principles themselves).

On the face of it these approaches have nothing to do with fairness but a good deal to do with power and freedom of manoeuvre in bargaining. In practice, commercial judgements on fairness do turn in part on what businessmen think can be obtained. Few firms will sacrifice much to assist an ex-owner, if the acquiring state appears willing and able both to take a firm stand on compensation and to meet its general contractual and payment obligations.

VALUE AND FAIRNESS

The issues of value and fairness are inextricably intertwined in any individual valuation exercise and especially in compensation.[13] The two interact. It is not fair to citizens of the acquiring state to pay more for acquired business or assets than they can earn in the future except in a very limited group of cases. The Tanzanian side in compensation talks has seen itself as responsible for ensuring fairness to Tanzania and Tanzanians. Normally the ex-owner can be expected to make his own case for what he believes is fair to him and what his assets were worth. Compensation discussions are partisan or adversary proceedings, not sessions of disinterested impartial arbitrators. This does not mean they need to be acrimonious or hostile; they are business (or in a sense diplomatic) dialogues and some regard for orderly procedure and personal politeness is usually profitable, so long as it is not allowed to hamper a clear statement and defence of one's case.

That said, fairness does have a meaning—otherwise there would be no case for paying any compensation to local ex-owners or to foreign ex-owners who could not mobilise effective government pressure on Tanzania. No state has ever taken quite that hard a line—the USSR paid some compensation to foreign firms with which it contracted under the New Economic Policy, and the socialist European states and China paid not inconsiderable amounts to some 'national capitalists' either formally or in high salaries and/or profit shares. In these cases fairness must probably be seen as a combination of avoiding unilateral repudiation of one's own agreements at the cost of the other party, taking account of the standards of fairness held by relevant domestic groups (classes, formations), and paying some attention to international legal and commercial opinion to the extent it could influence action.

The Tanzanian position has been that in principle some compensation is payable for assets acquired (including meeting liabilities associated with the assets). Debts or hostile acts may eliminate any particular claim, but are seen as offsets not a denial of the principle. This is a political principle which lies in the hands of the President, the National Assembly, the party and the people, not of civil servants. So long as it remains policy the problem for negotiators, analysts, and managers is applying it.

EXTERNAL STANDARDS CONSIDERATIONS

The domestic aspects of fairness, as perceived in Tanzania, turned partly on value, partly on past actions of the owner, partly on public policy.

Two external aspects of fairness arise—what official bodies not predisposed either to condemn the nationalising state or to accept uncompensated confiscation as a general principle will agree to be fair; and what an ex-owner or other foreign firm from whom the nationalising state still needs certain services will accept and then provide (sell) the needed goods or services and do so in a manner more or less analogous to standard commercial practice.

These areas can be misunderstood. It is not valid to surrender the national decision-taker's view of fairness, once clearly stated, to 'buy' international or company acceptance; principles are not for sale. On the other hand, it is not prudent to take a rigid stand providing no room for bargaining and no scope for 'hardship' cases. The use of principles is not, after all, to serve as spears on which to impale oneself. If possible, debate on specific cases and specific possible adjustments is preferable to a confrontation on principles. The latter is a test of right and wrong, good and evil, and really cannot be gracefully compromised once set in those terms. The former is a discussion on whether valuation computations and procedures and consideration of overall fairness as applied to a specific case were correct, and a compromise merely admits a procedural or mathematical mistake or a lack of full data in respect of fairness. Anybody can (and sensible people will when appropriate) admit to the occasional mistake with no loss of principle and minimum loss of face.

Basically International Law and official international opinion at present accept that:

(a) nationalisation may be for virtually any public purpose, if
(b) compensation is computed in relation to some version of the 'value' of the assets (possibly with some offsets based on past conduct, although this is less generally accepted);
(c) this value is explained in a rational way; even if
(d) the ex-owner feels aggrieved;
(e) considerable delay occurs in reaching an agreed figure; so long as
(f) some semblance of negotiation and evaluation is proceeding;
(g) deferred payment over several years, if
(h) some interest (not necessarily market rate) is paid, some fairly definite payment schedule provided, and some means of remitting proceeds to the ex-owner's home country allowed as part of the arrangements.

Problems arise not so much with a harsh formula whose offsets make most computed net values negative as with apparent confiscation however it may be justified. Even here it is clear that most governments will accept a blurring of the edges, e.g. appeals procedures, hardship cases, a few ex-gratia payments which really sidestep the issue of principle. A government can by such means assert (and in the bulk of cases literally apply) its own principle, and foreign governments can say that they did something for some of their citizens.

This point is illustrated by the U.K.-Tanzania confrontation (with the World Bank a rather unwilling bystander in the middle) over properties taken over under the Buildings Acquisition and Absentee Landlords Acts. After initial vague queries, the U.K. took a hard 'anti-confiscation' line. The Bank, by its own regulations (which the Board would not wish to abandon, even if a majority of its management and Executive Directors probably view them as out of date) is forced to stop recommending loans in cases involving confiscatory nationalisation. In this case it accepted a delay in acting on a loan proposal and sought to clarify the then existing position. Tanzania took a hard line:

(a) no retreat on principles of right to acquire and to determine a fair value;
(b) the inherent fairness of the formula phasing compensation down to zero for buildings owned over ten years;
(c) the adequacy and equity of appeals and hardship procedures which existed and had not been used;
(d) support for the U.K. position by blocking IBRD/IDA lending (whether by the Bank or a government) to be seen as a general act of economic hostility to Tanzania and responded to on that basis.

The last two points were crucial. Nobody wanted any such result as severing IBRD and major bilateral links with Tanzania. The point that appeals and hardship provisions existed gave the Bank and the Executive Directors representing other capitalist industrial economies a basis for saying that any complaint was premature.

The second U.K. challenge in 1973 was met in the same way with the added point that Tanzania could point to several buildings given back on hardship grounds or because, while legally correct, acquisition was not intended (e.g. accidental or incidental landlords). In 1973 the U.K. retreated more rapidly as apparently no other country supported their attempt to use blocking World Bank loans as a means of pressing for compensation in this case. After this victory on principle it was easier for Tanzania to take two actions (which did not alter principle) to defuse the issue:

(a) the President ruled that buildings not built for landlordism (e.g. staff flats, group property companies, blocks basically used by ex-owner for his own business) should be returned or compensated;
(b) the President further directed that a group of hardship cases should be paid the rather small sums due on a normal valuation more or less ex gratia, without further regard for secondary details.

Tanzania could not have gone this far in 1972 without apparently retreating on principle. After having twice succeeded in avoiding blocking of loans without any change in the Act it could afford to be more flexible on specific cases. However, the problems of 'accidental landlords' (e.g. cases in which previous nationalisations had caused unintended landlord status) and 'hardship cases' (e.g. an eighty-year-old lady in a nursing home and a seventy-five-year-old petrol pump attendant whose only retirement income had been rent) should have been foreseen and machinery set up to deal with them. The failure to foresee and raise these issues was basically a technical one; there is no reason to suppose political decision-takers would not have made provision for them if alerted in good time.[14]

EX-OWNERS' FUTURE INVOLVEMENT

If a need exists to keep foreign management or technical services, marketing arrangements, or purchasing facilities, and the most suitable interim route is through the ex-owner, then partial nationalisation and/or a greater emphasis on relatively agreed payment may be appropriate. However, this is not always either necessary or even desirable:

(a) it is sometimes possible to nationalise 100 per cent and still secure the needed services by contract (e.g. J. K. Chande at the Tanzania National Milling Corporation was probably the best of the ex-owner managers, even though the firm in which he had been a shareholder had been 100 per cent nationalised);

(b) replacement management can be procured by direct hire (e.g. Bora Shoe) or contract (e.g. Printpak)—thus there is no necessity to accept unreasonable terms of compensation as a price for continued technical or managerial cooperation.

Even if a 'joint venture' is chosen two critical points require attention if it is to be 'in the public interest', even on narrow grounds:

(a) if a significant stake (e.g. 40 per cent) remains, then profit on that plus management fees are enough that the former 100 per cent owner can be bargained down to a modest premium on book value (perhaps fixed assets plus a limited addition partially offsetting the inflation impact on historic cost of fixed assets), or five to seven years average recent past post-tax profits (e.g. in Tanzania initial cigarette, can, cement, brewery, and pyrethrum extract cases);

(b) nothing in such a first step prevents a subsequent 100 per cent takeover when one is in a position to dispense with all or most of ex-owner's services (e.g. in Tanzania by 1976 cement, pyrethrum extract, and in principle cigarettes). This implies a high degree of attention to citizen training clauses and/or a careful location of replacement management (failure to do either in the cement case led to an unsatisfactory gap between 100 per cent takeover and new management arrival).

So far as Tanzania was concerned these cases did not involve 'fairness' but were perceived as a 'value of continuous operation' issue. What extra, if any, it was worth paying for acquired assets in order to keep enough goodwill in relations to conclude arrangements providing continuity of management or services can only be answered on the facts of specific cases, since it could be 25 per cent and it could be nothing.

It is critical to consider nationalisation (or partial nationalisation) settlements as a whole. A former 100 per cent owner is concerned not solely with the amount and phasing of compensation, but also with possible future profit flows on a continued minority share in a joint venture and/or on management, technical, and sales contracts with the new public sector unit. If the minority shareholding and contract profits are likely to be significant, this will reduce the amount seen as acceptable for the majority ownership; a fact the government negotiators should bear in mind and include in their calculations. Similarly if the continued involvement of the former 100 per cent owner has some real value to the acquiring public sector (if not, then 100 per cent nationalisation and no contracts are appropriate), then presumptively it increases probable future earnings of the public sector unit and the total compensation which can be agreed without unfairness to taxpayers, workers, and consumers.

Both the ex-owner's and the acquiring public sector's perceptions may, therefore, make nationalisation plus joint ventures and/or special contracts a situation in which compensation is easier to agree—a conclusion Tanzanian experience in brewing, cement, cigarettes, tin, and pyrethrum extract in 1967 – 8 seems to bear out. It says nothing about the more basic question of whether in any given case continued special relations with the former 100 per cent owners are consistent with and conducive to attaining the goals which led to the decision to nationalise. If they are not, then ease of settling compensation will have been purchased at a very high price; e.g. the 1974 Zairean, 1967 Chilean and 1969 Zambian full or partial nationalisations of copper, and perhaps the 1967 Tanzanian cement case.

HARDSHIP CASES

A final area falling under the rubric of fairness rather than value proper is that of hardship or compassionate treatment cases. Where practicable, returning the asset—e.g. an aged person's rental houses, tenant-purchasers' flats—is better than compensating on a special basis. However, this is not always practicable and some special guidelines for assessing what to pay and why is then needed. It requires underlining that while compassion is a virtue it is hardly being compassionate to the taxpayers of the acquiring state or its consumers to pay an excessive amount of compensation. It is to Tanzania and Tanzanians that the political, administrative, and technical team representing Tanzania owe their primary duty of compassion as of fairness. There have, however, been cases in which compassion has been seen in Tanzania to be properly exercised because it was not at the expense of Tanzania or Tanzanians:

(a) if return of property initially nationalised to residents of Tanzania will avert hardship for them, but will not basically affect the degree of public sector control or efficiency;

(b) if the letter of the nationalisation legislation has (often inevitably if loopholes were to be avoided) caught assets which were not within the government's intention and can thus be returned with no damage to basic aims;

(c) if the compassion can be exercised at the expense of a third party and with his consent. The British Government's provision of grants or soft loans to buy out British farmers in Kenya, even if not in a *de jure* nationalisation context, is a case in point.

Appeals to compassion are often mixed with appeals to Christian or Islamic principles in general. That claim is not very convincing especially as usually made. The Old and the New Testament provide rather sounder cases against generosity to well-off ex-owners, much less to ex-exploiters.[15] Similar Koranic cases can be made like the prophet Mohamed's nationalisation of foreign property in Mecca for the communal use of the faithful.

With these varied approaches to fairness, and the fact that post-nationalisation negotiations are rarely totally amicable, and virtually always adversary proceedings, it is hardly surprising that settlements cannot always be agreed in any meaningful sense, and that some 'agreed' settlements are perceived as unfair by one party (or on occasion both parties). In the Tanzanian case probably 90 per cent of the assets (other than rental properties) acquired became the subject of what could meaningfully be termed agreements and perhaps 75–80 per cent of agreements in which both sides believed some degree of fairness had pertained.

4. VALUE: BASIC PRINCIPLES

The value of a firm or a collection of assets is basically what the acquiring public sector can reasonably expect to gain by owning them, in terms of the present discounted value of future benefits; i.e. the sum of future net cash flows discounted to the present at some rate of interest.[16] For purposes of compensation only discounted net cash flow to the firm is relevant, and benefits—such as employment, regional balance, providing markets or raw materials for other local firms, improving the foreign exchange balance—which do not accrue to the firm but to other economic units are not relevant, because the ex-owner could not have secured them for himself had he continued in possession.

Basically valuation of any particular set of assets is an exercise in estimating a future net-income-stream's present value, even though some convenient forms for computation (e.g. net book value) do not at first examination seem to do that. It is critical to bear that fact in mind, because one can only decide whether a method like net book value is reasonable by considering whether in the actual case under valuation it will give a reasonable approximation of the earnings flow value.

Similarly, because one cannot know future net cash flows (taken after all expenses including capital asset replacement) the first-approximation method often used is to assume that they will bear a fairly close relation to past net cash flows and it is necessary therefore to secure the data from which these can be computed. Computed, not simply read off—the differences in accounting presentations and in competence between firms are great enough to require careful analysis of and cross checks on all figures submitted. After that, adjustments can be made if there is good reason to expect the future to be very different from the past, or if some alteration (down or up) is appropriate on grounds of fairness.

Because the financing of working capital (current assets, e.g. spares, raw materials, work in progress, finished goods, prepaid expenses, debtors) varies widely, and because in principle such capital can be secured on a loan basis (e.g. from banks or suppliers), it is often appropriate to add net current assets to the basic discounted cash flow valuation figure; i.e. to take earnings flow as deriving from fixed assets only.

It is not appropriate to deduct long-term liabilities from a value reached in this way, because the interest on them is a charge before the net cash flow is reached. However, one can add loan interest back into the net cash flow; recompute the gross cash flow value for net worth and medium or long-term loans together; deduct the loans at face value, and arrive at an alternative future cash flow valuation for the net worth.

Thus in the case of a small farming, trading, or manufacturing firm with an average net cash flow (post-tax profit) of $200,000; net current assets of $100,000; and outside long term loans of $500,000 on which interest had been paid at $50,000 a year *before* net profit, one could calculate:

(a)	Six times (say) net profit	$1,200,000
(b)	Net current assets	$ 100,000
(c)	Value of net worth	$1,300,000

or

(a)	Adjusted net profit ($200,000 plus $50,000 less pro-forma tax of $20,000, *if* that had been profit not interest)	$ 230,000
(b)	Times six	$1,380,000
(c)	Plus net current assets	100,000
(d)	Less outside loan	500,000
(e)	Alternative net worth value	$ 980,000

The first approach is usually more appropriate to large, stable businesses in which outside loans are normal and prudent; the second may be better for small, risky, cyclical firms for whom large non-equity finance is imprudent or unusual.

The question of the discount rate on future earnings—or its approximation, the 'profit multiple' basis—needs examination. Basically it turns on the question: 'What would a prudent investor consider an acceptable average profit after tax on an investment of this kind?' The higher the rate specified the lower the earnings multiple, and therefore the lower the value for any given level of profitability.

Basically a large or medium-sized firm can reasonably expect and seek to earn $10 - 12\frac{1}{2}$ per cent on all assets employed, and by prudent use of debt to secure $15-20$ per cent on net worth. Net worth is total assets less total liabilities at nominal or paid up value of equity shares alone. That suggests that the earnings multiple should normally be in the range of five to seven times average post-tax profits of the years (say three to five)prior to acquisition, unless inflation has been so severe as to make past money figures no guide to present values, in which case some form of 'inflation adjustment' may be appropriate.

For a firm in a risky or cyclical business (with very wide swings in profits) a lower multiple, say three to five, plus care to use a base period including both bad and good years are needed. For example, in the case of coffee estates the cyclical element is present in Tanzania both on price and output, but risk is not abnormally high; in the case of sisal both cyclical and risk elements are very high.

However, at this point a short-cut method suggests itself. If a firm is actually earning say $12\frac{1}{2} - 22\frac{1}{2}$ per cent on net worth then it has normal profits and its net book value is likely to be a good estimate of its total value (discounted cash flow plus net current asset less medium and long-term liability). Because net book value is relatively easy to determine definitely by audit (granted that the process is tedious and sometimes slow), it has the advantage in normal profit record cases of side-stepping disputes on future or 'true' past profits. In Tanzania, Tanganyika Millers (grain-milling) was precisely such a case in 1967 and Tanganyika Portland Cement was in a similar position at the time of acquiring the final 50 per cent.

'Adjusted book value' is again a short-hand route to sidestep a formal earnings estimation. If profits are clearly far above or below normal and no special fairness issue arises against adjustment, one can formally adjust asset values to or towards market or replacement cost (which may mean raising or lowering them) to arrive at an acceptable value. What is critical is to remember that the earnings flow is basic, and not be beguiled into thinking asset replacement cost has any inherent value meaning (e.g. in the Bird and Co. sisal case an ex-owner offer on a replacement cost basis would have been about Sh125–50 million, not the Sh11 million actually negotiated five years later). The following example may be useful:

A trading company owned shipping-agency franchises and a large part of its profits came from them. These franchises can be bought and sold for three to five years net earnings, but were not listed as assets in the balance sheet. Evidently they were of value to Tanzania, and adjusting net worth by valuing them at slightly under three years net income gave a new value figure consistent with cash flow and acceptable both to Tanzania and the ex-owners.

For a concern which will be operated as such after acquisition it may be simpler to assume depreciation and asset replacement will cross-cancel and compute value on profit flow only. In that case value equals net discounted profit flow. This is usually most closely related to post-tax profit. Occasionally, however, a calculation using an appropriately lower multiple on pre-tax profit will be more convenient. In a normal profit-and-tax case there would be no difference in the results:

Pre-tax profit	1,000,000	
Post-tax profit	600,000	
Post-tax multiple (say)	6	
Value	3,600,000	(or 6 × 600,000)
Pre-tax multiple (post-tax multiple times the standard ratio of post-tax to pre-tax profits, e.g. 0·6 if company tax rate is 40 per cent)	$(6) \times (0·6) = 3·6$	
Value	3,600,000 (or 3·6 × 1,000,000)	

The point is that the tax position for the recent past may not have been normal:

(a) earlier losses may have been carried forward against current profits;
(b) initial allowances on investment may have caused abnormally low effective tax rates;
(c) corrections of past over (under) payment of tax may have raised (lowered) apparent post-tax profit.

If such elements seem to be present to a significant extent, a pre-tax multiple valuation should be made as a check. If it is very much lower than the post-tax valuation the pre-tax should be used.

COMPLICATIONS AND ADJUSTMENTS: FAIRNESS AND CALCULATION

Two broad categories of adjustments are often needed. The more basic does not *per se* query the value as derived by an earnings flow method, but queries whether that value is a fair price to pay. The less difficult consists of special circumstances affecting not whether it is, in principle, fair to pay at valuation, but whether discounted cash flow based on past or immediate future earnings is an adequate estimating method.

On the face of it future earnings flow is a basis for valuation which combines value and equity. True, disputes could arise as to what future earnings were likely to be (with the 'buyer' cautious and the 'seller' optimistic) but these would be technical questions. Even the rough rule-of-thumb method that past earnings are a good guide to probable future earnings can be modified when appropriate in determining value: why then does it cause problems in respect of fairness? The special plea for asset cost (in cases in which historic or replacement cost exceeds the value of future earnings) can readily be dismissed as a 'true value' claim. No willing buyer would accept it; nor could any seller secure it. Equally the plea that past earnings have been understated to avoid tax hardly creates much of a fairness case—that the tax avoider is caught in his own trap is surely an example of ironic justice. Where then lies the problem in deciding what is fair at the micro or case-by-case negotiating level?

Firstly past earnings may be a very bad guide to future earnings in specific cases, for reasons which do involve fairness. This can be true in both directions. If a firm has been built up, met its initial losses, won through to profits, and has a fairly assured future profit growth, average past earnings are not a fair guide to value but give too low an estimate. An evident case in point was Chande Industries which had just broken the Kenya-based Unga group's monopoly in wheat flour, and had had only one even approximately normal year prior to nationalisation. Thus it was paid ten times the post-tax profit of the last year before nationalisation versus perhaps six times for the ex-Unga group subsidiary. On the other hand, if a firm has earned monopoly profits by exploiting a captive market while the regulation officials were inactive, average past earnings will give an unfairly high figure. Dar Municipal Transport was a near-classic example with an average post-tax profit of 75 per cent a year on initial capital and 35 per cent on net worth including retained earnings. These levels would have been regarded as 'the unacceptable face of capitalism' by Mr. Heath and 'obscene' by any U.S. regulatory body. Thus no fair evaluation could start from them, even though they had involved no violation of the law or the company's charter.

Secondly, there may be general policy reasons why the future will not be like the past. Buildings Acquisition was an example: landlordism was viewed as a social evil and the 'earnings' of landlords as unfairly high. Thus a 5 per cent rent tax had been introduced in 1970, with a clear intent to raise it year by year to at least 25 per cent and perhaps 40 per cent. Therefore, the future net earnings of rental property were very unlikely to equal those of the past.

Thirdly, fairness requires considering all circumstances surrounding a firm or asset. Again, this may affect the valuation up or down. Two examples may help clarify:

(a) the insurance company funds in a large acquired building were invested under pressure from the Tanzania Treasury and under assurances by the Treasury that they would qualify as approved investments in terms of the insurance regulations. As the building was new no problem of compensation arose, but clearly in this case fairness could have required consideration of the negotiations leading to its construction;

(b) highly profitable companies which had paid high dividends (e.g. British American Tobacco) were not given generous profit multiples because of a feeling (which even they did not totally reject) that past remitted profits over a long period did reduce what it was fair to pay on acquisition.[17]

Fairness as perceived in Tanzania related partly to value, partly to general public policy, and partly to the past actions of the ex-owner. Since the overwhelming majority of these factors (even if by no means all) resulted in a reduction from the future earnings (or even average past earnings) valuation, they do give rise to arguments of unfairness which relate to different national and ex-owner concepts of what is right (in principle), and not just varying calculations of what is correct. It is important to understand the distinction, both to know when to introduce a special adjustment (down or up) to achieve fairness, and to comprehend the nature of disagreement with an ex-owner. On figures and calculations an official can and must seek to reach an accurate and agreed position. On principle he must obey the law as written, and seek legal advice if unsure what it means. This is especially true where, as in case of the Tanzania Abandoned Sisal Estates Act, the question of fairness was explicitly considered at Cabinet Committee level and in Parliament.

A second category of complexities is more common but involves less hard issues of principle. In every major firm there are likely to be some reasons for arguing positive or negative adjustments—the reason they are not usually central to compensation negotiations is that they are not normally certain enough or large enough to have a major impact on the value figure. In that event auditor's checks will usually provide a basis for agreed adjustments, if any. However, in some cases the situation is unusual enough to require special *ad hoc* formulae.

Short of special formulae, major adjustments to earnings multiples or to book net worth may sometimes be needed. In passing it should be noted that high management (or consultancy, or technical, or selling agency) fees or director's fees do not constitute a case for adjustment. If they were earned, then it will cost an acquiring public sector about the same to provide the services. If they were a tax avoidance or exchange control avoidance device the ex-owner is morally (and sometimes legally, e.g. if 'adjustment' would create a tax fraud or exchange control violation case) estopped from claiming his past profits were too low. He cannot be allowed to have his cake at nationalisation after having eaten it in earlier years.

Claims for adjustment should be considered on their merits. They may be valid. However, if one is to consider major upward adjustment claims it is necessary to inquire into whether major downward adjustment counterclaims are available to offset them. The counterclaim is a very useful negotiating tactic, even if the real aim is to achieve a dropping of all adjustment claims and counterclaims and reach agreement on the basis of a standard profit multiple or book net worth.

Tanganyika Packers is a Tanzanian example in which counter adjustment claims can be expected to arise. Taking all claims and counterclaims at face value the result would be to suggest a valuation of less than book net worth. (Pre-1974, Packers was a joint venture with the state.)

(a) past profits at acquisition in 1974 had been very low, but the firm was inherently viable and expansion was planned—thus an initial case could be made out for book net worth;

(b) the ex-partners in the joint venture claim Sh15 million was lost on the domestic meat trade because the government *de facto* insisted on subsidising consumers and the Dar Development Corporation at the packing plant's expense. This assertion is true in substance if not necessarily as to amount;

(c) but the ex-partners made their profits on the 15 per cent selling fee on exports. They systematically bid up cattle prices—probably by up to Sh50 a head in 1971 – 3—to get a few thousand more head to tin and export; an action totally contrary to Packer's commercial interest as opposed to that of other units in the partners' company group. On 200,000 head this comes to a negative adjustment of Sh10 million, just as valid in principle as the previous positive one, and just as subject to debate as to exact amount.

This example illustrates the need for coordinated positions and data. Ministry of Agriculture livestock personnel can give more extensive and more authoritative technical detail on questions of marketing, procuring, and processing procedures than can economic and financial analysts no matter how expert.

Assets acquired for purposes other than continued normal use form a rather special class. No normal value rule will apply because their past earnings are no guide to the future (which is likely to be demolition). Nor are the equity considerations which apply very similar to those pertaining to rental buildings or foreign banks, because the acquisition usually has little to do with the past conduct—or at least with the past exploitative conduct—of the ex-owner.

Because they do not really relate closely to other types of nationalisation, and are often very special indeed, they will not be examined in any detail here. In Tanzania the general goal—not always well pursued—has been to put the ex-owner in a position neither much better nor much worse off than he was before. For example if he has lost a house to a road, a factory, or a rural resettlement scheme he should be enabled to build a similar house or—if the old one was very poor—assisted toward building a better one.

5 VALUING AS A FINE ART

Valuing, on whatever formula, is not an exact science. There are several reasons:

(a) there can be real disagreement about facts. For example, how much of the cost of operating a sisal estate relates to short-run production, and how much to keeping up fields and factories for the medium and long term?;

(b) very different assumptions about the present can be used. For example, does one value used printing machinery at replacement cost for modern machinery of the same capacity less wear and tear, or does one go to the U.K., determine the actual cost of used machinery, and then add on shipping/installation costs?;

(c) projections of the future can vary quite remarkably. In the sisal example one ex-owner's representative really thought £140 was a reasonable average London price projection for standard grade over 1967–71, while two government technical personnel thought £70–75 (i.e. the early 1968 London price) a better forecast of the average to be expected;

(d) because of these differences a range of reasonable and professionally honest value estimates will be possible for most individual assets and all production units. The range can be very wide. The assumptions in the printing example were such as to give about two to one differences for the value of the relevant printing machinery, and in the sisal example to give a divergence between minus Sh3 million and plus Sh17 million for the net value of an estate group;

(e) the duty of a valuation advisor to his client means that he will—at least as a starting-point—choose out of reasonable views as to the facts, assumptions as to asset valuation, and projections of the future, those which favour his clients' interests. In the printing case a professional valuation firm hired by the ex-owners with an able and honest valuer and a highly competent public service valuer were involved. Each looked for an approach both professionally reputable and appropriate to his client's interest;

(f) only a jointly appointed valuer can be expected to weigh up approaches and judgements to give equal weight to the interests of both sides. For example, when the same valuation firm as in the printing machinery case valued Tanzanian assets of a petroleum company on an arm's length basis its figure was about 50 per cent over book value and about 25 per cent under the petroleum company's own valuation personnel's estimates, because of assumptions on construction cost and wear and tear on specialised assets which were between those a buyer's and a seller's representative would have chosen;

(g) even for an independent valuer jointly appointed the terms of reference (because they set down certain key assumptions and procedures) will play a very large role in determining the figures reached. For example, in the case of machinery usable for only four years because—say—a new plant will supersede it, does one take replacement less wear and tear or four year's 'rent' plus scrap metal value? At what rate does one discount future net cash flow from growing perennial crops—e.g. sugar cane—to arrive at present value, and how does one estimate future tilling, cutting, and overhead expenses to arrive at that figure? How does one value the basic clearing, levelling, bringing into cultivation of land – at historic cost? or present cost? or some compromise rate?

This is not to say there are not procedures for arriving at reasonably accurate valuations. Nor is it to say one cannot discuss, analyse, and evaluate assumptions about the present and projections of the future to show that certain assumptions and projections are 'better' (more probably correct) than others.

For example £140 for sisal was a mad projection, £70–75 came rather close to being correct for the relevant 1967–71 period but was a trifle low, a caution not inappropriate on the side of government evaluators. However, one of them rather unwisely added: 'I'll eat all the sisal we can export at £140 a tonne or more' without adding 'before the end of 1971', thus illustrating that the longer the time period the more difficult it is to make reasonably accurate projections.

PROCEDURES FOR VALUING

Valuing is not an occult art based on mystic texts or the entrails of a chicken any more than any other branch of business. The valuer who claims that it is either does not understand his own craft or does not wish his audience to understand it. Because of the ultimate inexactitude of knowledge, especially about the future, certain procedures are needed to limit error, especially when government figures and assumptions will be confronted with ex-owner valuations, and a real attempt made to resolve the difference on a basis more jointly participatory than 'take it or leave it'. The latter may be an appropriate stance at the end of prolonged discussion, and was used by Tanzania in certain sisal estate and industrial acquisitions, but rarely is it a desirable starting-point.

The combination of real areas of uncertainty and reasonable differences of opinion, together with the possibility of eliminating unreasonable assumptions and projections and arriving at reasoned judgement on remaining areas of doubt, has procedural implications.

(a) Basic assumptions and bases for projections should always be explicitly stated and explained. They should normally also be conveyed to the other party, so a reasoned discussion on method not a stubborn haggling on figures can ensue. For example in the case of sisal the normal assumptions were:

(i) the best result for a private owner would be to cut out over four years, sell residual assets, and liquidate. This was concluded from examining operating costs and probable revenues. The amount of sisal available to be cut was determined by Sisal Research Station experts soon after nationalisation, who also prepared a technical agronomic report on estate quality and condition;

(ii) the price of sisal over 1967–71 would average £70–75 ex-U.K. for standard grade on the basis of late 1967 and early 1968 prices and trade estimates of no likely early and sustained upturn;

(iii) costs for cutting out would be about the same as recent past estate by estate operating costs, less replanting and depreciation plus some capital replacement (e.g. lorries) needed to keep running;

(iv) from sisal available, price estimate and cost estimate, it was possible to compute net cutting-out cash flow over 1967–71. To get value at nationalisation, cash flow items should be discounted at 10 per cent a year (an interest rate for a risky business at that date; in 1974 a higher rate might have been seen as appropriate), e.g. 1967–8 95 per cent of undiscounted cash flow, 1968–9 85.5 per cent, 1969–70 77 per cent, 1970–1 69.25 per cent;

(v) to this was added residual value of fixed assets for other uses in 1971, e.g. value of used lorries on market, value of town godowns, houses for general use, value—if any—of estate buildings and works for—say—a cattle ranch. To it also was added (subtracted) net current assets (liabilities). Also to be subtracted would be long-term liabilities and to be added non-sisal investments valued at sale price. Current assets were valued at what could be collected, i.e. bad debts were to be written off, not paid for.

(b) Artificial assumptions may be useful for valuation: sisal illustrates this. Tanzania did not nationalise to cut out but to prevent cutting out. But, Tanzania could hardly 'charge' the ex-owners for the losses it expected to incur to preserve foreign-exchange earnings, employment, and the Tanga Region and Kilosa/Morogoro District economies by keeping sisal in production. Neither could the ex-owner properly ask book value by saying the government should pay the ex-owner for the expected foreign-exchange, employment, or regional economy gains.

One firm tried precisely such a claim, but admitted in discussion it really was unreasonable. Thus the 'artificial' estimation of what would have happened on cutting out was the most rational and 'realistic' basic assumption available.

(c) Alternative calculations based on other reasonable assumptions should be made to test one's own basic assumptions and projections and to be able to meet points made by the ex-owner. For example, in the Tanzanian printing and publishing case, after revaluing buildings at replacement less wear and tear and machinery at cost of buying and installing used machinery, a net value figure of about Sh6 million (really a range from say Sh5.9 to Sh6·2 million) was reached. An alternative evaluation was made on an earnings record basis (adjusting actual profits to add back interest and rent paid to associated companies, and to compute tax on resultant adjusted profit to get adjusted net profit). Using multiples of six to seven years average post-tax profits gave Sh5·5 to Sh5·9 million net value. This served two purposes. Firstly it confirmed that the asset valuation approach was giving a sensible figure, and secondly it allowed Tanzania to meet the ex-owner's claim for up to Sh9 million on a profit basis by showing it to be factually unrealistic.

(d) Ranges of values should be computed for internal evaluation, and as a basis for knowing what to offer in a compromise when negotiating. This is especially true in the case of artificial assumptions and values based on investible surplus or cash flow projection. Evidently, initial offers should be at the bottom of a reasonable range, but having an idea of the most likely value and the highest likely is helpful in deciding what ground, if any, to give in negotiations.

(e) Where the ex-owner or his representative are responsible people preliminary discussions should be held before a definite offer is made. It is helpful to know what the other side's assumptions and arguments are before committing too specific a position to paper. One may see—and plug—a loophole in one's case or see that one actually has undervalued (or, more seriously, overvalued). The initial discussions with the ex-owners of Tanganyika Millers were what actually convinced the two Tanzania technical personnel that their tentative view that book net worth was the top limit for compensation was the correct one. There is usually no need to shout and make 'take it or leave it' proposals from the start; open discussion and at least a partially agreed final result are better. In one major case the formal offer came after at least ten discussion sessions over two years and after the gap had been narrowed from Sh4 million vs Sh9 million to Sh6 million vs Sh6·5 million. Had the initial position been firmly and 'finally' committed to paper before the first meeting matters would have been much harder to resolve. At the end of extensive discussions a single 'take it or leave it' proposal may be appropriate. This is especially true if discussion turns into quite ludicrous haggling over such matters as who damaged a particular machine when, or other questions equally trivial (in amount) and inherently insoluble.

TOWARD A USABLE PRO-FORMA

It is desirable to draw up a standard pro-forma for the organisation of data in all acquisition valuation cases. Where a number of similar cases involve consistent special features an adjusted version of the pro-forma can be constructed.

Five basic elements must enter into any satisfactory pro-forma:
1. Balance sheet analysis (preferably for at least five years)
   (a) Book net worth
   (b) Book net current assets
   (c) medium and long-term liabilities
   (d) Notes on possible bad (or grossly over or undervalued) assets, unexplained year to year changes, etc.
2. Profit and loss analysis (also five years or more)
   (a) Pre and post-tax profits (annual and average)
   (b) Whether a trend (up or down), a static, or a cyclical pattern
   (c) Pre and post-tax profits, adjusted by adding back interest on medium or long-term debt to pre-tax profit, and using that figure less pro-forma company tax to estimate adjusted post-tax profit
   (d) Notes on special features—e.g. loss carry-forward, initial allowance effects on taxation, significant non-recurring profits or losses on—say— devaluation, bad debt or inventory writeoff, etc.
   (e) Notes on any special reason to suppose past profits will be a poor guide to future profits.
3. Adjustments to acquisition date
Needed only if balance sheet and profit/loss account either at or approximately at date of takeover are not available from the acquired firm. In that case a reconstructed balance sheet (especially as to current assets and outside liabilities) is needed. Minor divergences in balance sheet and acquisition dates for large firms with good accounting systems can usually be handled on an *ad hoc* basis.
4. Alternative valuations
   (a) Ex-Owner's claim (and how computed)
   (b) Book net worth
   (c) Pre-tax profit multiple plus net current assets
   (d) Pre-tax profit multiple (adjusted for interest as at 2-c) plus net current assets less medium long-term liabilities
   (e) and (f) Post-tax parallels to methods (c) and (d). In each case the reason for the earnings multiple used should be stated.
5. Special features
Notes on any special characteristics of firm (or assets) which may be relevant to valuation.

No pro-forma can ever be a substitute for analysis, evaluation of data, and judgement. What it can be is a means of organising and presenting data to make analysis, evaluation, judgement easier, more systematic, and less likely to miss any key point.

FACE VALUE, INTEREST, PERIOD: ELEMENTS OF A SETTLEMENT

Because no single formula has any particular claim to universal applicability, let alone universal superiority, selecting a valuation formula is a matter of choice. The logical basis of that choice for the public sector negotiator is economy to the state and its institutions. Primarily that means economy of payments to be made, subject to three constraints: that the formula can be explained and defended domestically to support groups critical to decision-takers; argued plausibly to ex-owners and other external parties with whose opinion one is concerned; and used to reach a settlement without undue delay and allocations of skilled manpower. For example literally revaluing every asset of a large firm after a physical check is not a plausible approach, because it fails to meet the last constraint.

Choosing the valuation formula is part of setting the framework of negotiations. Framework-setting is critical, because once a general pattern is set by one side the other is engaged in seeking marginal adjustments and limited in what gains it can make without appearing to be 'unreasonable' in demanding to go back to the beginning and start anew. It is of course still more difficult to withdraw a framework proposed by oneself if it turns out to be advantageous to the other party. At an early stage the loss of face in such a retreat may be a lower cost than continuing down an unpropitious route. Therefore it is critical to run rough checks on the figures likely to result from alternative valuation formulae before formally proposing or agreeing (as opposed to discussing in general while reserving a position on their acceptability) which to use in any particular case. This is not an area in which rigid adherence to one formula or set of formulae is likely to be prudent.

Valuation proper affects but does not uniquely determine the cost of a settlement. Two other factors are integral in all cases: interest paid on outstanding balances; and period of payment. The lower the interest rate and the longer the average period of repayment the lower the true cost of any given principal sum agreed as compensation will be to the acquiring state. All three factors—valuation, period of payment, and interest—should therefore be kept in mind during negotiation. Changes in any one affect the true cost of acquisition, but it is often easier to adjust the period and phasing of payment than the amount of compensation.

For the period to affect total true cost, the interest rate must be below the normal international borrowing rate facing the acquiring state.[18] Otherwise an international loan to finance a cash settlement would be just as advantageous. In the Tanzanian case almost all formal nationalisations involved 6 per cent interest, defended on the ground that it was the going rate for Tanzania's medium-term public debt. It was argued that the acquired assets were in Tanzania, so that this was a relevant rate and that it was below the 10–15 per cent discount rate implicit in most of the settlement figures because government securities are less risky than equity investments and therefore always yield lower rates of return. In some quasi-nationalisation settlements 7 per cent interest was negotiated. Whether rates below 7–8 per cent could have been negotiated on nationalisation settlements in 1973, as opposed to 1967, is unclear, because the market rate for Eurodollar loans to small governments with weak economies had risen from—say—9 per cent to the order of 15 per cent over that period.

Once an interest rate below a market rate is agreed as part of the settlement, then extension of the repayment period lowers the true cost of the acquisition. In the Tanzanian case a downpayment of 20–30 per cent—usually about fifteen to twenty-four months after acquisition because of the time required by negotiation—and the balance (with accrued interest) over five to fifteen years was achieved. Beside reducing the true cost this phasing had two further advantages:

(a) for almost all individual acquisitions public sector earnings on the investment exceeded compensation payments in all years except that of the downpayment (and for that year were often covered by the previous year's profit);

(b) for the foreign exchange balance as a whole, compensation payments in every year were exceeded by the profits which would have been owned by foreign ex-owners (but which now accrued to the public sector), and were probably exceeded by the portion of those profits which would otherwise have been remitted.

Therefore both national surplus and the foreign account balance were improved even during the period of maximum compensation payments. Indeed by the early 1970s the 1967 acquisitions were yielding after tax profits in excess of Sh100 million on a total principal sum of compensation of the order of Sh250 million and against an annual (principal and interest) compensation flow which had never exceeded Sh50 million and by then had fallen to about Sh30 million.

The basic goals to be sought in as many individual cases as possible and for all acquisitions taken together are:

(a) public enterprise profits in excess of annual interest and principal compensation payments;

(b) balance of payments savings on remitted profits also in excess of annual compensation.

This does not necessarily mean a formal tying of payments to profits. Especially where no joint venture is created, it is probable that such a formula will be costly, because ex-owners will estimate future profits pessimistically and thus overestimate the period before they will be paid off, thereby raising the minimum valuation they will accept. The only profit-tied settlement in the Tanzanian case was a quasi-nationalisation of 50 per cent of the oil refinery. In that case the facts of a joint venture and of a refinery charge formula to the user companies, which guarded profits against cost increases, meant that the repayment flows could be calculated fairly accurately and with limited risk even under a profit-tied formula.

Whether the profits are literally used to make compensation payments is equally a matter for case-by-case evaluation. If an acquired firm requires expansion it may make little sense for it to pay funds to the Treasury to meet compensation instalments and then borrow the funds back. It may in general be more sensible to treat compensation as equity investment in the public sector firms and to collect dividends on the basis of firm surplus generation and approved investment needs. In Tanzania most compensation has been turned into state equity capital, although a portion has been treated as medium term loans to the new public sector firms.

If special contracts—e.g. for management or technical services—and/or a continued minority private ownership stake accompany nationalisation, these also affect the compensation bargaining. The ex-owners would not contract to provide services unless they expected to make a profit on them, and will expect to secure profit flows on a minority stake. The expectation of these profits will normally make them ready to agree to a lower price than they otherwise would for the acquired assets (or shares).

EXPLAINING THE RESULT

One final feature of a settlement which is critical is that it must be in a form each party can defend to his own principals (e.g. Party Executive, Board of Directors) and supporters (e.g. urban workers, shareholders). Thus a set of numbers picked at random are not usually adequate, even if bargaining itself at times seems little more organised than that. It is not necessary that each party put the same interpretation on the settlement (that might hamper its chances of acceptance) beyond a joint statement that it has been agreed and a joint commitment to defend it against criticism and to implement it.

On occasion the need to defend a settlement may lead to otherwise peculiar provisions. In one Tanzanian quasi-nationalisation case the departing owners insisted on $9 million principal payments while

Tanzania valued (conservatively as it turned out) the net assets as worth $6 – 7 million. The sellers disclosed a need to avoid a capital loss on their books in respect of debt, but a willingness to forego interest if the face value of the compensation could be at least $9 million. In the end phased payments over fourteen years (with an average period of about six years) totalling $9 million were agreed. At a discount rate of 7 per cent the present (date of settlement) value of the compensation was slightly under $7 million. The ex-owners had avoided a book loss on the principal sum of their loans, Tanzania had avoided paying over $7 million. A $7 million principal sum paid with interest at 7 per cent over the same period would have cost Tanzania the same amount (and been equally acceptable to Tanzanian negotiators or decision-takers) but would have posed problems for the ex-owners in respect of their Boards. This illustrates the value of considering the other party's particular goals to see whether an agreement can be reconstructed—at the same cost to one's own side—to be more acceptable to and defensible by the other side.

6. POLITICAL-TECHNICAL INTERACTION: TOWARDS NEGOTIATION AND OPERATION

How to proceed with a nationalisation exercise depends to a considerable extent on whether technical and managerial capacity is called in to implement it after a basic political decision has produced a fairly detailed list of what is to be acquired and in what way, or earlier as an input into reaching the political decision. There can, of course, be mixed cases. In Tanzania, Treasury personnel advocated acquiring grossly neglected sisal estates with a high yield potential as early as 1970, on the basis of Treasury and Sisal Corporation managerial/financial analysis. However, in the event, their acquisition over 1971 – 3 was basically politically determined with only details of implementation (including legislation) left for technical-level action.

To all intents and purposes any government acquisition is a nationalisation so far as appropriate procedures for valuation, coordination, and parallel measures are concerned. The reason is simple—refusal to accept terms of the type a state would offer after nationalisation will usually lead to statutory nationalisation, even if initial discussions were technically of a 'willing buyer' and 'willing seller' type. If the same results can be achieved without legislation and with a more cordial relationship with those acquired, then it may be as well to avoid statutory nationalisation. Legislation is extra work; statutory acquisition may have some marginal publicity effects. However, the gains are usually minor; it is rarely worth paying much to obtain them. Whatever the sequence, it is imperative to maintain coordination and full information flows in the public sector, among all the Ministries and public corporations concerned with the technical and negotiation questions. Regular consultation and clear resolution of differences or ambiguities as soon as possible is important. In Tanzania the Treasury's assumption of the leading role in valuation and compensation meant that it was responsible for coordination. In any country some central coordinating point is needed for all acquisition cases.

Lack of a coherent national position prevents negotiators (and for that matter analysts) from knowing what they are seeking. When carried to the point of vehement intra-public sector debate, it often suggests a confusion between the (presumably) common interests of the public sector units and the (presumably) more divergent ones of the ex-owners. Such divergences are especially damaging when carried into negotiations with the former owner. At best he is unable to frame any consistent response, because he is unable to determine which public sector position he should respond to; at worst he pursues an effective set of divide-and-rule tactics. In one Tanzanian case confused public sector positions at initial negotiations certainly increased the length and reduced the coherence of negotiations, and made an agreed settlement much harder to secure, even after an agreed Tanzanian position had finally been evolved.

This does not mean all institutions must or should attend all internal procedural or external negotiating meetings. The former may be desirable, but sometimes (e.g. at legislative drafting stage) is unduly cumbersome. The latter is likely to be counterproductive; negotiating teams with more than three or four speaking members are likely to prove unwieldy and harmfully confusing both to the other party and to themselves.

A political decision may take the form of a list of firms acquired at once with all legislation and organisation to be done after acquisition or a decision to acquire certain stated firms or categories of firms by a given date with exact details (including particular firms in some cases and legislation in most) to be prepared before formal publication and acquisition. Whenever practicable, the latter exercise is preferable. It does not prevent political decisions or announcement of action, but it does allow a more coherent set of actions and possibly even a more carefully articulated set of political decisions. In cases of initially *ad hoc* acquisitions it is a critical responsibility of civil servants to mobilise action to organise, regularise, and detail acquisition and related issues at once, and not to let matters drag on for years—as is by no means unknown. Operational efficiency, even more than expeditious settlement, requires clarifying what has been acquired and who is responsible for running it.

In many cases the exact list of firms needed to be acquired in order to implement a decision to take effective control of a sector is unclear before analysis or the actual units covered by a very general definition; this will require securing both a workable technical rule-of-thumb method and political clarity on intent. The Tanzania Acquisition of Buildings Act illustrates the second case. It also appears to illustrate inadequate liaison. It was never intended either to acquire genuine tenant-purchase flats or buildings not built for landlordism but subsequently partially let—that was clear from presidential statements. The prolonged and complex steps needed to give retrospective effect after acquiring these types of building (or parts of building) could and should have been minimised by securing clear political directives on types of building not to acquire and embodying them either in Regulations to the Act or administrative instructions to administering officers. The first case is illustrated by grain mills and sisal estates. A draft list of over one hundred mills was in existence but was cut down to two major units, a medium-sized food processing company, and six small mills (subsequently irreverently called the 'six dwarfs') believed to be adequate to dominate the industry without imposing major managerial and compensation complications. In the event, it is probably true that at least three of the six were also unnecessary and certainly the bother and cost in time of negotiations in relation to business volume or asset value was incredibly high for all six. Management proved uncontrollable too, until all public sector milling units were consolidated—a situation causing some losses of revenue and surplus, and nearly resulting in a Sh1.5 million loss (or straying away) of assets. This experience suggests that nationalisation for centralised operation of a large number of small units poses special problems. If it cannot be avoided (e.g. by using decentralised or cooperative public sector operators) speedy reorganisation in a more consolidated structure is needed.

In the case of sisal, detailed pre-acquisition studies were made with the following guidelines finally agreed:

(a) the new Tanzania Sisal Corporation and an existing joint venture to have about 60 per cent of total production capacity;
(b) the three largest private groups to be left intact, because they were well run and would not go out of business or slaughter-cut;
(c) no hopelessly unviable estates to be acquired.

PROBABLE SCENARIOS

It is perhaps useful to outline the cases in which a political decision which is followed by technical implementation and those in which technical advice which is followed by a political decision leading to implementation are more probable. In the first group fall:

(a) a basic shift toward a socialist mode of production; e.g. the Arusha package in Tanzania comprising banking and insurance, most foreign trade, and a majority of large scale manufacturing plus the one large plantation-dominated export crop;
(b) taking total control of critical sectors, because they can or do dominate the rest of the economy (e.g. banking);

(c) providing adequate public sector size in an industry or group of industries to make the public sector dominant;

(d) redressing what has come to be seen as a particularly unacceptable form of exploitation (e.g. the Tanzania Building Acquisition Act 1971, when rental property had become conspicuous as the one area not affected by the 1967–70 steps towards a transition to socialism);

(e) moving to end a situation which has become inconsistent enough with the general political economic and sociopolitical patterns to create serious tensions (e.g. Tanzania Acquired Coffee Estates legislation in 1973 when a foreign plantation enclave had become clearly incongruous in the context both of transition to socialist villages as a rural strategy, and of the sharp reduction of real income differentials as a strategy for concentrating resources on meeting basic material needs);

(f) dealing with specific cases of misconduct of an economic nature other than those directly called to decision-takers' attention by officials.

On the other hand, technical proposals are likely to precede political action in cases of:

(a) a sector having become important and buoyant enough to make acquiring direct control through ownership newly critical (e.g. the aluminium/steel products company—ALAF – in Tanzania in 1973);

(b) past success with part of a sector indicating desirability of completing the takeover (e.g. Tanzania acquisition of remaining private shipping agencies in 1973);

(c) conflicts of interest with partners or simply feeling they have come to be too costly or no longer needed (e.g. in Tanzania Cement 1973 as a conflict case, and cigarettes over 1974–6 as a more amicable phasing out);

(d) basic divergence of interests between Tanzania and the partner on production and development requiring buying out partner (e.g. meat packing in Tanzania in 1974 where Tanzania's concern both for the domestic market and for the welfare of growers and the technical requirements of expansion on a new site conflicted with basic partner interests in maximising a particular export to related companies serving traditional markets);

(e) lack of technical competence by the existing partner to play a dynamic role in the development of the industry leading to need to buy out partner and buy needed knowledge elsewhere.

IMPROVING TECHNICAL PREPARATION

These categories suggest that over time in most countries technical preparation before political decision is likely to become more general.

They also suggest that more serious attention at the technical level to logical (economically, socially, or politically) extension of the public sector by acquisition would be useful to political decision-takers and ease the problems of implementation. The problems of abandoned sisal estates in Tanzania should have led to joint agriculture, lands, treasury, sisal corporation proposals in 1970; the evident need to phase out the settler farmers should have led to technical background on how to acquire, operate, and pay studies before a political decision became urgent.

The fact that public sector expansion by acquisition will continue in many countries has implications for public sector financial institutions. This is not necessarily to argue that no finance should be provided to the private sector, or that it should necessarily take equity as its initial form. One logical conclusion may often be that loans to private sector companies should be convertible into equity or accompanied by rights to buy 60 per cent of the equity on or after a stated future date; i.e. build in a route to national ownership dominance. Such a policy would facilitate orderly future expansion by acquisition.

Some relevant issues for the cases in which technical study and advice precedes the political decision to acquire (or to move from joint ventures to wholly controlled units) can be illustrated by looking at two Tanzanian examples:

The operations of the Commissioner for Public Investment, price control bodies, and the industrial promotion ministerial coordinating committee clearly showed that ALAF was becoming the key company in the metal products sector and was integrating backward into heavy rolling as well as moving laterally into important new products notably steel pipe and potentially scrap smelting. In effect it was one of the key heavy industries in Tanzania, and one whose development could assist or damage public sector plans for an integrated basic steel capacity to come into production about 1980.

The initial reason for not acquiring 60 per cent of ALAF in 1967 had been its very weak financial position and the great managerial and technical effort necessary to achieve recovery. By 1972 the owners had achieved a dramatic turnaround, so that this problem was no longer a deterrent.

Therefore socialist transition dictated moving to a dominant position in ALAF and integrating it as a central part of the metal sector. However, because ALAF was critically dependent on imports of scarce raw materials bought through the owner's group management company, and on exports sold largely to other group companies, immediate 100 per cent takeover was not advisable. This conclusion was reinforced by the management company's evident expertise in planning expansion and backward integration, which for at least a few years would be clearly superior to (and more based on experience than) any possible Tanzanian substitute.

From a decision to advise nationalisation and to advise an initial joint venture form, another question arose—whether to act by buying existing shares or by creating (and buying) new shares to provide the equity base for more rapid expansion? Given the key role of the metal products industry which justified large investment in expansion and the need to ensure a serious interest on the part of the former 100 per cent owner in how ALAF prospered as a joint venture, the latter course was adopted.

Two logical consequences of this package were accepted but with somewhat slow implementation. Firstly expansion (and integration into an overall metal sector programme) needed to be agreed and implemented rapidly, both to secure the desired structural gains and to bolster the investible surplus flow to the joint venture which was limited so long as the payment for new shares remained in 5 per cent government paper and was not transformed into new production units. Secondly dividend approval at reasonable levels was critical to maintaining live minority partner interest in the company.

Serious conflicts over management style, worker relations, expansion plans, sources of equipment, price levels for output, and fees characterised Tanzania relations with Tanganyika Portland Cement's expatriate management contractor. The results included loss of planned output, very poor labour participation and morale (leading to overt sabotage in some cases), and very high management fees. The latter included a high per tonne element, perhaps reasonable when output was at 160,000 tonnes but not when it was set to reach 400,000 tonnes with no major consequential cost increase to the managing agents (one of two private partners in the joint venture).

Continued disagreement in these areas led to a decision to complete nationalisation, thus terminating the joint venture. Originally, direct hire of managers (not a new agreement) was planned, but an interim management agreement with a Pakistani firm was eventually thought safer. However, coordination among public sector bodies was weak. Despite the fact that the reasons for completing nationalisation urgently required the immediate installation of a new management, a lag of about eight months ensued and handover arrangements were not particularly smooth or effective; neither was effective control over the new management's performance secured.

7. MAKING ACQUISITION EFFECTIVE: INITIAL STEPS

A checklist of major implementation areas following political decisions is crucial because failure to proceed in a coherent, complete, and orderly fashion hinders making the political decision effective, and proceeding in a technically unsound manner instead of finding a sound one is to be gravely disrespectful to politicians by implying they wish their decisions to be implemented ineffectually rather than efficiently and effectively.[19] Among the key items on the list are:

(a) establishing an effective physical and data collection presence in the acquired unit. Ideally this means at least some senior local manager from the start (e.g. a deputy general manager with an agricultural background in the Sisal Corporation case who became general manager about a year later) and at a minimum it means regular collection and checking of data from a retained or newly hired outside management. Following this pattern gave effective control over banks in 1967, and avoided a deposit panic or interruption of their operations. Failure to do the same with the six small grain mills led to significant waste of funds and innumerable problems of unscrambling data and recovering funds at a later stage;

(b) taking steps to insure that no breakdown in operations occurs. Instructions must be issued to the new or old top management as to how to proceed, and in particular instructions to carry on normal day to day business—subject to any specified rectrictions—until directed otherwise. In normal takeovers, the ex-owner's management rarely leaves at once, so that this aspect poses no problems if directions are given and a national supervisory presence installed. The situation is different if the acquired units are entrusted to totally inexperienced local units and the ex-owner (or his manager) sent away at once or if acquisition follows an owner's departure. In such cases a watching brief is needed to ensure that breakdowns in operation are identified and put right promptly;

(c) determining the form of management and ownership requires consideration of the nature and size of the firm, how it relates to the sector of which it is a part, and how that sector relates to national goals and plans. This issue needs to be settled rapidly, both to avoid jurisdictional disputes and to allow reorganisation and development on the new basis to begin as rapidly as possible. For large firms in Tanzania the only real option is attachment to a sectoral parastatal or creation of a new sectoral parastatal. However, for smaller units allocation to either regional or district level control, or to a cooperative or an Ujamaa village is now both consistent with Tanzanian sociopolitical policy and with rather general economic and technical realities. A holding company for forty small, scattered coffee farms would not be sensible technically any more than politically. The identification of future public sector ownership and control bodies need not mean immediate transfer of title to them—interim ownership by the Treasury Registrar or other acquiring agency may prove convenient—but it should mean immediate transfer of management responsibility;

(d) the intended basis of payment needs to be determined promptly because it will determine whether special legislative provisions are needed. This means working out a draft compensation formula and its

rationale, even if Cabinet approval on specific settlements is taken later;
(e) the form of compensation may need to be considered at once,
although this is not usually imperative. A general power to the Minister
of Finance to set terms and conditions (as given in most of Tanzanian
legislation) will usually be adequate. A power for a single body—usually
a Treasury—to review proposed compensation, whoever negotiates it, is
critical. Special means of payment require early decision. If it is
intended to pay in a special government stock issue, this does need to be
decided promptly. Payment for new shares made in government stock
cashable for approved new investment has also been used. The real
decision was to expand by acquisition, locking in the old 100 per cent
owner's funds to ensure his continued concern with the firm's welfare
and to guard continued purchases from the acquired unit by group
companies outside Tanzania;
(f) where and in what currency to pay is normally simple—in the ex-
owner's country of residence in its currency, but with the amount
payable expressed in the nationalising country's currency. The problem
of inadequate reserves to make transfers need not block settlements and
schedules. A settlement is a contract and is subject to exchange control
rules in force from time to time. Therefore, it is possible to suspend
remittances until the situation in respect of foreign exchange improves,
in the same way as remittances of dividends or of loan principal can be
suspended. A negotiated settlement and a suspension of remittance
resulting from a general tightening of exchange control is likely to raise
less difficulties than a specific negotiated but not ratified settlement or a
deliberate dragging out of negotiations. Inability to remit on time (i.e. *de
facto* rescheduling) does not raise either private or public international
response as serious as suspicion of unwillingness to negotiate or to pay
agreed settlements;
(g) finally, the form of legislation needs to be determined promptly and
with full participation of all concerned public sector bodies including
the future public sector ownership and management units. The
substantive issues noted earlier must be resolved before legal personnel
can be asked to draft and the nature of the decisions should be explained
to them, to allow legislation which is consistent with the substantive
intent. A lawyer with experience in prior nationalisation exercises can
be of significant value in discussing substantive issues and should, if
available, be involved at that stage, not simply brought in to draft at the
last minute.

ACQUIRED NET LIABILITIES: LOSS MINIMISATION

A special problem arises when examination of an acquired firm shows
negative true net worth. This is possible even in the case of companies

technically appraised before takeover, but is more common in cases of broad political selection of target firms. The problem arises because nationalisation normally involves acquiring firm liabilities as well as assets, especially when the acquisition is hurried and little or nothing is done about handover because, in such cases, the ex-owner is unlikely to be able, or particularly eager, to satisfy his creditors. Several possible courses of action to minimise acquiring deficits exist, and, except for the last, were used in Tanzania:

(a) debts to ex-owners or close associates can be treated as equity;

(b) specific liabilities can be disallowed and 'returned' to ex-owner if they are not arm's length transactions or were clearly irrecoverable before nationalisation:

(c) the firm can be denationalised, a local creditor can file for receivership, the assets can then be sold free of liabilities and the receiver pays the creditors on a pro-rata basis. This was done *de facto* with one tea estate and was suggested—and perhaps should have been done—in respect of a construction firm;

(d) the deficit—if minor in relation to the damage of repudiation—can be treated as a cost of taking greater control of the economy;

(e) the ex-owner can be pressed to make good the deficit. This is rarely practical unless a pre-existing guarantee or contractual violation can be proved and the ex-owner has other assets in the country;

(f) the acquisition legislation can specify that government acceptance of liabilities should be limited to a sum not exceeding the value of assets acquired, and that in the case of liabilities exceeding this amount pro-rata distribution under standard receivership and liquidation principles would be carried out.

Which approach is most appropriate will need to be judged on a case by case basis. Accepting the deficit is not usually appropriate if large sums are involved, but if the losers from repudiation would be public sector bodies or a significant number of innocent normal citizens then it may have to be accepted even though the deficit is large. Massive and frequent repudiation of debts can be very damaging if it is confused with inability or refusal of parastatal bodies to meet their own subsequent obligations.

The acquisition of assets only leaving all liabilities to be settled by the ex-owner, is a superficially attractive course. However, it has serious drawbacks. If the creditors are domestic parties unrelated to the ex-owner it will cause maximum domestic economic dislocations and possibly erosion of political support for nationalisation. If the creditors are foreign third parties (e.g. banks, manufacturers, commercial houses) they are likely to react by refusing to contract new business with the public sector and possibly the private sector on normal commercial terms. This is not a reaction to nationalisation as such but to the fact that it has been carried out in a way making all normal commercial contracts—not merely those related to foreign investment as such—uncertain and in an unusual and unpredictable way. This damage to commercial credibility and credit-rating is usually not one a nationalising state will find it prudent to accept (a conclusion reached by Chile and—in transactions with most non-U.S. firms—Cuba as much as by Tanzania).

IN THE PUBLIC INTEREST: BEYOND ACQUISITION AND INITIAL OPERATION

Nationalisation is not simply a matter of buying and paying for assets. In this sense too it is analogous to a takeover bid. A takeover bidder rarely plans to run his acquisition in the same way with the same personnel. No more has Tanzania seen nationalisation as a means to citizenising the neo-colonial ownership, production, expansion, management, worker re-lationship, and customer service structures, and by so doing to perpetuate them in African dress. To do so is not perceived by Tanzanian decision-takers as 'nationalisation in the public interest'. They have seen the basic purposes to be served by nationalisation as:

(a) achieving effective control over the economy through broadening the public directly productive sector;
(b) maintaining and improving the existing operations of the acquired firm, with respect both to the type, volume, and quality of service provided to the public, and with respect to the generation of investible surplus. The latter point is no less critical than the first if the public enterprise sector is large in Tanzania three quarters of company tax comes from the parastatal sector, as does over Sh100 million a year in dividends to the Treasury with about Sh300 million retained earnings available in 1973 and more in later years toward parastatal gross investment;
(c) developing operations in such a way as to strengthen national economic integration, i.e. provide increasing markets for products of other domestic productive sector units and an increasing range of inputs into their operations;
(d) expanding and diversifying output in accordance with mass needs for consumer goods and services and/or specific national plan require-ments for expanded production of capital intermediate, and export goods.
(e) serving as a means to developing technical, technological, and managerial knowledge under national control and a route to training citizens to have and use that knowledge;
(f) creating participatory work patterns based on internalised (as opposed to external authoritarian) discipline; (a goal perhaps less

generaliseable from Tanzanian to other groups of national decision-takers);
(g) extending the areas of activity effectively coordinated into the national planning process.

Therefore whether it orginates from technical advice or from political decision it is critical that implementation be based on a detailed understanding of why nationalisation has taken place; what gains are to be expected from it, and what complementary measures will be needed to realise them; and which areas, if any, require urgent attention to limit interim difficulties. Different cases are very different indeed in these critical elements. The basic reasons why continued partial private shareholding and management inputs were seen as useful to Tanzania for at least an interim period at ALAF are very similar to those counselling immediate 100 per cent takeover and new management in the cement case. Different objective realities require different courses of action; to try to draft action without studying the underlying realities of the case is to run a very grave risk of making expensive mistakes.

To ensure that nationalisation does further basic aims requires careful attention before, at the time of, and just after takeover, to key operational and management areas as they pose problems for the firm. This exercise of review, control, and planning does not, of course, cease six months or a year after acquisition, (just as, ideally, it does not begin only on the day of acquisition) but it then becomes integrated into the overall structure of planning for, regulating, operating, and reviewing the public directly productive sector.

TOWARD EFFECTIVE CONTROL

Key areas include:

(a) general operating management;
(b) financial management;
(c) technical management;
(d) domestic marketing;
(e) external marketing;
(f) external purchasing;
(g) technological backup both in respect of personnel to cope with emergencies, of special testing and research services, and of a flow of data on new technological and technical possibilities applicable to the firm;
(h) short-term forward-planning capacity in respect of ongoing operations and short-term development;
(i) medium-term forward-planning capacity, especially in respect of significant changes in scale and potential new products or services.

Not all of these areas are likely to pose serious problems in respect of any single acquired unit. Nor are the problem areas likely to take identical form for a large, technologically complex and sensitive unit (e.g. an oil refinery); a large, but technologically routine unit (e.g. a group of sisal estates); or a small, simple technology unit (e.g. a single coffee farm). Once the problems are identified it is necessary to determine:

(a) what can be done with internal public sector institutional, personnel, knowledge, and financial resources;

(b) by direct hire of personnel and purchase of knowledge;

(c) through acquiring the services of a new contractor, whether as a managing contractor for a broad range of services or on a more limited basis to supplement direct public sector inputs;

(d) by retaining some form of services contract with the former (or former majority) owners, whether in a joint venture or some other relationship.

The fourth approach normally looks easiest for large firms. Over the short term (say six to twelve months) it has a great deal to recommend it in the majority of cases, because it avoids a break with technical/managerial continuity, provides a period to learn the business better, and a probability of avoiding serious initial errors through inexperience. However, there is a real danger in extending that argument to the extent of making out a general case for joint ventures and long-term management agreements. That route hampers serious change and medium-term planning. With the growth of experienced citizen managerial, professional, and technical personnel (e.g. in Tanzania in 1973 as opposed to 1967) it may often be no longer evidently desirable even as a first stage. In Tanzania the National Bank of Commerce has been a major success at least as much because of as in spite of the very rapid withdrawal of most expatriate staff and the lags in securing a much smaller group of direct hire expatriates to fill initial voids in staffing and knowledge. True, concentration on NBC direct management did mean other nationalised firms had to make very extensive use of ex-owner services, but that was a constraint imposed by shortage of personnel, knowledge, and institutional capacity, not by any inherent superiority of contract management. Certainly when major reorganisation and innovation is required, continuity of management has serious limitations. In general, the greater the changes in the nature of the operation after nationalisation or the more central the nationalised unit to overall political economic control and strategy, the stronger is the case for direct management. Banking in the Tanzanian context was the extreme case on both criteria.

The first question should be what can be done from public sector capacities to meet the problem. The answer is usually that a good deal more than nationalising states may suppose can be achieved in this way;

especially if they can locate a company with experience in parallel fields and the capacity to hire staff directly or through technical assistance.

The Tanzanian practice of moving at least one experienced citizen with a record of managerial success (whether in the parastatal or the government sector) to significant new acquired firms as general manager, deputy general manager, or controller is a good example to follow, even when significant direct hire or contract management components will also be needed. Especially if—as is usual in Africa or the Pacific—the newly acquired firm has had little citizenisation, a number of middle-level managers should also be moved into place at once.

Usually some gaps in available national personnel and knowledge will exist. In Tanzania both NBC and the Sisal Corporation (the outstanding successes of immediate direct control) did use a handful of key direct hire expatriates selectively chosen from their predecessors' staffs or newly hired from abroad. Similarly, planning and internal consultancy capacity has usually been (and will usually be) weak and not easily created rapidly within the firm. NBC was an exception because it had to create research and planning capacity rapidly to be at all effective; TSC's planning department was very weak for several years. However, local interim options exist, e.g. use of public sector holding or production group company to provide planning capacity, securing ministerial and financial institution advice on firm planning, hiring local institutions (e.g. in Tanzania the National Institute of Productivity and Institute of Finance Management), or creating local *ad hoc* bodies (e.g. restructuring of import and wholesale sector, price commission creation) for provision of specific planning, management, training, and consultancy work. The cases have included some of the best consultancy work done in Tanzania on institutional planning and restructuring, while some of the worst has been done by high powered, expensive international firms. In one case a prior foreign consultancy exercise on the same sector led to the situation of utter chaos requiring the local consultancy and reorganisation.

Direct hire of foreign personnel is a means of strengthening a local institution. So is direct purchase of a limited study—e.g. a technical plant design—or service—e.g. a raw material buying contract. These methods leave control much more securely in national hands than do more general contracts and also tend to give rise to more rapid training and promotion of citizens. They do suffer from the fact that, unless under technical assistance auspices, a good manager, especially on the technical side, will be unwilling to take a short-term contract except at a very high salary because of career damage and domestic professional re-entry problems. Thus to secure an entire senior management by direct hire could well prove more expensive and less satisfactory in terms of personnel competence than a management contract.

Whether a new contractor will be preferable to the ex-owner depends on why the nationalisation has occurred, how well the firm was being run, what other competent 'bidders' there are, and whether a contract very different in structure from (probably, but not necessarily, also narrower than) the former arrangements, is sought. In the case of the Tanzanian cigarette company no evident purpose would have been served by switching management, and considerable dislocation of operations would have been likely. Given the reasons for ending the joint ventures, the reverse was true in the cement case.

EVALUATING CONTRACTORS

Before deciding on a management, technical, or export sales contractor several questions should be asked:

(a) can it do the basic operating job well?
(b) what is its experience and record in the country considering hiring it and/or relatively similar countries?
(c) what reputation does it have in its home country? The proponents of new managements often seem not to have asked that question, nor indeed even the question as to competence. A new contractor is not better simply because it is new to a country, much less new to a line of production, and being on less than the best of terms with major firms in its home country is not necessarily evidence in its favour;
(d) can it provide a regular technical backup and knowledge flow which is adequate for exploring new developments by the firm as well as continuing ongoing operations?
(e) on the record (in the firm, elsewhere is the country, abroad) will the proposed contractor be willing and able (if pushed by the Board) to train citizens rapidly and competently?
(f) what is the proposed contractor's probable response to Board or other public sector policy directives—intelligent compliance, blind following, bland obstruction, or open hostility?
(g) how much will be charged compared both to firm size and profit and to what the other prospective candidates would charge? This is very far from being the only and may well not normally be the proper dominant issue. A firm ranking high on the previous points is worth more than one with a lower rating. Certainly the fee should be bargained down and constructed to provide incentives for performance, but to get a second rate contractor for marginally less than a first rate one is a bad 'bargain';
(h) is there a better prospective contractor in sight?
Even if no long-term continued relation is envisaged there will always be certain things wanted from the ex-owner or ex-partner. The first and most obvious is an orderly handover. This should not normally be hard to achieve—'downing tools' before handover is likely to embitter com-

pensation talks and damage the owner's compensation settlement as well as general commercial relations with the acquiring state—results major firms usually wish to avoid.

Secondly a transitional management may be sought for a six to nine month period while more basic reorganisation is carried out—in Tanzania the import/export/wholesale sector was a case in point; the British banks (as opposed to Dutch, U.S., Indian, and Pakistani) were cases in which such an arrangement, while desired, was not acceptable to the ex-owners.

Thirdly there may be a need for some seconded staff as individuals not as part of an outside management team. This may be harder to achieve—especially if the individuals one desires to keep are highly competent and usable elsewhere in the group—but is sometimes possible.

Fourthly, a longer continued management agreement may be needed if the acquired firm has complex technology or technical business demands and the initial number of expatriates is high.

Finally, the ex-owners of one of a group of acquired firms may be appropriate as contract managers for a consolidated group spanning their own former firm and others: e.g. the managers and former part-owners of the second largest milling firm served as general managers of the consolidated National Milling Corporation.

TOWARD CONTROLLING THE CONTRACTOR

Once it has been decided that a contract is needed and who is likely to be the most satisfactory contractor, care must be taken to ensure that all the elements needed by the public sector are written into the agreement. Among the more important elements are:

(a) ensuring that the power to exercise effective control is vested in the Board, and that a Board with members capable of identifying key issues and exercising control over decisions on them is appointed;
(b) providing for adequate data flows to (and direct access to data by) the Board, the holding parastatal, the parent Ministry and specialised government analysis units (e.g. the Commissioner of Public Investments in Tanzania). Without such data no Board can be more than a tool in the hands of the management;
(c) provisions guaranteeing the effective transfer of knowledge through training programmes, technological data, and specifications, etc. Without such a transfer—the most obvious and often the key element of which is the citizen-training programme—the need to hire a management services supplier will grow greater, not less, over time;
(d) a clear listing of duties with penalty clauses for default and payments so structured as to encourage high performance: e.g. a low fixed fee, a fee on physical volume of activity above a normal target

level, a share in profits or trading profits as contrasted with a high fixed fee, and a unit fee on all output from the first tonne forward;

(e) a built-in process of citizen takeover of duties flowing from the training programme and, like it, having specific target dates for certain posts and certain functions to be performed by citizens. The exact dates and functions are normally best left to the Board. What it does need is a clause requiring the contractor to submit, secure Board approval for, and act on such a devolution process;

(f) safeguards against gross overpayment, especially in cases in which the probable results of the proposed formula are unclear because the sales or profits or both are hard to project, or the revised structure is likely to create large economies or diseconomies of scale. The milling management contract illustrated this. Profit depended on controlled grain and bread prices and the previous record as to setting a logical series of prices from farmer to bakery was weak. Thus a fee related to turnover not profit was agreed, but one with a ceiling on the total fee payable. In the event the National Milling Corporation management performed well enough to receive each year the ceiling fee; without such a cutoff they might have had about twice as much;

(g) renegotiation and review clauses ideally avoiding tying the public sector for longer than three years before a contractual right to review arises. Had such a clause existed in respect of the cement contract in Tanzania, the Tanzanian public enterprise side could probably have forced a lowering of the per tonne fee, and certainly avoided facing the significant claim for compensation in respect of breach of contract resulting from nationalisation and change of management during the validity of a long-term contract. Joint ventures and overall management agreements should never be seen as permanent forms; they are transitional. The sole exceptions to that rule are ones in which integral portions of logically combined operations take place in more than one country, or in which there really is an underlying broad common interest among the partners. A joint Tanzanian-European company producing, shipping, roasting and packing, wholesaling coffee might be an example of the former, and the Zambia-Tanzania oil pipeline of the second.

THE LIMITS OF NEGOTIATION AND OF CONTRACTS

Like valuation, contract negotiation is not an exact science. Best estimates of what will serve public sector interests best are needed, not utopian visions of perfect decisions based on perfect predictions about the future. Checklists of main points are more satisfactory than the fruitless quest for a draft contract complete with standard training and fee provisions suitable for all cases.[20] Experience—whether direct or gained by studying the past record of others—and coordination with other informed parties on the public sector side should lead to relatively good contracts. The implementation of contracts is at least as critical as their formulation and negotiation. However, that is neither something which can be ensured in the negotiating process nor is it, except in its preliminary stage, a part of acquisition, initial operation, and valuation. Similarly, joint ventures—unless they have very detailed and precise phase-out agreements in respect of the foreign (or domestic private sector) partner—will eventually give rise to a subsequent nationalisation exercise or something like it. That should be foreseen—and arrangements likely to maximise difficulties in a final takeover should be avoided—in negotiating a partial nationalisation settlement; it is not, by itself, a case against joint ventures. The operation of almost any set of agreements will diverge in some respects from the expectation of any of the parties (e.g. in one Tanzanian case it diverged so radically against the external partner as to cause it to seek major alterations on grounds of equity not wholly without justification), because the commercial future is always uncertain even in a context of economic planning. A need to alter arrangements because of new conditions or knowledge which was not available, and could not reasonably have been expected to be secured by the public sector negotiators, is neither a criticism of the initial arrangements nor comparable to bargaining mistakes and failures to secure and analyse data.

Even taken as a whole acquisition, initial operation, and valuation are the first steps in a process. The subsequent steps are part of other—and in most respects broader—aspects of public sector management and control and of national political economic development planning. What the first steps do is assist or hinder, set a course for, or require a change of course in, the subsequent ones. Therefore the importance attached to them is real; their impact continues long after they are in a formal sense complete, and their physical results consigned to dusty (or circular) files.

Notes

1 In fact, I deal here only with mainland Tanzania. Zanzibar—the other partner in the United Republic—also operated a sweeping series of nationalisations, but one more parallel to than linked with the mainland's and also one not considered in this study.

2 The data and views are not in themselves viewed as confidential or as secret by the United Republic. Many have been openly stated by senior politicians and public servants and are in fragmentary form included in various documents notably the 1967–8 through 1974–5 *Budget Speeches* (Dar es Salaam: Government Printer). However, there is no coherent single study, and use of materials is hampered by their being filed with materials which are viewed as

confidential or secret (or in some cases included in memoranda and papers whose other paragraphs are in part confidential or secret). This study is based on the author's recollections and working notes including those for an internal training paper for public servants engaged in future nationalisations. Any evaluations, judgements, or conclusions are those of the author and are not necessarily the same as those of the Tanzanian Treasury whose economic advisor he was over the period 1967 – 74.

3 'The Arusha Declaration' in J. K. Nyerere, *Freedom and Socialism* (Dar es Salaam: Oxford University Press, 1968). See also related speeches at chapters 27, 28, 29, 32, 35, 39 in the same volume. See also L. Cliffe and J. Saul (editors), *Socialism In Tanzania* (2 volumes), (Dar es Salaam: East African Publishing House, 1972); and R. H. Green, 'Political independence and the national economy', in C. Allen and R. Johnson (editors), *African Perspectives* (Cambridge: Cambridge University Press 1970).

4 A 50 per cent stake in Tanganyika Packers (with Liebig) was part of the deal which led to the firm's establishment. A 50 per cent stake in Williamson Diamonds was acquired as a settlement of estate duty on Dr Williamson's death and held to yield revenue.

5 The existing government stakes were largely transferred to the National Development Corporation which promoted a number of joint ventures. One textile mill provided on Chinese aid was the only major 100 per cent public sector productive unit founded while another privately financed one had 40 per cent NDC and 20 per cent cooperative ownership. A number of joint ventures in finance and commerce were founded over 1961 – 6 but with mixed micro results and no macro tendency toward a dominantly public directly productive sector.

6 Technically all that was nationalised were the private shares in the National Insurance Corporation which was then given the sole right to carry on new business. Existing private firm policies were not directly affected or their assets and liabilities acquired. So far as subsequent operation of the insurance business was concerned, however, this was *de facto* nationalisation.

7 In form existing provisions to take a 50 per cent government share were used in respect of the refinery. In practice the terms and conditions were not those of the original contract but of the parallel cases of nationalisation (or settlement negotiated subject to nationalisation).

8 For a fuller account see J. S. Saul, B. Van Arkadie, R. H. Green chapters in D.P. Ghai (ed.) *Economic Independence in Africa* (Nairobi: East African Literature Bureau, 1973); R. H. Green 'Income Distribution and the Eradication of Poverty in Tanzania' in I. L. Horowitz (ed.), *Equity, Income and Policy* (New York: Praeger, 1977) and bibliography to same.

9 The term is perhaps not very helpful but no less obscure substitute is widely accepted. Its use here in part relates to an early 1967 internal Tanzanian memorandum (still secret) on initial operation, compensation, and worker-participation measures for implementing the nationalisation measures following the Arusha declaration entitled 'Nationalization In The Public Interest' and critical of certain alternative proposals which were perceived by its authors as inconsistent either with the political economic aims of the Arusha declaration, with keeping the nationalised units operating, with medium-term surplus generation or with all three.

10 For a fuller account see C. Pratt, *The Critical Phase in Tanzania 1945 – 1968* (Cambridge: Cambridge University Press, 1976).

11 The present writer cannot claim to be an outside observer. He was involved to too great an extent for that. Further his analysis is within the broad goals of TANU (set out in more detail in Nyerere *op cit*; Pratt, *op cit*; Green, *op cit*.), not on the premises of either a 'right', a 'left' or a 'technocratic' basic critique of those goals. Finally it accepts that nationalisation was a necessary means toward TANU's goals and examines its requirements and problems, potentials, and limitations rather than questioning it root and branch—neither a transition to socialism or national political economic decision-taking appears practicable without ending private, and especially foreign private, dominance of large and medium-sized economic unit ownership.

12 What they did do was disinvest. However, that had more severe impact on sectors not nationalised, e.g. retail commerce, construction, road transport, than on those which were the object of nationalisations because in the 'non-nationalised' sectors there were far less adequate national or local public sector enterprise capacities to replace the retreating private capitalists.

13 This section owes a large debt to Roland Godfrey Brown—the chief legal consultant in the first five years of Tanzanian nationalisation exercises. It also—ironically—owes much to the British personnel who forced a crisis over the Buildings Acquisition Act and thus caused a much more explicit Tanzanian consideration of what we meant by 'fair'. Neither Mr. Brown nor, especially, the British are responsible for the conclusions drawn here.

14 A number of other implementation problems were forseen and did result in reformulations in the articulation of the buildings nationalisation. It can, however, be argued that in this case more time to review formulation could have been given officials—landlords could not go off with the buildings and were unlikely to damage them. As an involved official the author must accept part of the burden of his own criticism.

15 A significant body of theological writing in Latin America, Asia and Africa is in this tradition as are most World Council of Churches studies and statements.

16 This section and the following one owe a major debt to the late H. C. Steen-Hansen the auditing consultant in the first six years of Tanzanian national-isation exercises, and a significant one to Messrs Wood and Aldridge then of the Government Valuers' Department. They are not responsible, however, for the balance of conclusions drawn here.

17 Transfer pricing and artificial accounting leading to artificially low (or negative) declared profits have been cited as a reason against discounted cash flow valuation, e.g. in the Ethiopian case. However, if past profits are used as a guide and these are artificially low or negative then the valuation reached from them will be low and thus penalise the past transfer pricing/accounting exploitation. Transfer pricing/accounting devices raise far more serious problems for an asset-value based exercise than a net-earnings based one. If, however, overcharging of (or underpaying) the local unit has been combined with high declared profits then a need to offset against the (high) profit based valuation does arise.

18 If the acquiring country has large external reserves (e.g. Nigeria) the relevant interest rate is the one received on reserves which could be realised to make a cash settlement. Tanzania never had external asset levels making that

calculation relevant.

19 Put this bluntly these points may appear to be truisms. Unfortunately in practice officials do have a tendency to justify sloppiness on the grounds that it helps speed politically taken decisions and to avoid the bother of working out a sound technical approach on the ground that a political decision is beyond their power to criticise or reverse and therefore beyond their need to understand.

20 This point too may seem self evident. It is not so in practice. Both academics on leave to government and management consultants have a distinct tendency to try to develop the perfect format and contract in which one need only fill in a few blanks to 'read off' the 'correct' result. Apart from misdirecting the time of those seeking these el Dorados, the process creates procrustean beds which distort actual analyses and contracts. In the Tanzanian context it has the further drawback that it quite consciously seeks to deter thinking, initiative, and proposals except at the top; i.e. the form constructor and reader is dominant and the operating personnel are mindless automata if the process works as designed.

3 A Decision Without A Strategy: *Excess Profits in the Nationalisation of Copper in Chile*

JULIO FAUNDEZ*

1 INTRODUCTION

Executive Decree No. 92, signed by President Allende on 28 September 1971, was the single most important decision taken by his government and the one which provoked the greatest international interest.[1] By virtue of this decree, the government determined the amount that should be deducted, by concept of excess profits, in the computation of compensation due to three mining companies owned by the Kennecott Copper Corporation and by the Anaconda Company. The exercise of this power was part of an intricate procedure established by the Constitutional Amendment of July 1971, which nationalised the copper industry in Chile. As one would expect, the left-wing parties in Chile greeted this reduction of compensation with enthusiasm, while the companies affected by this measure described the action of the Chilean government as confiscatory.[2]

The excess profit deduction had an enormous impact on the amount of compensation that the nationalised companies expected. Indeed, the 774 million dollars deducted as excess profits made it impossible for three out of the five nationalised companies to receive any compensation at all. Furthermore, given that the book value of these three companies was

* I am grateful to Professor Richard Parker of the Universidad Central in Venezuela and to Professor Henry Steiner of Harvard University in the United States for their helpful comments on an earlier version of this paper. I acknowledge the generous financial support of the Joint Committee on Latin American Studies of the American Council of Learned Societies and the American Social Science Research Council which made possible the writing of this essay.

about 627 million dollars, in the final computation these companies ended up as debtors to the Chilean state. Anaconda's debt amounted to 78 million dollars and Kennecott's debt was close to 300 million dollars.[3]

Because of the impact which this deduction had in the compensation due to the nationalised companies, most of the studies which have dealt with the problem of excess profits have generally concentrated on analysing its significance as an international precedent. Some have analysed it as a problem of international justice linking it with the notion of unjust enrichment. Others have analysed it as a purely legal issue due to its relationship with the concepts of sovereignty and self-determination. The issue has also been explained in terms of the new wave of economic nationalism in the Third World.[4]

Due to the emphasis which all these studies place on the international aspects of the deduction of excess profits, they fail to raise the fundamental question which emerges from President Allende's decision: what factors led Allende to take a decision which apparently went beyond the limits of his own definition of the Chilean road to socialism and which later on provoked serious international complications for his government? In order to answer this question, it is necessary to study carefully some of the factors which underlie Allende's decision.

Even a superficial analysis of the political factors surrounding the excess profits deduction reveals a variety of apparently paradoxical circumstances. In the first place, the excess profit deduction was contrary to the general contours of the government's foreign policy. While the deduction decision was likely to generate conflict, Chile was simultaneously attempting to implement a conciliatory foreign policy. In the second place, the changes which Congress introduced to the excess profits provision radically altered the political meaning it had in the proposed constitutional amendment. While in the government's bill the notion of excess profits played a secondary role in the overall nationalisation procedure, the modifications introduced by Congress transformed this deduction into the central issue assuming even greater importance than the very act of nationalisation. In the third place, Congress' stand on the question of copper nationalisation sharply contrasted with the role that this body played throughout the Allende administration. While Congress systematically refused to approve any of Allende's major legislative proposals, it not only supported the amendment proposed by the President in regard to copper nationalisation, but did so unanimously.

In attempting to answer the various issues which arise from the situation described above, I shall divide this paper into four sections. In the first part I will briefly describe Allende's foreign policy as a means towards understanding its relationship to the government's copper policy. I will also examine the political implications brought about by the changes introduced by Congress. In the second section I will examine the legislative process concerning the excess profits provision in order to interpret the political rationale underlying the behaviour of the various political parties. In the third part I will identify the various factors which may explain why Allende was compelled to take such a drastic decision regarding excess profits. I will also examine some policy options open to the President, even after Congress had changed the political nature of the original proposal. Finally in the fourth part I will make a brief reference to the international repercussions of excess profits deduction.

This paper does not purport to offer general conclusions concerning the overall question of compensation in the nationalisation of foreign-owned property. I do not share the view held by many academic lawyers and by the United States government, that International Law requires adequate compensation assessed in terms of the market value of the nationalised property.[5] On the other hand I do not agree with those left-wing academics and politicians, who believe that the amount paid as compensation is an indication of the revolutionary will of a given government.

The notion implicit in this work is that the question of compensation is more complex than it appears, and that the decision for or against the payment of compensation is shaped by factors which are often beyond the control of the most committed revolutionaries. This complexity should not signify that the question of compensation has to be determined by mere opportunistic considerations. What needs to be kept in mind, however, is that any policy regarding compensation which a government attempting a revolution may adopt, must be subordinated to the overall strategy of the revolutionary programme.

I hope this paper will prove that it is erroneous to interpret the excess profits deduction as an arbitrary decision typical of a Marxist politician, or to interpret it as a decision having an important revolutionary content. In his decision to deduct excess profits, President Allende had to confront two types of pressures: those arising from the way in which Congress approved the nationalisation of copper; and those arising from the conception which some left-wing parties had about the nationalisation.

These conflicting pressures brought about a disruption of the copper policy of the government and eventually undermined the foreign policy strategy which Allende had so carefully formulated. The dilemma which Allende confronted in this particular case was part of the more general problem of reconciling his role as upholder of legality with his role as leader of his own coalition. This problem was to reappear in different forms during the Allende years, and the government's failure to resolve it affected the coherence of its overall strategy. I hope, therefore, that the study of this particular decision—the excess profits deduction—may be useful in clarifying some of the more general questions about Chile's road to socialism.

2 COPPER AND THE FOREIGN POLICY OF THE UNIDAD POPULAR

NON-CONTENTIOUS FOREIGN POLICY

The political programme of Salvador Allende was an attempt at initiating a process of transition to socialism within the institutional framework of the Chilean state. This attempt later became known as the Chilean road to socialism. The domestic political aspects of the Chilean road to socialism are generally well known, but its international aspects are quite often ignored. According to the strategy of the Unidad Popular, the eventual success of the domestic political programme was closely dependent upon the policy pursued at the international level. Thus a non-contentious foreign policy constituted an essential component in the Chilean strategy of peaceful transition to socialism.

President Allende's non-contentious foreign policy was basically aimed at safeguarding the formal status of the Chilean state in the international arena. In general terms, this meant avoiding a sharp confrontation with the industrialised capitalist world to which Chile was bound politically. According to the *Programma Basico*, the government of the Unidad Popular would try to achieve the following foreign policy goals: (a) maintain a broad ideological consensus in the international field; (b) contribute to the development of an effective solidarity among third-world countries, particularly among Latin American countries; and (c) resolve the border disputes with Chile's neighbours, establish a framework to carry out political and commercial relations with socialist countries, and strengthen Chile's relation with Western Europe and Japan.[6]

The need to avoid international isolation is unambiguously expressed in the political programme of the Unidad Popular. Yet the possibility of maintaining the international position of the Chilean state was dependent upon the nature of the policies which the government would implement in the domestic field. President Allende was certainly aware that any attempt to bring about an effective change in the power structure of Chilean society was bound to meet with serious resistance abroad. The challenge that Allende's non-conflictive foreign policy had to resolve consisted of assuring that the potentially disruptive effects of a negative international reaction should not be allowed to become an obstacle in implementing the initial stages of the political programme.

From the very beginning of his administration, President Allende clearly expressed his intention of putting into practice this non-contentious foreign policy. The most aggressive points contained in the programme were either forgotten or substantially modified. Thus, for example, although the programme proposed that Chile should denounce the military agreements with the United States and withdraw from the

O.A.S., United States military aid was maintained in practice at suspiciously normal levels,[7] and Chile continued to participate in all the inter-American Organisations. The programme also proposed that tied loans should not be accepted because they were offensive to Chile's sovereignty. Nevertheless, the government ignored this part of the programme and accepted tied loans, including some from socialist countries.[8]

During his first year in office, President Allende showed a special interest in consolidating Chile's position among the Latin American countries. His interest in Latin America was two-fold. On the one hand, he wanted to take precautionary measures against the danger of some Latin American countries forming an anti-communist alliance against Chile, similar to that established against Cuba in the decade of the sixties; and, on the other hand, he wanted to increase the economic links between Chile and its neighbours, in order to give a more definite political content to the joint policies which they may want to pursue. In the context of this 'Latin-americanist' policy, it was no mere coincidence that in his first Presidential address, before quoting Marx, Lenin, or Castro, Allende quoted the words of President Velasco of Peru.[9]

In July of 1971, President Allende and President Lanusse of Argentina reached an important agreement concerning the border problem of the Beagle Canal.[10] In August of the same year, President Allende visited Peru, Ecuador, and Colombia. Each one of these countries acknowledged that they would respect ideological pluralism in the region, and agreed not to accept external economic pressures infringing on their independence and sovereignty.[11] During this same period, while Allende's Foreign Minister travelled to the Soviet Union and to other European socialist countries in order to obtain credit and technical assistance, the President of the Central Bank was putting forward the contents of Allende's economic policy to officials in Western Europe with a view to furthering Chile's ties with the EEC countries.[12]

The non-contentious nature of Allende's foreign policy was more clearly expressed in the government's transference of foreign-owned enterprises operating in Chile to the state sector. The mechanism employed by the government to takeover foreign-owned enterprises was remarkably different to that employed for enterprises owned predominantly by Chilean capitalists. In the case of Chilean-owned enterprises, the government employed two administrative mechanisms: requisition, in the case of a drop in production; and intervention, in the case of a labour dispute. From a strictly legal point of view, the exercise of this administrative power only had the effect of transferring to the government temporary control over the enterprises affected by these measures; thus postponing the settlement of property rights and compensation to a later stage. The settlement of these questions remained dependent upon favourable action by Congress which Allende was unable to secure.[13]

Compared to the procedure described above, the government's policy towards foreign-owned enterprises was much more amicable. The government aimed at excluding foreign investment from certain key sections of the economy, such as mining and banking. With regard to other sectors of the economy, the government favoured the creation of mixed enterprises where the state would control at least half of the shares and the foreign investors the rest.[14] In order to takeover the existing foreign-owned enterprises, the government chose the path of direct negotiations. The recourse to this procedure enabled the government not to appear as if it was exercising an act of authority over the foreign-owned enterprises, thus avoiding the accusation of discrimination against foreign investors. By means of this friendly procedure, the government assumed control of banks, steel, and several other industries in different sectors of the economy. Incomplete statistics indicate that a total of eighteen foreign-owned industries were transferred to the state sector by means of this 'reasonable' procedure.[15]

THE PLACE OF THE NATIONALISATION OF COPPER IN ALLENDE'S FOREIGN POLICY

Upon taking office, Allende had to decide on the details of his copper policy. In general terms, the copper policy had to satisfy two requirements: it had to fit within the framework of the government's non-contentious foreign policy; and it had to obtain substantial support in Congress. These two requirements were fully satisfied by the proposed Constitutional Amendment (hereinafter referred to as the government's bill) submitted to Congress on 21 December 1970. The terms of the government's bill reveal its two-fold objective: that the copper policy should enjoy international respectability as well as widespread domestic support. In order to achieve these objectives, the government stressed the international legality of the act of nationalisation itself and emphasised the nationalistic elements involved in the bill.

The government made use of Resolution No. 1803 of the United Nations General Assembly in order to support its claim regarding the international legality of its decision to nationalise the copper industry.[16] Resolution 1803 acknowledges permanent sovereignty of peoples and nations over their wealth and natural resources, and in case of nationalisation, it provides that compensation shall be paid in accordance with the domestic legislation of the state carrying out the act of nationalisation, and in conformity with International Law. The resolution is purposely ambiguous on this point; it does not draw a clear distinction between the jurisdiction of the state and of International Law. The ambiguity of the resolution has provoked a great deal of academic controversy which will not be dealt with in this paper.[17] It should be borne in mind, however,

that according to the interpretation by the Chilean government, Resolution 1803 did not, in any way, limit the jurisdiction of the state with
regard to the choice of legal procedure for the implementation of the policy
of nationalisation.[18]

The government also aimed at presenting the Act of Nationalisation as a
sovereign decision of the Chilean state, and not as an arbitrary measure
taken by a Marxist government. To achieve this objective, the government
needed the institutional support from other branches of the state,
particularly from Congress. This support could only be attained if the bill
was drafted in terms which would not offend the ideologies and political
interests of the opposition. To overcome the ideological resistance of the
traditional right-wing party (Partido Nacional), the government had to
emphasise the nationalistic elements involved in the notion of incorporating
the copper industry into the public sector. To obtain support from the
Christian Democratic Party, the government had to make sure that its
proposal would not be interpreted as a total reversal of President Frei's
(1964–70) copper policy.[19]

The terms of the government's bill to Congress reveal that the
government was trying to put forward a formula whereby the copper
companies would receive as compensation an amount which would
certainly not have met their expectations (i.e., market value), but which
would have been higher than the negative amount which was eventually
determined. However, it is more useful to consider the bill as a bargaining
device than to speculate about the eventual compensation. Given the fact
that the opposition controlled Congress, President Allende could not have
expected Congressional behaviour to be very generous. It is then safe to
assume that the government's bill should be regarded as the upper limit
from which the parties of the Unidad Popular would try to strike a
compromise with the opposition.[20]

The government had no problem in securing the support of Congress
and surprisingly enough, the support was unanimous.[21] Apart from the
problem of assuring the backing of Congress, the government was also
concerned with that of sharing the international political responsibility for
the nationalisation with other sectors of the Chilean state. President
Allende's intention was that those parts in the copper nationalisation
process likely to create international problems should be regarded as the
legitimate exercise of power by a democratic state, and not as an arbitrary
decision of a Marxist government.

The terms of the original proposal confirmed the government's intention
of sharing political responsibility with the other branches of the state.
Indeed, the two decisions designed to have the greatest incidence in the
determination of the amount due as compensation were conceived as
decisions by two branches of the state over which neither President Allende
nor the Unidad Popular had any control. The government's original
proposal provided that the state would not assume responsibility for the

debts of the nationalised enterprises. As the government's bill did not require any further action in order to implement this provision, the decision was in fact meant to be attributed to Congress. On the other hand, the decision concerning excess profits was entrusted to the Comptroller General.[22]

At the time of Frei's administration the copper companies had incurred debts amounting to the sum of 700 million dollars. These debts were contracted under guarantees given by the Chilean state as part of a programme to increase production.[23] The bill which Allende submitted to Congress provided as a general rule that the state would not be responsible for the payment of these debts, except in specific cases to be determined by the President. Thus, according to the government's formula, the decision not to pay the debts would have derived directly from the approval of the bill by Congress, while the President was empowered to determine in which cases the rule would not apply. This provision not only would have managed to take away the political responsibility for this decision from the Executive, but would have also given the President a great amount of flexibility to bargain with the copper companies, had it been necessary.

The manner in which the government conceived the deduction of excess profits also revealed its original intention of sharing political responsibility for the nationalisation. In the government's bill the deduction of excess profits was more a technical than a political decision. The following factors account for the technical character of the deduction. In the first place, according to the government's original proposal, the excess profit deduction was entrusted to the Comptroller General. The main function of this official in the Chilean political system is to control the legality of the Executive decrees, orders, and regulations. The Comptroller General is appointed by the President subject to Congressional approval, and can only be removed from office through impeachment.[24] The man who held the office of Comptroller under the Allende administration had been appointed by Eduardo Frei, and his political sympathies were clearly with the right. Allende therefore, could not have counted upon any influence over the Comptroller's decision in regard to excess profits, given the nature of the post and the right-wing sympathies of the man in office. In the second place, according to the government's bill, the Comptroller would have had to follow rather rigid guidelines in order to take this decision.[25] In the third place, as the Comptroller's decision was to some extent a ruled decision, it was not final and could have been appealed before the Special Tribunal set up by the Constitutional Amendment.[26]

All these factors indicate that the government did not expect the excess profits deduction to have a decisive impact in the determination of the compensation. The technical nature of the Comptroller's decision, combined with the possibility of an appeal, made it highly unlikely that the amount deducted as excess profits would have cancelled out the amount due as compensation. The government was apparently only interested in including the excess profits clause as one more element which would make the amount due as compensation less onerous for the state. It is also possible that the government envisaged the notion of excess profits as having the value of a precedent for future nationalisations. In any case, to the extent that the government did not want to assume direct political responsibility for the consequences of this deduction, its intentions were clear.

THE SIGNIFICANCE OF THE CHANGES INTRODUCED BY CONGRESS

On 11 July 1971, Congress unanimously approved the Constitutional Amendment nationalising the copper industry.[27] The Unidad Popular parties expressed their satisfaction at the way Congress had handled the government's proposal.[28] In a recent study, a Chilean left-wing politician has asserted that the most positive feature of the role played by Congress in the copper nationalisation had been the broad delegation of powers to the President.[29] I believe, however, that the changes introduced by Congress cannot be interpreted as signifying solidarity towards the Executive. Indeed, these changes radically altered the political meaning that the government had wanted to give to nationalisation and, eventually, brought about the disruption of its non-contentious foreign policy. In the following paragraphs, I shall examine the reasons which support this interpretation.

The crucial changes introduced by Congress relate to the clause concerning the companies' debts and to the clause concerning excess profits. With regard to the outstanding debts, the government had proposed that Congress should decide that the state was not responsible for any debt, unless a decree to the contrary was issued by the President. But the clause approved by Congress provided that the state was liable for all the outstanding debts of the companies, unless the President specifically decreed that a debt would not be paid.[30]

In regard to excess profits, Congress introduced three changes: (a) it transferred the power from the Comptroller to the President; (b) it set extremely flexible guidelines empowering the President to determine the notion of normal profits and to decide the amount, in excess of normal profits, that ought to be deducted from the amount due as compensation; (c) it established that there could be no appeal against the Presidential ruling on excess profits.[31]

The changes introduced by Congress acquire a very important political significance against the background of the government's original intention to share the international political responsibility for the nationalisation of copper with other branches of the state; Congress in fact drew a very clear line identifying the responsibility for the nationalisation which lay with the Executive. Congress transferred to the office of the President the two decisions which were meant to have an important impact in the determination of the compensation. Such an act constituted an unambiguous sign that Congress had refused to share political responsibility with the government for the nationalisation of copper.

The government had sought institutional solidarity from other branches of the Chilean state in order to confront the international complications which were likely to develop. Yet Congress, while voting unanimously in favour of the nationalisation, also made it very clear that its solidarity with the government ended precisely at the moment the government had wanted it to begin.

The sharp distinction introduced by Congress between that part of the copper nationalisation which was the responsibility of the Chilean state, as a whole, and that part which was the exclusive responsibility of the President, restored to the issue of excess profits and to the entire nationalisation process, its true political significance. The government had tried in vain to conceal this political significance by means of a complicated legal formula. In practical terms, the amendment meant that the companies affected by this measure were in a position to characterise Chile's action as an arbitrary act of the government alone, while the participation of other branches of the Chilean state went unquestioned. In other words, Congress had brought about a situation whereby critics could focus their attacks on the Marxist government of President Allende which nationalised foreign-owned enterprises, without having to make their criticism extend to the legislative process which had generated the act of nationalisation.

In the domestic arena, political consensus—which had made the nationalisation possible—forced the government to share with the opposition the 'political privilege' of having recovered for Chile its basic natural resources. Thus the opposition managed to annul the domestic political dividends which the government had expected to obtain through the nationalisation, while it refused to accept any international responsibility for its consequences.

3 THE PARLIAMENTARY BACKGROUND OF THE EXCESS PROFITS DEDUCTION

In the first part of this chapter, I examined the place of copper in the context of Allende's foreign policy. I also discussed the meaning of the changes introduced by Congress to the government's bill nationalising copper. Up to this stage, my argument has concentrated on the analysis of factors which suggest that Congressional action in the nationalisation had the effect of disrupting Allende's international and copper strategies, thereby bringing about serious international complications which the government had tried to avoid. So far, however, my interpretation has been limited to attributing a very general political significance to the changes introduced by Congress. It is now necessary to clarify some equally important, but more complex questions. What was the political background to the legislation under analysis? To what extent were the political parties and government officials aware of the political import of the changes they were introducing?

These questions have been generally ignored by specialists who have dealt with the problem. Some have informally asserted that the changes introduced by Congress to the nationalisation bill must be attributed to the impressive legal skills of President Allende's legal advisor, Eduardo Novoa. According to this interpretation, the democratic naivety of the opposition permitted unscrupulous Marxists to obtain unexpected political advantages. Other observers have maintained that the stand taken by Congress, with regard to the copper nationalisation, constitutes an example of the new economic nationalism among the developing countries.[32]

Neither of these interpretations are satisfactory. A study of the political background of the legislative process leading to the approval of the copper nationalisation will show that the behaviour of Congress cannot be explained in terms of democratic naivety or in terms of economic nationalism. In this section, I will try to show that the changes introduced by Congress can only be explained as a product of the very structure of parliamentary processes. I will suggest that the action taken by Congress in this particular instance was not the consequence of a parliamentary manoeuvre ascribable to any particular group. The detailed examination of the successive stages in the parliamentary process of the copper bill will show how various conflicting strategies and political tactics coalesced, thereby bringing about a legal form, the full implications of which no-one had foreseen and perhaps only few would have desired.

In order to study the political background of the action taken by Congress, I will divide this section into three parts. In the first I will examine some political antecedents concerning the notion of excess profits. In the second, I will analyse the successive amendments moved to the clause concerning excess profits in the various Congressional stages. Finally, I will attempt to reconstruct the political rationale which may explain the position taken by the main political parties represented in Congress.

EXCESS PROFITS AND CHILEAN COPPER

The notion of excess profits is intimately linked to the history of copper in Chile over the past twenty years. During that entire period, the regulation of the copper industry occupied an important place in the political programmes of several administrations. The successive attempts to formulate comprehensive policies towards the copper industry constitute a good indication of their limited success. The political debate concerning copper was accompanied by abundant literature providing useful insights about the real nature of the relationship between the Chilean state and the United States multinational copper companies.[33]

The preceding government of Eduardo Frei put forward an ambitious and comprehensive copper policy which was central to his political programme. It involved agreements with the copper companies, whereby the companies were granted incentives and franchises in exchange for an expansion in the level of production.[34] Shortly after the accord of these agreements the price of copper sustained an important rise. Moreover, due to the terms of the agreements, the Chilean state did not benefit from this price rise in the same proportion as its foreign partners. The left-wing opposition denounced this imbalance, pointing out that, in view of the unscrupulous behaviour of the companies, the only solution was to proceed immediately towards total nationalisation of the copper industry.

The criticism put forward by the left was shared by the right-wing parties and by some groups within Frei's Christian Democratic Party.[35]. During the parliamentary debate over the Budget in 1968, two Christian Democrats moved an amendment which provided that any profits resulting from the sale of copper at an average annual price in excess of 0·40 U.S. dollars per pound would be passed on to the state. In its National Assembly of January 1968, Frei's Christian Democratic Party supported the idea embodied in this amendment. But President Frei was less sympathetic.[36] He claimed that the copper agreements could not be amended by law, as this would violate the contractual obligations of the state towards the companies. Moreover Frei pointed out that the approval of this amendment could bring about a substantial decrease in foreign aid.[37] Eventually the Christian Democratic Party gave in to Frei's pressures and the amendment was withdrawn.

However the debate was reopened in 1969 when two members of the Christian Democratic Party alleged that Anaconda had breached its contractual obligations under the copper agreements. This new allegation, together with the persistent problem of the inflated profits received by the North American associates, contributed towards creating a favourable climate for the total nationalisation of the copper industry. President Frei himself was forced to acknowledge that the copper agreements had to be modified, and promised that a bill would be submitted to Congress in order to deal with this problem.[38] Frei never sent the promised bill to Congress and, instead, chose to negotiate new agreements with the companies. These new agreements contained clauses determining the level of production at which the state's share in the copper price would increase.

Frei's solution satisfied neither the left nor many groups within the CDP. There were mainly two sources of grievance. In the first place, the left-wing parties resented the fact that Frei had chosen to deal directly with the companies, thus avoiding public debate in Congress which would have certainly focused on the issue of nationalisation; in the second place, not everybody was convinced that the formula of the surtax was favourable to the interests of the Chilean state.[39]

As a result of the 1969 debate, two bills for nationalisation were introduced into Congress: one of these was presented by the parties of the left,[40] and the other by the Radical Party.[41] The bill introduced by the Radical Party contains for the first time the idea of deducting from the amount due as compensation a sum equal to ten per cent of the profits received by the companies in the preceding decade. Both bills presented, however, were not considered by Congress due to the proximity of the Presidential elections of 1970. In the 1970 electoral campaign, the nationalisation of copper occupied a prominent place both in Allende's programme and in that of the CDP.

In order to obtain Congressional approval for its nationalisation bill, the government needed the support and votes of the CDP. The CDP promptly announced that it would support the general idea of nationalising the copper industry, but that it would move amendments to the bill in the committee stage. In fact, the CDP did not object to the idea of introducing the excess profits deduction in the computation of the compensation, but objected to the legal mechanism chosen by the government to carry out the proposed nationalisation. This is the reason why the debate on the excess profits clause did not occupy a very prominent place in the parliamentary debate over the nationalisation.

The government's bill provided that the nationalisation would cover the fixed assets necessary to the normal operation of the copper industry, and that the amount due as compensation would be the original cost of the said fixed assets less certain deductions, which included the excess profits deduction.[42] The CDP objected to this procedure, suggesting instead that the nationalisation could be carried out simply by expropriating the shares held by the U.S.-owned companies in the joint ventures created by Frei's copper agreements. The CDP claimed that their proposed formula acknowledged the legal validity of Frei's copper agreements and, what was more important, they argued it also recognised the political continuity between the Frei and the Allende administrations.[43]

Negotiations between the government and the CPD were established shortly after the bill had its second reading in Congress. The government was represented in these negotiations by the Minister of Mining. The negotiations were on the whole successful. According to Allende's legal adviser, the government gave in to the demands of the CDP in order to ensure that the nationalisation bill would receive solid support in Congress.[44] The agreement between the Executive and the CDP was later approved by Congress with only a few, although important, changes.[45]

The terms of the agreement between the government and the CDP were contained in amendments moved by the CDP at the committee stage in Congress. These amendments provided that the nationalisation would include the joint ventures created under Frei's government, rather than the assets necessary to the normal operation of the copper industry; and that book value, instead of the original cost of the assets, would be used as the basis for determining compensation. These amendments had the effect of making the state liable for the debts of the companies nationalised. These debts amounted to 700 million dollars.[46]

The CDP also moved an amendment on the subject of excess profits. This amendment differed in some respects from the idea contained in the government's bill. The government had proposed that the Comptroller General should deduct the excess profits obtained by the company since 1955.[47] The CDP's amendment added to this idea a clause whereby the President was empowered to apply retrospectively, up to 1965, a surtax which Frei had applied to the companies in 1969. In other words, the CDP had in fact taken up the idea of excess profits, but sought to apply it to a situation created under the administration of President Frei.[48]

The CDP's amendment was agreed to at the committee stage in the Senate. However, the approval of this amendment did not have the effect of rejecting the clause proposed by the government. Consequently, the nationalisation bill now contained two clauses providing for an excess profits deduction. The committee, considering that the differences existing between these two clauses were purely formal, decided to entrust a CDP Senator and the Chairman of the State Copper Agency with the task of redrafting these clauses into a single clause.[49] The committee then proceeded to approve the following text:[50]

> The President of the Republic is hereby empowered to deduct from the amount due as compensation the excess profits earned annually by the nationalised companies, beginning with the entry into force of law 11,828, giving special consideration to the normal profits which they themselves, their affiliates and subsidiaries may have obtained in their international operations as a whole. Likewise, the President is empowered in this matter to apply those rules agreed upon between the State and the nationalised companies with respect to preferential dividends for the Copper Corporation, when the price of the metal has risen above the levels established by the present rules, as from the date when the said companies were established.

The new drafting of the clause had effectively transferred the power to deduct excess profits from the hands of the Comptroller General to the President. The members of the committee do not seem to have noticed this fact. The Senate approved the new draft version, but referred it back to the committee for further formal clarification. At this stage, the committee added several new ideas, all of which were eventually approved by Congress. These new ideas were included in three separate amendments moved by CDP Senators. The first amendment purported to give more flexibility to the President in the exercise of his power. It provided that the President was free to decide whether he would deduct all or part of the excess profits. The second amendment provided that the President should take a decision on the excess profits deduction before the Comptroller General completed the computation of the compensation. The third amendment set a limitation of thirty days to the exercise of the President's power.[51]

The new draft was approved by the Senate with no votes against, but with the abstention of the Partido Nacional, the right-wing party.[52] In the Chamber of Deputies, the Partido Nacional again abstained. The amendment which was finally approved and incorporated into the Constitution is the following:[53]

> The President of the Republic is hereby empowered to order the Comptroller General, in computing the compensation, to deduct all or part of the excess profits earned by the nationalised companies and their predecessors annually beginning with the entry into force of Law No. 11,828, giving special consideration to the normal profits they have obtained in their international operations as a whole, or resulting from agreements which the Chilean State may have concluded on the matter of maximum profitability of foreign companies established in the country. Likewise in this matter, those rules agreed upon between the State and the nationalised companies with respect to preferential dividends for the Copper Corporation, when the price of the metal has risen above the levels established by the present rules, may likewise be considered.

> The President of the Republic shall exercise his power and report to the Comptroller his decision on the amount of the aforesaid deductions within 30 days of the Comptroller's request. After expiration of that time limit, the Comptroller General may determine the amount of the compensation without further formalities, whether or not the President has exercised his power.

THE POLITICAL INTERESTS AT STAKE

The various changes undergone by the excess profits clause would seem to indicate that its final form was the result of pure chance. Indeed if one takes into consideration the relatively short period of time (seven months altogether) which Congress took to pass the bill, as well as the fact that the debate over the excess profits discussion occupied a very marginal place in the overall nationalisation debate, then it becomes plausible to argue that mere chance can explain the outcome of the legislative process. I believe, however, that this legislative product can be explained in terms of the political interests of the parties represented in Congress. This explanation is not simple, because in this particular instance the interests at stake were not always made explicit by all the parties concerned.

Although all the political parties were independently pursuing their own political strategy, several conjunctural factors allowed them to arrive at a consensus on the legal articulation of these interests.

The position of the Partido Nacional, representing the traditional Conservative interests, was ambiguous.[54] Even though ideologically, the representatives of the Partido Nacional could not agree to the notion of deducting excess profits, certain developments in the course of the debate forced them to abandon the defence of the U.S. companies and finally to abstain.

Initially, the Partido Nacional put forward several objections to the idea of incorporating this type of deduction into the text of the Constitution. These objections were approximately the same as those later used by the companies abroad.[55] The Partido Nacional started by arguing that the retrospective application of the excess profits provision would constitute a violation of basic principles of private morality.[56] They also claimed that in this particular case the deduction was most unfair because of the high risks involved in mining.[57] One of the Partido Nacional Senators pointed out that the implementation of this clause would have the effect of making compensation illusory.[58] He also pointed out that the excess profits deduction was particularly inappropriate, since the activities of the U.S. companies in Chile could not be described as being a case of economic exploitation. He based this argument on the fact that foreign companies had sold the copper extracted from Chile in the international market; he reasoned that the activities of the companies did not involve the exploitation of Chileans. According to this Senator, economic exploitation exists only when an enterprise such as a soap factory or a bakery sells its produce on the national market.[59]

The Partido Nacional tried to draw the CDP into an open debate over the questions arising from the excess profits clause. Aware of the ideological advantage which the Partido Nacional would enjoy in a public debate of this nature, the CDP managed to pass a resolution whereby debate on the excess profits clause was made secret.[60] This resolution, however, did not prevent the members of the Partido Nacional from publicly expressing their views on this matter.

However, the Partido Nacional changed its position as the debate over the nationalisation bill progressed. In spite of its very strong views about the excess profits clause, the Partido Nacional ordered its members to abstain at the time of voting. The Partido Nacional's seemingly incoherent attitude can be explained in terms of its own evaluation of the relationship between the Unidad Popular and the CDP. The Partido Nacional seems to have been extremely concerned that the copper nationalisation could provide a focus for a long-term agreement between the government and the CDP. The Partido Nacional was also particularly worried that, in the future, the mechanism of profits deduction would be employed in the nationalisation of other sectors of the economy. In order to take precautions against this danger, the Partido Nacional sought to circumscribe the application of the excess profits deduction to the nationalisation of copper.

One of the members of the Partido Nacional summed up his party's position in the following way:

I admit that over the past few years the U.S. companies have earned excessive profits, but these excessive profits do not warrant that we should now establish a general rule which tomorrow may affect a huge number of miners in this country.'[61]

Thus, the Partido Nacional gave up the defence of a lost cause, and concentrated on the more limited objective of restricting the effects of the excess profits deductions to copper nationalisation. To such an extent, the tactics of the Partido Nacional were successful.

The position of the CDP is more difficult to elucidate. Although the notion of profits deduction was not originally formulated by the CDP (as some have erroneously maintained[62]) there is no doubt that the CDP members were more aware than supporters of the government about the political consequences involved in entrusting to the President the task of exercising this power. However, the vast majority of the members of the CDP taking part in the debate seemed to have been unaware of the implications involved in the changes which Congress introduced to the excess profits clause.

At the time of the copper nationalisation debate, the CDP was still trying out an opposition strategy which would allow them to distinguish themselves from the more militant right-wing line of the Partido Nacional, but which would not alienate their electoral appeal among some left-wing voters.[63] The nationalisation of the copper industry posed a very special dilemma for the CDP. On the one hand, the party could not risk opposing a policy which had been part of its own candidate's presidential platform in 1970 and which enjoyed widespread backing throughout the country. On the other hand, the CDP could not support a bill which could reasonably be read as an implicit rejection of a policy which, only recently, President Frei had enacted. It is, therefore, mistaken to interpret the response of the CDP to the government's bill as an act of mere political 'vanity'[64].

I have already described how Allende, in order to ensure the approval of the copper bill, accepted the amendment moved by the CDP providing that the joint ventures created by the Frei government would be respected by the new legislation. The CDP also moved an amendment containing an excess profits provision, but this provision was linked to a surtax imposed by Frei on the companies in 1969.

The CDP were clearly searching for a formula which would prevent the Allende nationalisation from being interpreted as a total break with the policies pursued by Frei. The terms of the amendment also reveal that the CDP were keen on making their stand appear unambiguously nationalistic. This explains why they included the excess profits clause in their own amendment, and tried to link it to a situation created under the Frei administration.

When it became necessary to harmonise and reconcile the ideas put forward by the government with those contained in the amendments moved by the CDP, the members of the CDP showed evidence of having a clear understanding of the implications of the changes which were being proposed to the excess profits clause. The amendments moved by the CDP at that stage had the effect of making the President fully and exclusively responsible for the implementation of the excess profits deduction.

The majority of the representatives of the Unidad Popular did not participate in this part of the debate. The legal advisor of the Presidency expressed some reservations about the drafting of the amendment moved by the Christian Democrats, on the grounds that under this new wording the implementation of the new drafting would require special legislation in order to implement the excess profits deduction.[65] The CDP explained that the legal advisor's reservations were ill-founded, as the new drafting was solely intended to give more flexibility to the President in the exercise of his power. The President's advisor accepted this explanation.

At no stage in the parliamentary process did the representatives of the Unidad Popular express any concern about the political consequences involved in this broad delegation of power to the President. Apparently, the Unidad Popular representatives shared the view held by the CDP that these changes signified an act of political trust by Congress in the person of President Allende.[66] It seems that the only politician of the Unidad Popular who realised the political dangers implicit in these changes was President Allende. According to his legal advisor, President Allende considered vetoing this part of the bill, but finally did not do so in order to maintain the unanimous support which the bill had obtained in Congress.[67] Moreover, at this late stage of the parliamentary process the exercise of the veto would have lacked political justification. Indeed, in exercising the veto power, the President would have been objecting to a provision delegating broad powers to him to complete the nationalisation process. This episode reveals that while President Allende may have had a clear idea of the best strategy for nationalising copper, the members of the Unidad Popular either could not understand it or simply did not agree to it. The impossibility of reconciling Allende's political strategy with the diversity of ideological conceptions within the Unidad Popular, continually recurred throughout the short-lived administration of the Chilean left.

Paradoxically, a right-wing Senator was the only person to warn against the risks involved in such a broad delegation of power to the President. In a speech on the Senate floor, he stated:

> We believe that it is improper to vest such powers in the President, because in exercising them the President will be forced to take decisions which will be highly controversial.

He also added that decisions of this type

> will surely be subjected to very severe criticism, justified or unjustified – *in this case I feel that they could be unjustified* – given the enormous economic interests involved.[68]

4 ALLENDE'S DILEMMA

The changes introduced by Congress to the excess profits clause created a serious dilemma for Allende. Although Congress had seemingly left the President entirely free to choose how to implement the excess profits clause, Allende's discretion was in fact severely limited. He was bound to alienate the support of some group with which he wanted to maintain good relations, whether or not he decided to exercise his power. On the one hand, the decision to deduct from the compensation a substantial amount as excess profits would have inevitably brought about a hostile international reaction. On the other hand, the option of declining to exercise the power delegated by this clause would have created serious problems among the more left-wing sectors in the Unidad Popular. In pursuing the latter alternative, the President's policy would have been described as 'soft on imperialism', and threats to break up the coalition would have followed. Thus, Congress handed over a particularly dangerous weapon to the President. On the one hand, the U.S. companies could be fairly confident of being able to describe almost any decision that Allende would take as an arbitrary act of a Marxist politician. On the other hand, intoxicated by the mirage of power, some left-wing groups within the Unidad Popular could demand that the government take vigorous action against the foreign companies.

Allende's dilemma was further complicated by other political factors. In this section, I will discuss in some detail some of those factors which may help to explain his decision concerning excess profits. I will then show how even the legal drafting of the excess profits clause was influential in determining Allende's decision. I will conclude this section by suggesting policy alternatives that could have solved Allende's dilemma.

POLITICAL FACTORS SURROUNDING THE EXCESS PROFITS DEDUCTION

Allende's excess profits deduction was regarded by many as unreasonable on account of the sheer magnitude of the sums involved. To some extent, the political climate of Chile in 1971 may help to explain Allende's decision. At that time, the Allende government was achieving impressive results in both the economic and political field. The government showed itself capable of initiating an extensive nationalisation programme as well as a generous policy of income redistribution, together with full employment and control of inflation. This initial economic policy brought about an industrial growth of nearly 12 per cent and an increase of 8·3 per cent in the GNP.[69] The success of the economic policy was reflected in the successful electoral results in favour of the government in the municipal elections of April 1971.[70]

But although the general political climate was auspicious to the government, the copper industry gave rise to a variety of controversies involving the government, the opposition parties, and the copper companies. One of these controversies concerned a slight decrease in the level of copper production in the first quarter of 1971. The government claimed that this fall in the level of production was due to mismanagement on the part of the U.S. companies. The opposition argued instead, that the politicisation of the workers, at the government's instigation, was the main cause of the poor performance.[71] Another point of controversy arose from the sale by the state copper agency, CODELCO, of 15,000 tons of copper to a Swiss cartel. The opposition alleged that the sale was contrary to public policy, and claimed that it constituted a good example of the corruption existing among highly placed government officials.[72] The government brought a criminal action against those involved in this sale, and maintained that this affair was part of an international conspiracy to damage Chile's reputation as a copper supplier in the international markets.[73]

These controversies only increased the bad feelings against the American companies. The definitive blow against the companies' public image came in August 1971, when the Eximbank refused to consider Chile's application for a loan to buy three commerical aircrafts for its national airline. The President of Eximbank explained that consideration of this application had been deferred because Chile's credit-worthiness was doubtful, since it had not been able to guarantee adequate compensation to the copper companies.[74] The Eximbank decision was criticised by all sectors of political opinion in Chile. Even the daily newspaper *El Mercurio*, the well-known champion of Conservative interests, joined sides with

Eximbank's opponents.[75]

President Allende, who, at the time of the Eximbank decision was visiting one of the copper mines, made the following statement:[76]

> We do not accept this type of pressure. . . . We shall defend Chile's right to act in accordance with its own legislation . . . we do not want to take possession of foreign capital invested in our country. We shall pay for the copper if it is fair to pay, and we shall not pay if it is not fair to do so.

Certainly, the controversies surrounding the copper industry must have influenced the views held by the Unidad Popular parties. However, except for the Socialist Party, none of the other parties issued any official policy statement on the question of compensation.

The official line of the Socialist Party on the question of compensation was approved by a National Convention of the party held in August 1971.[77] At that meeting, the party adopted the following resolution:

> **Nationalisation** without compensation is a fair policy because of the enormous wealth which the imperialist firms have already seized, and because they have left the mining sites in terrible operating conditions.[78']

The importance of the position adopted by the Socialist Party should not be underestimated. The Socialist Party had become, by April 1971, the most powerful political force within the government coalition, contributing almost half of the total electoral support (49·7 per cent) obtained by the government in 1971[79] Moreover, Salvador Allende was a member of the Socialist Party. But the position of the Socialist Party was also important because although the resolutions adopted by the party did not mention the excess profits deduction, they were in fact conceived so as to put pressure on Allende in the implementation of this deduction. Indeed, given that the bill approved by Congress in July provided that the amount of compensation would be book value less certain deductions, and given that— except for the excess profits deduction—the determination of these deductions had been entrusted to an official who was not under the political control of the government, the only way that Allende could satisfy the demands put forward in August by the Socialist Party was by means of the excess profits deduction.

The Socialist Party justified its position arguing that the companies should not receive compensation, because imperialism had already obtained enormous profits in Chile. According to this argument, the act of nationalisation acquired the character of a penalty for the historical misbehaviour of the copper companies. But the Socialists also put forward another type of justification. An article published in *Indoamerica*,[80] a non-official magazine of the party, argued that a nationalisation programme not involving direct confrontation with the imperialist companies would lack any meaning, as it would not be the outcome of the 'struggle of the masses'. The article goes on to argue that, 'the compensation paid to foreign investors . . . brings into question conclusive truths which have constituted the most precious anti-imperialist banner of the left in Chile and in the rest of the world'.[81] Thus, both conceptions—nationalisation as a particularistic notion involving a penalty and nationalisation as a general principle of anti-imperialism—led to the same conclusion: President Allende should not pay compensation for nationalisation.

LEGAL FORMALISM AS AN INSTRUMENT OF PRESSURE—THE POLICY OPTIONS

Besides the political factors influencing Allende's decision, the very wording of the excess profits clause affected the outcome of the decision. The Constitutional Amendment approved by Congress provided that the Comptroller would determine the amount of compensation in a time limit of ninety days which could be extended. On the other hand, the amendment only gave the President thirty days wherein to implement the excess profits deduction:[82]

> The President of the Republic should exercise this power and report to the Comptroller his decision on the amount of the aforesaid deductions within thirty days of the Comptroller's request. After expiration of that time limit, the Comptroller General may determine the amount of the compensation without further formalities, whether or not the President of the Republic has exercised his power.

Although the Constitutional Amendment provided that the time limit given to the Comptroller could be extended, it did not contain any provisions authorising the extension of the thirty days' term given to the President. The government seems to have regarded this term as a 'term of the essence' (*plazo fatal*), in the sense that the term could not be extended and that the power granted therein could not be exercised after the thirty day period of limitation had expired.[83] Thus, the government interpretation of the thirty day time limit forced Allende to take a delicate decision at a very difficult political moment. The political circumstances described above, combined with the euphoria generated by the approval of the nationalisation bill, made it difficult for Allende to exercise his power in any other way but drastically. Thus, the government's interpretation of the wording of the excess profits clause deprived the President of the possibility of using the excess profits deduction as a flexible bargaining device. In a sense, the large amount of the excess profits deduction could be regarded as having been predetermined by the wording of the clause.

The excess profits clause was also drafted in such a way that, by exercising his power, the President would exhaust his jurisdiction over the matter. In other words, the President's decision not only could not be the object of an appeal, but even could not be modified by him.[84] Thus, the wording of the excess profits clause affected the outcome of the decision in two ways: on the one hand, the thirty day time limit, interpreted as a term of the essence, forced the President to take a decision at a very unfavourable time for the government; on the other hand, the nature of the President's jurisdiction made it impossible for him to change his mind.

So far, my interpretation of the excess profits clause could lead to the conclusion that Allende was so conditioned by political and legal circumstances that the large amount of the deduction was almost inevitable. Undoubtedly, Allende's options in the exercise of this power were very limited. Nevertheless, even after Congress had amended the government's bill, there still remained alternatives open to the President. In the following paragraphs I shall briefly examine two alternative policies which Allende could have chosen, and which would not have involved abandoning the power to deduct excess profits.

The first alternative policy presupposes that the question of a time extension was central to the government's strategy, either because the government wished to exercise its power at a more favourable time, or because it wanted to use this power as a tool in future negotiations with the copper companies or with the government of the United States. In this event, the Executive would have needed to extend the thirty day time limit fixed by the Constitutional Amendment. The Special Copper Tribunal would have been the appropriate organ to apply for such an extension.[85]

The Special Copper Tribunal was established by the Constitution for the purpose of dealing with any claim or controversy that could arise in connection with the copper nationalisation.[86] On the basis of the Tribunal's broad jurisdiction, the government could have requested the Tribunal to interpret the nature of the thirty day time limitation fixed by the Constitutional Amendment. The government could have argued that the procedure established by the Constitutional Amendment to determine the amount due as compensation was of a different nature from the Presidential power over excess profits.[87] If the Tribunal had accepted the existence of a basic distinction between these two procedures, then it would have been easy for the government to obtain a ruling from the Tribunal along the following lines: firstly, providing that the thirty day term fixed for the implementation of the excess profit deduction was not linked to the ninety day term established for the determination of the compensation by the Comptroller; and secondly, that the President could therefore extend his thirty day time limit.

But the government may have considered it too risky to involve the Tribunal in a procedure of the type described above. In this event, the government could have resorted to another alternative policy. This second alternative flows from the text of the excess profits clause.

According to the text of the excess profits clause, the President had several options. In the first place, he could decide whether or not to deduct excess profits. In the second place, if he chose to deduct profits, he was still free to decide whether to deduct all or part of the excess profits. This second option presupposed that the President would first determine the amount of normal profits and then, on this basis, proceed to deduct any amount which he considered appropriate. This distinction enabled the President to issue a decree ordering the Comptroller to deduct any amount in excess of a specific percentage of profits. The President would have thus avoided the determination of the exact amount of the deduction.

This second alternative would have had the advantage of limiting the President's involvement in the excess profits deduction to a minimum. A Presidential decision stating that the acceptable rate of profit in the copper industry should not exceed 10 per cent or 12 per cent of the book value would have had a more positive character and would have been difficult to describe as confiscatory.[88] Moreover, this second alternative would have facilitated an upsurge of international solidarity with the Chilean government. Indeed, the separation of the principle of deducting excess profits from its actual application to a particular case, would have made it easier for the government to promote the idea of excess profits at the international level.

In an earlier section, I described how Congress had frustrated the government's original intention to present the excess profits deduction as a merely technical operation. This second alternative policy would have had the effect of partly restoring the technical character of the deduction, by placing the accounting responsibility on the Comptroller. This division of functions would have forced the companies to make their criticisms extend to other branches of the state. Likewise, this procedure would have forced the Comptroller into taking sides in the controversy with the copper companies.

The two alternatives outlined above would have enabled President Allende to deduct excess profits and to avoid premature international complications. Neither of the two alternatives would have involved compromising the substance of the political programme of the Unidad Popular.

5 CONCLUSION

In this paper I have attempted to elucidate the various factors which influenced Allende's deduction of excess profits in the copper national-isation process. I described the compatibility between the government's non-contentious foreign policy and its original nationalisation proposal. I went on to suggest that the changes introduced by Congress fundamentally altered the government's underlying political strategy. Congressional action had the effect of transferring to the President full political responsibility for those aspects of the nationalisation which were likely to provoke international controversy.

The form chosen by the government to exercise the excess profits deduction contradicted its overall diplomatic strategy. Chile's failure to pay compensation incited a hostile international reaction which the government had intended to avoid. I am not suggesting that payment of prompt and adequate compensation would have allowed the Allende government to pursue its programme without outside interference. The government of the United States and the U.S. companies operating in Chile and the rest of Latin America were certainly not interested in the procedural subtleties of International Law. Their objective was simply to prevent Allende from implementing his economic programme. This simple objective allowed for a variety of tactics ranging from efforts to persuade Allende to compromise his programme to the well-documented plots instigated by the CIA and ITT.

Despite the predictability of the international reaction to the Allende government, I would suggest that neither the form it took nor its timing were inevitable. The implementation of the excess profits deduction provided the United States government with an excuse to assume a more openly anti-Allende policy. This policy included 'legitimate' obstruction in bodies such as the International Monetary Fund and the World Bank. For the Chilean government, the excess profits deduction brought about exactly the type of result that the government had wished to avoid: it transformed the question of compensation into the central issue of Chile's foreign policy.

The evidence examined in this paper does not suggest that the Members of Congress were fully aware of the changes they were introducing. Instead, I suggested that the behaviour of Congress—immediately linked to a variety of disparate technical and political factors—objectively constituted a manoeuvre which can only be ascribed to the operation of the parliamentary system itself.

If indeed the government did possess a well-defined strategy to achieve nationalisation, there are two questions which still remain to be answered: why did the government allow Congress to place it in such a difficult situation? Why did President Allende not choose an alternative policy to deduct excess profits? The answer to these questions is connected to the nature of the Unidad Popular as a political body, and to its relation with President Allende.

The strategy originally contained in the government's bill reflected the centrist line of President Allende and the Communist Party. Other parties in the Unidad Popular doubtlessly approved the terms of the bill before it was sent to Congress. Yet, the behaviour of the Members of Parliament belonging to the Unidad Popular reveals that they did not understand that the underlying purpose of the bill was to extend the political responsibility for the nationalisation to other branches of the state. Because the Members of Parliament of the Unidad Popular disregarded such a critical element in the overall strategy of the government, they were pleased to approve each one of the clauses whereby Congress delegated power to the President. But this delegation of powers, which in the Chambers of Parliament appeared as a victory for the left, openly contradicted the political strategy of the President. Thus, the contribution of the revolutionist Members of Parliament to the parliamentarian revolution of President Allende became most problematic. According to Mr Novoa, President Allende was aware of the political implications of the changes introduced by Congress and considered using the veto. But at this late stage, the veto was no longer politically possible because of the unanimous support that Congress had given to the nationalisation. Thus, the unexpected stand taken by Congress made it impossible for the government to resume its original strategy.

The position of the Socialist Party, requiring non-payment of compensation, severely limited the President's flexibility to deduct excess profits. Allende could not ignore the pressures of his own party without jeopardising the very existence of the Unidad Popular. Moreover, in view of the electoral strength of the left in the middle of 1971, the President's refusal to exercise his powers would have been construed as a sign of weakness.

In the exercise of his power, President Allende was confronted with a dilemma: in order to resolve it he would have had to either resort to his veto power or simply choose to ignore the pressures from within the Unidad Popular. But these two alternatives would have forced him to abdicate his role as leader of a revolutionary movement. This dilemma continued to persist in different forms throughout the short-lived administration of Salvador Allende.

Unable to frame the excess profits decision within its original political strategy, the government had to resort to moralistic justifications. The decree ordering the deduction asserted that this decision was undertaken in order to rectify 'an historic past that permitted exploitation of basic natural resources of the major copper mines by private investors'. This justification neglected to take into account that the government, while referring to Chile's historic past, was simultaneously trying to make a revolution and that revolutions are not made to improve the past.

NOTES

1 'Decree Concerning Excess Profits of Copper Companies', 10 *International Legal Materials*, 1235 (1971).

2 See, e.g., *Ercilla*, No. 1870, 6–12 October 1971, at 21.
3 'Comptroller General's Resolution on Compensation,' 10 *International Legal Materials* 1240 (1971). The Chilean government's view on the profits earned by the nationalised companies is found in CODELCO, *Resumen Informativo Especial sobre la Nacionalización del Cobre*, Circular No. 187 (18 October 1971).
4 See, e.g., Eduardo Novoa, *La Batalla por el Cobre: Comentarios y Documentos* (Santiago: Editorial Quimantu, 1972); note, 'Nationalization -International Minimum Standard- Chilean Excess Profit Deductions Held Non-Reviewable', 14 *Harvard Journal of International Law* 378 (1973); Kennecott Copper Corporation, *Confiscation of El Teniente: Expropriation Without Compensation* (New York, 1971).
5 *Restatement (Second) of Foreign Relations*, 185–189 (1965); Frankin R. Root, "The Expropriation Experience of American Companies," 2 *Business Horizons* 69 (1968); Ramón Vega, "Expropriation" (U.S. Treasury Department, unpublished discussion paper, 1971).
6 The Programme of government of the Unidad Popular can be found in Salvador Allende, *Chile's Road to Socialism*, Joan Garcés (ed.), (England: Penguin Books, 1973) pp. 23–51.
7 Paul Sigmund, 'The "Invisible Blockade" and the Overthrow of Allende,' 52 *Foreign Affairs* 334 (1974). On military aid to Chile during the Allende government, see the interesting exchange between John Crimmins of the State Department and Senator Fulbright in *Hearings on S. 748 before the Committee on Foreign Relations of the U.S. Senate*, 92nd Congress, 1st Session, 45–50, 59–60 (1971).
8 *Ercilla*, No. 1875 (23–29 June 1971) p. 47.
9 Salvador Allende, *op. cit.*, p. 52.
10 *Ahora*, No. 15, (27 July 1971) p. 10–15.
11 *Ahora*, No. 20, (31 August 1971) p. 50–52; *Ahora*, No. 21, (7 September 1971) p. 50.
12 *Ercilla*, No. 1875, (23–9 June 1971) p. 47–8.
13 On the legal strategy of the government see, e.g., Jose Antonio Viera Gallo, 'The Legal System and Socialism,' 3 *Wisconsin Law Review* 754 (1972).
14 Sergio Bitar, 'La Presencia de la Empresa Extranjera en la Industria Chilena,' 13 *Desarrollo Económico* 243 (1973).
15 Universidad de Chile, *La Economia Chilena en 1972* (Santiago, 1973). In October 1971, the Department of State sent the U.S. Congress a list detailing the situation of the American companies operating in Chile. This list distinguished between two types of companies: those which had been transferred to the government through negotiation, and those which were still subject to negotiation. The first group included Companies such as ARMCO Steel, Bank of America, Bethlehem Steel, Northern Indiana Brass Co. (NIBCO), Parsons and Whittemore, and RCA. The second group included companies such as Anglo-Lautaro Nitrate, Dresser Industries, Dupont Chemical, First National City Bank, Ford Motor, ITT Telephone Company, North America Rockwell, and Ralston Purina. Cf. *Recent Developments in Chile (October 1971)*, Hearings before the Subcommittee on Inter-American Affairs, of the House Committee on Foreign Affairs, 92nd Congress, 1st Session, p. 16 (1971). Even in those cases where the foreign enterprises were confiscated or intervened—for example, the case of Ford— the government promptly entered into negotiations to arrange

for the payment of compensation. Further details on the background of the situation of the foreign enterprises during the Allende administration can be found in Bureau of Intelligence and Research, U.S. Department of State, 'Nationalization, Expropriation and Other Takings of United States and Certain Foreign Property Since 1960' (Doc. RECS-14) November 1971, p. 23; North American Congress on Latin America (NACLA), *New Chile*, p. 24–5 (Berkley, California, 1973); *Chile Hoy*, No. 16 (29 September 1972). In the case of ITT, the government attempted, unsuccessfully, to arrive at a negotiated settlement. It was only after the breakdown of these negotiations, in September 1971, that the government decided to intervene ITT. A law confiscating ITT was passed in 1972 only after the famous ITT documents were revealed: see, *Chile Hoy*, No. 39 (9 March 1973). The government persisted in its amicable treatment towards foreign-owned companies up to the middle of 1972. At that time, on the occasion of the employers' lock-out, the government proceeded to intervene industries by means of decrees affecting groups of industries irrespective of the nationality of their owners.

16 17 U.N. GAOR Supp (No. 17) 42, U.N. Doc. A/5217 (1962). Konstantin Katzarov's book *The Theory of Nationalisation* (The Hague: Nijhoff, 1964) was very influential among the government officials in charge of drafting the nationalisation bill.

17 Karol N. Gess, 'Permanent Sovereignty Over Natural Resources: An Analytical Review of the U.N. Declaration and Its Genesis,' 13 *International and Comparative Law Quarterly* 398 (1964); Stephen M. Schwebel, 'The Story of the U.N.'s Declaration on Permanent Sovereignty Over Natural Resources,' 49 *American Bar Association Journal* 463 (1963).

18 Novoa, *op. cit.*, p. 167–9.

19 On Frei's copper policies, see: Luis Maira, 'El Camino de la Nacionalización del Cobre,' *Revista de Derecho Económico* (Univ. de Chile), Vols. 27/28 (1969); 29/30 (1969–70) and 31–2 (1970); Note, 'The Chileanizàtion of the Copper Industry,' 2 *New York University Journal of International Law and Politics* 158 (1969); John Fleming, 'The Nationalisation of Chile's Large Copper Companies in Contemporary Interstate Relations,' 18 *Villanova Law Review* 595 (1973).

20 The notion of the government's bill as a mere bargaining tool for further negotiations with the opposition is suggested by Novoa in his book *La Batalla por el Cobre*, p. 147. He does not however elaborate on this point.

21 The procedure to amend the Constitution involves two stages: In the first, each Chamber votes separately on the different sections of the proposed amendment. In the second stage, the two chambers take a joint vote on the Amendment (Article 108, Constitucion Política). With regard to the copper nationalisation, Congress unanimously approved the amendment at the second stage, but at the first stage, dissident votes were cast with respect to particular sections of the bill.

22 'Proposed Constitutional Amendment Concerning Natural Resources and their Nationalization,' 10 *International Legal Materials* 430 (1971). Hereinafter referred to as government's bill.

23 The copper agreements that took place under the Frei administration appear at 6 *International Legal Materials* 424, 1146 (1967); and at 9 *International Legal Materials* 921 (1970).

24 Enrique Silva Cima, *La Contraloría General de la República*, (Santiago: Imprenta Nascimento, 1945) p. 132.

25 Government's bill, Transitional Article Sixteenth, subparagraph *d*:

> Said compensation shall be decreased by a sum equivalent to the excessive income production that said persons or enterprises, or their predecessors have enjoyed since 1955 over the normal revenues which they themselves, or similar enterprises may have obtained in their total international operations.

Compare this provision with the text finally adopted by Congress. See text accompanying Note 53, *Infra*.

26 Government's bill, Transitional Article Subparagraphs *i* and *j*.
27 'Constitutional Amendment Concerning Natural Resources and Their Nationalization' 10 *International Legal Materials* 1067 (1971). Hereinafter cited as Amendment. The procedure provided by the Constitution for the determination of the compensation entailed several measures: the amount of the compensation was to be determined on the basis of the book value of each enterprise; this amount was then subject to several deductions. These deductions included: any revaluation made by the companies or their predecessors after 31 December 1964; any amount representing assets that the state fails to receive in good operating conditions, or property turned over without service rights. These deductions were determined by the Comptroller General. The excess profits deduction was, on the other hand, undertaken by the President in a separate procedure. The Comptroller was given a time limit of ninety days in which to make this calculation. The President, on his part, was given a thirty day term which was part of the ninety day term given to the Comptroller. The decision of the Comptroller—unlike that of the President— was subject to appeal before a Special Tribunal established by the Constitution (see: Notes 31 and 85, *infra*). Five days after the Special Tribunal handed down its decision the President was supposed to determine the amount that would actually be paid as compensation. Such payment could not exceed thirty years with an interest that could not be less than 3 per cent per annum. At the time of the military coup in September 1973, the proceedings before the Special Tribunal were still pending.
28 *El Mercurio*, (12 July 1971)
29 Luis Maira, *La Nacionalización del Cobre en Chile: Algunas de sus Repercusiones Jurídicas y Políticas* (Universidad Católica, CEPLAN, 1973).
30 Amendment, Transitional Provision Seventeenth, sub-paragraph *h*.
31 Amendment, Transitional Provision Seventeenth, sub-paragraph *b*. The Constitutional Amendment did not expressly provide that the Presidential decision concerning excess profits could not be subject to an appeal. Based on the ambiguity in the drafting of the Amendment, the nationalised companies requested the Special Copper Tribunal to review the President's decision on excess profits. The Tribunal ruled against their request on the grounds that the excess profits deduction was a Presidential prerogative and as such, not subject to judicial review. For the nationalised companies, this decision constituted denial of justice. 'Fallo del Tribunal Especial del Cobre,' *Diario Oficial*, (19 August 1972) p. 3383.
32 See note 4, *supra*; see also Henry Landau, 'Economic and Political Nationalism and Private Foreign Investment,' 2 *Denver Journal of International Law and Policy* 169 (1972).

33 See e.g. Mario Vera and Elmo Catalán *La Encrucijada del Cobre* (Cuba: Instituto del Libro, 1967); Mario Vera, *Una Política Definitiva para Nuestras Riquezas Básicas* (Santiago: Prensa Latinoamericana, 1964); Mariano Puga, *El Cobre Chileno* (Santiago: Editorial Andres Bello, 1965). In English, the best introduction to the recent history of copper in Chile is Theodore H. Moran, *Multinational Corporations and the Politics of Dependence: Copper in Chile* (Princeton: Princeton University Press, 1974). See also George M. Ingram, *Expropriation of U.S. Property in South America* (New York: Praeger Publishers, 1974). The contributions by Mikesell and Mamalakis in R.F. Mikesell *et. al.*, *Foreign Investment in the Petroleum and Mineral Industries* (Baltimore: The John Hopkins Press, 1971) provide useful background information and analysis of the economics of the copper industry in Chile.

34 See notes 19 and 23 *supra*.

35 Theodore H. Moran, 'The Alliance for Progress and the Foreign Copper Companies and Their Local Conservative Allies in Chile, 1955–70,' 25 *Inter-American Economic Affairs* 15 (1971).

36 The 1964 agreements between Frei and the Companies were negotiated on the basis of a price of copper of U.S. $0·40 per pound. By 1969, the price of copper had reached $0·66 per pound. Cf. *La Economía Chilena en 1972, (op. cit.)* p. 400.

37 Luis Maira, 'El Camino de la Nacionalización,' 29–30 *Revista de Derecho Económico* 117 (1969–70).

38 *Ibid*, 118.

39 *Ibid*, 119.

40 *Cámara de Diputados, Boletín 36–69–1*, (13 June 1969).

41 *Cámara de Diputados, Boletín 36–69–1*, (12 June 1969).

42 Government's bill Transitional Provision Seventeenth.

43 *Senado Boletín 25073*, Informe de la Comisión de Constitución Legislación Justicia y Reglamaento, (17 January 1971) p. 269. Hereinafter cited as *Boletín 25073*.

44 Novoa, *op. cit.*, 143.

45 See Amendment No. 13, Senado, *Boletín 24486* Segundo Informe, (31 January 1971) pp. 5–7. Hereinafter cited as *Boletín 24486*.

46 Novoa, *op. cit.*, at 143.

47 Government's Bill, Transitional Provision Sixteenth, sub-paragraph *b*. The government's bill refers to the date (1955) when Law 11828 came into force. That was the date when the Chilean state established its copper agency and began to exercise control over the companies' activities.

48 *Boletin 24486*, p. 12

49 *Boletin 24486*, pp. 107–8

50 *Boletin 24486*, p. 111

51 *Diario de Sesiones del Senado*, 37th Meeting, (10 February 1971) p. 2203.

52 *Diario de Sesiones del Senado*, 38th Meeting, (10 February 1971) p. 2274.

53 Amendment, Transitional Provision Sixteenth, sub-paragraph *b*.

54 The political right has in fact expressed very strong anti-United States feelings. See, for example, Moran's article cited in note 35, *supra*. The reader must however be careful to distinguish between the interests of the traditional political right and those of the national bourgeoisie. Unless this distinction is taken into account, the central role played by the Christian Democratic Party in Chile over the last fifteen years may be easily overlooked.

55 Kennecott Copper Corporation, *Confiscation of El Teniente*, (Supp. 2, New York, 1972).
56 'We do not want our country to do, collectively, what an honourable individual would not do in his private relations.' Speech of Senator Bulnes, *Diario de Sesiones del Senado*, 26th Meeting, (20 January 1971) p. 1414.
57 *Diario de Sesiones del Senado*, 32nd Meeting, (3 February 1971) p. 1857.
58 *Ibid.*
59 *Ibid.*
60 *Ibid*, 1867.
61 *Diario de Sesiones del Senado*, 38th Meeting, (10 February 1971) p. 2243.
62 Radomiro Tomic, 'Cobre: Lecciones del Pasado y Riesgos de Hoy,' *El Mercurio*, (19 October 1971).
63 *Ercilla*, No. 1869, (12–18 May 1971) p. 8.
64 Novoa, *op. cit.* p. 141
65 *Boletin 24486* at XXI.
66 *Diario de Sesiones del Senado*, 37th Meeting, (10 February 1971) p. 2181.
67 Novoa, *op. cit.* p. 220–1
68 Speech by Senator Pedro Ibáñez, *Diario de Sesiones del Senado*, 38th Meeting, (10 February 1971) pp. 2274–5. (Emphasis mine)
69 6 *Bank of London and South America Review* 31 (1972).
70 In September 1970 the Unidad Popular coalition won the Presidential elections obtaining 36·3 per cent of the vote. In April 1971, the Unidad Popular obtained 49·7 per cent of the vote compared to 48 per cent by the opposition: cf. 5 *Bank of London and South America Review* 287 (1971).
71 *El Mercurio*, (25 May, 8 July, and 9 August 1971). The decline in production only affected some of the mines. The total production of the Gran Mineria del Cobre increased from 540,658 metric tons in 1970 to 571,223 metric tons in 1971. However during this period the price of copper fell from 64·2 cents per pound in 1970, to 48·5 cents in 1971. In 1972 copper production reached 588,083 metric tons and the price per pound was 48 cents. The phrase Gran Mineria del Cobre refers to the copper mines nationalised by the Allende government.
   See e.g. *La Economia Chilena en 1972, op. cit.* p. 400.
72 *El Mercurio*, (13 March 1971)
73 *Ibid.*
74 5 *Bank of London and South America Review* 543 (1971).
75 *El Mercurio*, (22 August 1971)
76 *Ahora*, No. 18, (17 August 1971) p. 14–15.
77 *El Mercurio*, (11 August 1971); *Ahora* No. 19, (22 August 1971) p. 8.
78 4 *Indoamerica*, 3 (1971)
79 18 *Keesing's Contemporary Archives* 24872 (1972)
80 'Revolucion con Indemnización,' 4 *Indoamerica* 14 (1971).
81 *Ibid.* p. 15.
82 Amendment, Transitional Provision Seventeenth, sub-paragraph *b*.
83 Novoa, *op. cit.* p. 222. The government's interpretation of the nature of the term stems from the drafting of the Constitutional Amendment. According to the Constitution, the President had to exercise his power *within thirty days*. When a time limitation contains the words *in* or *within*, in Chilean civil law, it is interpreted to be a term of the essence. The expiration of a term of the essence

has the effect of extinguishing a right *ipso iure*. The Supreme Court upheld the view that the term of the essence cannot be extended. *See* 42 *Revista de Derecho y Jurisprudencia* 225 (n.d.). At first glance, it would seem that the time limit given to the President to deduct excess profits should have been governed by principles of Public Law, and hence such a term should not have been regarded as a term of the essence.

84 The Chilean government used this argument in its negotiations with the United States government over Chile's foreign debt. In those negotiations the government maintained that the copper companies had to wait for the outcomes of the legal instances established by the Constitutional Amendment. The government of Chile also argued that the decision on excess profits could only be modified by another Constitutional Amendment: cf., *Chile Hoy*, No. 21, (3 November 1972) p. 13.

85 The Special Tribunal was established by the Amendment to deal with all matters arising from the nationalisation. The Tribunal was made up of five members: three High Court Justices and two officials appointed by the government.

86 Chile's Civil Code (Art. 1494) provides that courts may interpret terms. The government in fact did make use of the broad jurisdiction of the Special Tribunal: See, Novoa, *op. cit.*, pp. 330–9.

87 The Special Tribunal ruled that the excess profits deduction constituted a type of procedure which was different from that of the computation of compensation by the Comptroller. See, 'Fallo del Tribunal Especial del Cobre,' *Diario Oficial*, (19 August 1972) p. 3383.

88 The President in fact only deducted profits exceeding 12 per cent per annum. See, Novoa, *op. cit.* p. 21.

4 The Cuban Nationalisations in the United States Courts: *The Sabbatino Case and its Progeny*

VICTOR RABINOWITZ

On 6 August 1960 stevedores at the port of Santa Maria on the southern coast of Cuba commenced loading 14,000 tons of sugar on board the S.S. *Hornfels*, a steamer bound for Morocco. The sugar had been produced by Compania Azucarera Camaguey de Cuba (referred to in the litigation which followed as CAV), one of Cuba's largest sugar companies. Like most of Cuba's sugar producers, it was owned by nationals of the United States. The sugar was to be shipped pursuant to a contract of sale between CAV and Farr Whitlock & Co., a United States sugar dealer.

The loading of the *Hornfels* was completed on 10 August. It was a routine matter, save for one fact. On 6 August, CAV was nationalised by the revolutionary government of Cuba. So started one of the most complicated and fascinating series of litigations in the history of International Law.

The nationalisation decree could hardly have come as a surprise to CAV or anyone else. A very short era of good feeling between the United States and Cuba may have greeted the success of the Castro forces which triumphantly entered Havana on 1 January 1969, but it had long since been replaced by hostility which increased daily. On 17 May 1959 the Cuban government enacted its first Agrarian Reform Law authorising the nationalisation of the latifundia in Cuba, with provisions for deferred compensation. Although no United States property was actually seized until October, the State Department, on 11 June 1959, had already protested that 'the wording of the . . . law gives serious concern to the government of the United States with regard to the adequacy of the provision for compensation to its citizens whose property may be expropriated'.[1] Cuba responded that agrarian reform was an essential feature of the economic programme of the new government and that deferred payment was the only kind of payment Cuba could afford.

Bad feelings had reached a high pitch by January and February 1960. Small single-engine planes were dropping fire bombs on Cuban cane fields and several, based in Florida, had crashed in Cuba. The United States either would not or could not stop these flights. There was a small, but steady, trickle of small planes and boats, many stolen from their owners, from Cuba to Miami and other points in Florida. The United States did nothing to discourage this either.

In the meantime, the United States Congress was considering amendments to the Sugar Act of 1948. For twenty years the act had provided large subsidies to Cuban sugar producers through the purchase of sugar by the United States at a price often in excess of the world market price.[2] Throughout the early part of 1960 it became clear that Congress intended to cut the quota of sugar purchased from Cuba, and to cut it sharply. It was equally clear that, as the United States Court of Appeals later found, 'the main purpose of the amendment was to impose a sanction against an unfriendly nation—*Banco Nacional de Cuba* v. *Sabbatino*, 307 F.2d 845 at 865 (1962). In vain, Cuba contended that such an economic sanction would be a violation of a series of inter-American treaties which prohibited any form of governmental coercion against the economic or political elements of another state. On 6 July 1960 Congress passed an amendment to the Sugar Act which gave to President Eisenhower the power to cut Cuban quotas and, on the following day, the President cut that quota sharply.[3]

Even before the President acted, the Cuban government reacted. On 6 July, a few hours after the amendment to the Sugar Act was passed, Cuban Law No. 851 was enacted, authorising the President and Prime Minister to nationalise property owned by nationals of the United States. The preamble of the law read, in part:

WHEREAS, the attitude assumed by the government and the Legislative Power of the United States of North America, which constitutes an aggression, for political purposes, against the basic interest of the Cuban economy, as recently evidenced by the Amendment to the Sugar Act just enacted by the United States Congress at the request of the Chief Executive of that country, whereby exceptional powers are conferred upon the President of the United States to reduce the participation of Cuban sugars in the American sugar market as a threat of political action against Cuba, forces the Revolutionary Government to adopt, without hesitation, all and whatever measures it may deem appropriate or desirable for the due defense of the national sovereignty and protection of our economic development process.

Five weeks later, Cuba announced the nationalisation of twenty-six large United States-owned enterprises, including CAV. The preamble to the resolution charged that the government of the United States had attempted to interfere with the revolutionary process in Cuba, and that the sugar industry, in particular, had taken possession of 'the best lands of our country under the protection of the Platt Amendment' of 1900, by which the United States had asserted the right to intervene in Cuba, and which had been the legal basis for repeated intervention by the United States in Cuba's internal affairs for over half a century. Cuba offered compensation to the owners of the property, but on a deferred basis and pursuant to a complex formula which the courts later found to be illusory.

Expected or not, the nationalisation decree had a profound effect on the shipment of sugar being loaded at Santa Maria. After the S.S. *Hornfels* was loaded, but before it was allowed to leave Cuba, Farr Whitlock was required to execute a new contract of sale with Banco Para El Comercio Exterior, an agency of the Cuban government. When the *Hornfels* sailed, the shipper received the usual bill of lading which it assigned to Banco Nacional de Cuba, the Cuban National Bank, for collection.

Banco Nacional sent the shipping documents, including the bill of lading and a sight draft drawn on Farr Whitlock for $175,250·69, to Societe Generale, a French-owned bank with an office in New York, which was acting as the local representative of the Cuban government. Societe Generale received the draft, the bill, and the other documents on 26 August, a Friday, and on that day presented it to Farr Whitlock for collection. Farr Whitlock refused payment, stating that only two copies of the shipping documents were presented whereas three were required. Societe Generale offered to guarantee production of the third set of documents in accordance with customary practice when such technical objections are raised, but Farr Whitlock refused the guarantee—a most unusual circumstance.

The events which followed can best be told in the words of Henri Blanchenay, manager and principal officer of Societe Generale in New York. He said:

On Monday, August 29, 1960, we were in receipt of the third set of the shipping documents and at about 10 A.M. presented them and the draft once again to Farr Whitlock for payment. The representative of Societe Generale was told by the Farr Whitlock & Co. representative that the latter wished to examine the documents to see if they conformed with the specifications of the contract and asked that the former return at 3 P.M. at which time Farr Whitlock & Co. would make payment of the $175,250.69 if the documents were found to be in order. In accordance with the usual commercial practices of collecting banks in New York, the papers were left with Farr Whitlock & Co. for inspection. When Societe Generale's representative returned at 3 o'clock, he was informed that Farr Whitlock & Co. would not make payment because they had been advised that [CAV] had claimed that the funds belonged to it.

In a documentary bank collection of this kind the collecting bank is entitled to receive either payment of the draft or return of the related documents including the bill of lading. Accordingly, when payment was refused by Farr Whitlock & Co., our representative demanded return of the documents but Farr Whitlock advised that they had already negotiated the documents and had received payment. Later that afternoon (August 29), Farr Whitlock delivered to us a letter concerning their refusal to pay.

Between 6 August and 29 August many things had happened about which Societe Generale knew nothing. On 16 August a receiver was appointed over the property of CAV in New York, without notice to CAV or anyone else, pursuant to the provisions of Section 977b of the Civil Practice Act of New York. The court appointed Mr Peter L. S. Sabbatino as a receiver over the properties of CAV; those properties included about three million dollars in cash, as well as a claim to the proceeds of the sale of the sugar on board the S.S. *Hornfels*.

Section 977b authorised the appointment of a receiver over the New York property of a 'foreign corporation which has been dissolved [or] nationalized . . . in the jurisdiction of its incorporation'. The purported purpose of this provision was to protect the stockholders and creditors of a foreign corporation which had been nationalised, and it may even accomplish that purpose on occasion. But the law has another purpose as well. Receiverships are as important to an urban political machine as oil is to an internal combustion engine. They provide fees, usually large ones, to deserving lawyers, accountants, printers, stenographers, and the rest of the paraphernalia of the court room, and this receivership over the assets of CAV was no different. The receiver, Mr Sabbatino, was a criminal lawyer, who had for many years been a part of the Democratic Party machine of New York. The attorney for the receiver was Harold L. Fisher, then a member (later chairman) of the Law Committee of the Democratic Party of Kings County.

By Friday 26 August, when Societe Generale first presented the draft and bill of lading to Farr Whitlock, the latter was aware of the appointment of Mr Sabbatino as receiver. On the same day, presumably after the Societe Generale representative had first presented the bill of lading and the draft to Farr Whitlock, the latter entered into an agreement with CAV, by the terms of which Farr Whitlock agreed that if it could get title to the sugar (i.e. the bill of lading) without paying for it, it would hold the purchase price of $175,000 and not pay it over to Banco Nacional or the receiver unless compelled to do so by court order; CAV on its part agreed that if it received the $175,000 it would hold that sum in escrow to indemnify Farr Whitlock against any claim from Banco Nacional or anyone else. CAV also agreed 'to defend, at its own cost and expense and by its own attorneys, any suit against Farr Whitlock'. For its services, CAV agreed 'to pay Farr Whitlock 10 per cent of the said approximately $175,000 . . . if and when [CAV] finally obtains possession and clear title to said funds'.

So, on 29 August, Farr Whitlock had both the purchase price of the sugar and the sugar itself, represented by the bill of lading. CAV was in receivership, and Mr Sabbatino, the receiver, would want the $175,000. CAV, contesting the receivership, also wanted the money. Banco Nacional had neither the sugar nor the purchase price, and claimed the right to one or the other. And, Societe Generale was potentially liable to a claim by Banco Nacional for negligence in giving up the bill of lading without getting payment for it. Obviously, all this was a fruitful prospect for the legal profession.

Litigation, and a lot of it, was inevitable, for the stakes were high enough to make it all worth-while. Even more important, at least for Cuba, was the basic issue behind the claims and counterclaims, namely, the legal effect of the Cuban expropriations.

On 10 October 1960 Banco Nacional de Cuba filed suit in the United States District Court in New York against Mr Sabbatino and Farr Whitlock & Co., seeking recovery of $175,000.

The parties before the District Court argued many issues, most of them technical in nature, and long since forgotten. An issue which was *not* argued was whether the act-of-state doctrine was applicable, all parties apparently being in agreement that it was. This doctrine dates from the end of the last century in United States law and has much more ancient antecedents in English jurisprudence. The simplest statement of the doctrine by the Supreme Court can be found in *Underhill* v. *Hernandez*, 168 U.S. 250 (1897) in which the court said:

> Every sovereign state is bound to respect the independence of every other sovereign state, and the courts of one country will not sit in judgment on the acts of a government of another done within its own territory. Redress of grievances by reason of such acts must be obtained through the means open to be availed of by sovereign powers as between themselves.

A decade later in *American Banana Company* v. *United Fruit Company*, 213 U.S. 347 (1909), Mr Justice Holmes held that 'the very meaning of sovereignty is that the decree of the sovereign makes law, and that for a United States court to look into the question of the validity of that law 'would be a violation of the sovereignty of the nation enacting it'. Other cases, such as *Ricaud* v. *American Metal Co.*, 246 U.S. 304 (1918), arising out of the Mexican Civil Wars of 1916 and 1917 and still others coming out of the nationalisation decrees of the Soviet Union following World War I repeated this same principle, not only in the federal courts, but in the New York state courts as well. The Cuban decrees appeared to fit squarely within these decisions; the standard act-of-state cases were relied upon by Banco Nacional and neither Farr Whitlock nor Sabbatino challenged them.

On 31 March 1961 the District Court handed down its decision dismissing Banco Nacional's complaint—*Banco Nacional* v. *Sabbatino*, 193 F. Supp. 375 (1961).[4] It quickly disposed of the arguments made by the parties, deciding all of them in favour of Cuba. However, it held that the act-of-state doctrine did not apply when the foreign decree violated International Law. It further held that the Cuban decree nationalising CAV's property was in violation of International Law on three separate grounds: the decree was discriminatory against the nationals of the United States; it was in retaliation for the acts of the homeland of the owner of the property; and it failed to provide adequate compensation to the owner.

On appeal, Banco Nacional argued that the District Court had no right to inquire into the validity of the Cuban decree under the doctrine of the act-of-state cases. It argued further that the rules of International Law enunciated by the District Court were without authority. It denied that the Cuban decree was either discriminatory or retaliatory, pointing out that it was not only United States-owned property which was being nationalised, but that all major Cuban industry had been nationalised in the course of turning the economy of that nation into a socialist economy.

Finally, it urged that compensation was not required by International Law. International Law was, by definition, the custom and practice of civilised nations, and, Banco Nacional argued, there was no well-defined practice or custom recognising any right to compensation for property nationalised. Indeed, it was contended, there was wide diversity of opinion on this subject, both in the writings of scholars and especially in the actual practice of the nations of the earth.

After briefs were filed, but before argument, an important incident occurred which affected the ambiance in which the case was presented. On 17 August 1961 the captain of the *Bahia de Nipe*, a vessel owned by the Cuban government, radioed to the United States coast guard that the ship under his command had been diverted by him from its course, that it intended to enter United States territorial waters, and that he and ten members of the crew wished political asylum. The vessel was met by the coast guard at the three-mile limit and taken to anchorage where it remained in custody. The captain and ten defecting crew members were permitted to leave the ship.

In the next five days, five separate writs of attachment were issued out against the ship and cargo. One was by the defecting crew members, who wanted their wages; another was by a judgement creditor of a Cuban agency who was attempting to execute on a judgement it had obtained in

Louisiana two years earlier; others were by longshoremen and suppliers claiming under old judgements. The most significant attachment was that filed against the cargo of sugar on board the ship by the United Fruit Sugar Company. That company claimed that the sugar belonged to it because it came from United Fruit's sugar plantation, and had been taken by a Cuban nationalisation decree which was contrary to International Law and hence invalid. The decree which nationalised United Fruit's sugar was the very decree involved in the *Sabbatino* case. In every respect the claim of United Fruit was identical with that of CAV, and United Fruit relied heavily on the District Court decision in *Sabbatino*.

On 19 August the Cuban government, through the Swiss government, advised the United States that the ship belonged to it, and as such was entitled to immunity.

For many centuries, most courts throughout the western world had adhered to the doctrine that a sovereign state was immune from suit, and its property immune from attachment. Early in the existence of the United States, Chief Justice Marshall had expounded this doctrine at length in *Schooner Exchange* v. *McFadden*, 7 Cranch (11 U.S.) 116 (1812), and such immunity was recognised by the courts of the United States throughout the nineteenth century. In the context of the times, the only property of a sovereign likely to be found in foreign territory was a public warship and the cases typically involved such vessels.

In the second decade of the twentieth century, and increasingly as the years passed, however, the situation changed. Many ships owned by sovereigns were not warships at all, but vessels engaged in trade. More and more frequently the property of the sovereign, which a suitor tried to attach, was a bank account or other personalty belonging to a foreign sovereign state. And, in time, sovereign states increasingly acted through state-owned corporations and trading companies. The existence, after 1918, of socialist states greatly increased the number of state-owned vessels and other property utilised in commercial enterprises.

And so, by the middle of the century, some dissatisfaction with the rule of sovereign immunity developed. In 1952, the United States State Department announced that henceforth the Executive Branch of the government would apply a 'restrictive' view of sovereign immunity, by which immunity would not be granted in litigation arising out of commercial enterprises, even when the defendant in the litigation was a sovereign.[5]

There is often much confusion as to whether any specific activity is a 'commercial enterprise', but there can be little doubt that the voyage of the *Bahia de Nipe* was well within that concept. Thus Cuba's demand for immunity presented the State Department with a most embarrassing problem, which made it impossible for the department to follow its own rules.

On 24 July 1961, shortly before the *Bahia de Nipe* came into Norfolk, an

Eastern Airlines plane had been hijacked and had landed in Cuba. The incident caused a great sensation in the United States. It was the first hijacking of a commercial plane to Cuba, and Congress, the press, and the public urgently demanded its immediate return. Cuba, on its part, called attention to the fact that for a period of some years, persons had been hijacking small boats and airplanes from Cuba and running them to Miami and Tampa, frequently with passengers who were seeking to leave Cuba. In fact, Cuba claimed there had been at least ten such incidents in the previous ten months and that the United States had, generally speaking, not returned those planes and boats. On 2 August 1961 the government of the United States made a formal declaration to the United Nations Security Council that it would promptly return all hijacked property if proper application were made to the State Department. Accordingly, Cuba released the Eastern Airlines plane on 16 August.

The very next day the *Bahia de Nipe* arrived at Norfolk. A day or so after receipt of the Cuban note, the State Department filed with the District Court its suggestion of immunity. Throughout the ensuing litigation the department made it clear to the court that the commitment made by the United States to the Security Council and Cuba's return of the Eastern Airlines plane required the immediate return to Cuba of the *Bahia de Nipe* and its cargo. As Secretary of State Rusk advised the court on the very day Cuba filed its claim: 'The release of this vessel would avoid further disturbance to our international relations in the premises.' Government counsel publicly stated that even the short delay of two weeks which had been caused by the litigation was proving a matter of serious embarrassment.

The District Court directed that the ship be released, pursuant to the request of the State Department—*Rich* v. *Naviera de Cuba*, 197 F.Supp. 710 (1961) aff'd 295 F.2d 24 (1961). This is in accordance with well-established principles of law. In at least two cases, *Ex Parte Peru*, 318 U.S. 578 (1943) and *Republic of Mexico* v. *Hoffman*, 324 U.S. 30 (1945), the Supreme Court had held that United States courts would be bound by a suggestion of immunity filed by the State Department. The court made it clear that the recognition of a sovereign's immunity was a matter of high political priority, and that the courts would not interfere with a decision of the Executive Branch of the government.

The case presented no real problems so far as the claims by the judgement creditor and the crew of the ship were concerned because they had attached the ship; the ship was the property of the government of Cuba and, therefore, it was entitled to immunity. But the same was not true of the claims of United Fruit, which had attached not the ship but the cargo. As United Fruit pointed out, the issue of ownership of the sugar on board the ship was in serious dispute. Therefore, it argued, while sovereign immunity might be applicable as far as the vessel was concerned, it could not be applicable so far as the cargo was concerned until a decision had been made as to ownership of the sugar.

The Court of Appeals heard the case in an emergency special session on 5 September and it affirmed two days later. All of the libelants immediately made application to the Supreme Court for a continuation of the attachment to prevent the ship from leaving until they had an opportunity to file petitions for writs of *certiorari*. Unless such a stay were granted the ship would sail off and once it left the jurisdiction, neither it nor its cargo would be further amenable to any order of the courts of the United States. The Solicitor General and the State Department had very little trouble with the claims of the judgement creditor and the crew members against the ship. *Ex Parte Peru* and *Republic of Mexico v. Hoffman* were dispositive. Quite different, however, was the claim of United Fruit Company. If the District Court in *Sabbatino* was right, United Fruit was entitled to recover its sugar; a claim of sovereign immunity could not be upheld except as to property of the sovereign.

The Solicitor General, in his memorandum opposing the granting of the stay, said:

> Petitioner, in effect, seeks redress in this proceeding for the expropriation of its property allegedly owned by it in Cuba. But no such redress is available here. It may be assumed that the confiscation is unlawful under international law, i.e., so far as relations between the governments of the United States and Cuba are concerned. But that does not mean that Cuba, as between itself and petitioner, does not have valid title to the expropriated property so far as our courts are concerned . . .

He then quoted *Underhill* v. *Hernandez* and the other act-of-state cases mentioned above.

Chief Justice Warren before whom these applications came on 11, 12, and 14 September denied all of the applications for stays. In denying the application for stay for the libelants other than United Fruit Company, the Chief Justice cited *Ex Parte Peru*, 318 U.S. 578, and *Republic of Mexico* v. *Hoffman*, 324 U.S. 30. In denying the application for the stay made by United Fruit, he additionally cited *Underhill* v. *Hernandez*, 168 U.S. 250, 252 and *Ricaud* v. *American Metal Company*, 246 U.S. 304, 309.

The *Bahia de Nipe* litigation has little value as precedent in act-of-state cases. The published decisions do not discuss act of state, and that aspect of the case is well-hidden in the briefs of the parties, and the unpublished records of the Supreme Court. Only the scholar has time for such esoterica.[6] But the case is nevertheless important, because it offered a good illustration of the importance of that doctrine in the management of foreign affairs, and it influenced the State and Justice Departments in their subsequent decision to support the act-of-state doctrine when the *Sabbatino* case came before the Supreme Court.

In July 1962 the Court of Appeals affirmed the District Court decision in the *Sabbatino* case holding the act-of-state doctrine not applicable because the Cuban decree was in violation of International Law—307 F.2 d 845. But its reasoning differed somewhat from that of the District Court. Lack of compensation alone may not be in violation of International Law, it said, and the court conceded much difference of opinion on this point. But, the court continued, in this case there was a combination of three elements— lack of compensation, discrimination, and retaliation—and that combination was enough to invalidate the nationalisation decree. No authority could be cited for this proposition—International Law is not so well-developed as to provide even analogous cases to situations such as that before the court.

During the pendency of the *Sabbatino* litigation, a great deal of interest in the case had developed among practicing lawyers and law school academics. Law review articles were turned out in large numbers; study of the case was (and still is) a part of every course in International Law and practising lawyers (especially those whose clients had large investments in Cuba or other parts of Latin America) followed every turn of the litigation with great interest. These *aficionados* of the act-of-state doctrine were known colloquially as 'the Sabbatino-watchers'[7] and they included the most influential members of the International Law bar, including at least three men who later became legal advisers to the State Department (John R. Stevenson, Carlyle B. Maw, and Monroe Leigh). They collected briefs on all aspects of the case, held frequent meetings in their law societies, often wrote *amicus* briefs and attended court hearings in the case and related cases.

A handful of the Sabbatino-watchers supported the act-of-state doctrine as urged by Banco Nacional. Prominent among these were Professors Wolfgang Friedmann and Louis Henkin of Columbia University, Professor Richard Falk of Princeton, and Professor Stanley Metzger of Georgetown. The late Harvey Reeves, a partner in Shearman & Sterling, lawyers for First National City Bank, also expressed his sharp disagreement with the lower court decision in the *Sabbatino* case.[8]

But the vast majority of the Sabbatino-watchers supported the CAV position, and their cheers were loud and long when the District Court made its decision. The Court of Appeals decision was greeted with modified rapture. Typical was the article by Mr Stevenson in 57 *American Journal of International Law*, 97 (1963) entitled 'The Sabbatino Case—Three Steps Forward and Two Steps Back.' John Laylin, a prominent Washington practitioner and partner in Covington & Burling, has signed five *amicus curiae* briefs attacking the act-of-state doctrine. Professors Cecil Olmstead and Myres McDougal have each signed three. Olmstead and McDougal both testified before Congressional Committees on the subject, and they and other International Law professors have lectured endlessly to their classes on the inequities of the doctrine.

When the case reached the Supreme Court, *amicus* briefs were filed by the American Bar Association, by the American Branch of the International Law Association, by the International Law Committee of the Bar Association of the City of New York, and by North American Sugar Industries, Inc., all urging affirmance of the Court of Appeals decision. The cream of the International Law bar was represented among the signatories to the briefs.

But Banco Nacional also picked up an ally at the Supreme Court level. Concerned by the role played by the Executive Branch of the government in the *Bahia de Nipe* case, the court requested the Justice Department to file an *amicus* brief and to argue orally. That brief urged full support of the act-of-state doctrine.

The Supreme Court, in April 1964, handed down its decision, holding that the act-of-state doctrine precluded a court of the United States from examining the legality of the Cuban decree (376 U.S. 398). The decision was one of great significance. Its support of the standard act-of-state cases was important, but much more so was the extended discussion by Justice Harlan, one of the more conservative members of the court, in an opinion concurred in by all members of the court except Justice White. For the first time, the court discussed the 'constitutional underpinnings' of the doctrine:

It arises out of the basic relationships between branches of government in a system of separation of powers. It concerns the competency of dissimilar institutions to make and implement particular kinds of decisions in the area of international relations. The doctrine as formulated in past decisions expresses the strong sense of the Judicial Branch that its engagement in the task of passing on the validity of foreign acts of state may hinder rather than further this country's pursuit of goals both for itself and for the community of nations as a whole in the international sphere.

Noting that where treaties were involved, or where there was a general consensus of opinion as to International Law, the act-of-state doctrine might not be applied, the court went on to say:

There are few if any issues in international law today on which opinion seems to be so divided as the limitations on a state's power to expropriate the property of aliens. There is of course authority, in international judicial and arbitral decision, in the expressions of national governments, and among commentators, for the view that a taking is improper under international law if it is not for a public purpose, is discriminatory, or is without provision for prompt adequate and effective compensation. However, Communist countries, although they have in fact provided a degree of compensation after diplomatic efforts, commonly regard no obligation on the part of the taking country. Certain representatives of the newly independent and underdeveloped countries have questioned whether rules of state responsibility toward aliens can bind the nations that have not consented to them and it is argued that the traditionally articulated standards governing expropriation of property reflect 'imperialist' interest and are inappropriate to the circumstances of emerging states.

The disagreement as to relevant international law standards reflects an even more basic divergence between the national interests of capital importing and capital exporting nations and between the social ideologies of those countries that favor state control of a considerable portion of the means of production and those that adhere to the free enterprise system. It is difficult to imagine the courts of this country embarking on adjudication in an area which touches more sensitively the practical and ideological goals of the various members of the community of nations.

Clearly expressed throughout the Court's opinion was the thought that nationalisation questions were political, not legal issues, to be handled by the political arm of the government. The fear that the independence of the judiciary, a cornerstone of the United States constitutional system might be compromised by the court's involvement in such questions was clearly uppermost in Justice Harlan's mind.

Justice White, in his dissent, argued that, under the Constitution, International Law as a part of the law of the land, and that 'part of the law American courts are bound to administer is international law.' He expressed doubt as to whether the majority was right in its finding that there were no areas of agreement as to International Law governing expropriations, but said that in any event the duty of a court is to clarify the law, rather than to abstain from decision. He saw no necessary conflict between the Executive and Judicial Branches, and suggested that the Judicial Branch should abstain only when specifically requested to do so by the Executive.

The case was remanded to the District Court for decision on a few routine and peripheral matters and for the entry of judgement, while the academic Sabbatino-watchers attacked the decision of the court with fury. But practical men of affairs turned their attention to Congress rather than to the printed page. Shortly after the decision, and before the District Court had had an opportunity to act, a bill was introduced into the Senate by Senator Hickenlooper, at the request of an *ad hoc* committee calling itself the Rule of Law Committee. Its spokesman was Professor Cecil Olmstead, one of the elder statesmen of the International Law fraternity. The committee, according to Professor Olmstead, 'represents a significant part of American business abroad,' and it included the following representatives of United States industry: Aluminium Company of America,

American and Foreign Power, Inc., American Metal Climax, Inc., Anaconda Co., Bethlehem Steel, Chase Manhattan Bank, Ford Motor Co., Gulf Oil Co., International Telephone and Telegraph Corp., Kennecott Copper Corp., North American Sugar Industries, Republic Steel Corp., Socony-Mobil Oil Co., Inc., Standard Oil Company of California, Standard Oil Co (New Jersey), Texaco Inc., United Fruit Company, United States Steel Corp., and Pan American Life Insurance Company.[9]

The list, while perhaps not a good cross-section of United States public opinion, certainly represented a good cross-section of United States economic power. All of these companies, as Professor Olmstead pointed out, 'have a common interest in the protection of overseas investment.' The members of the committee were 'deeply disturbed' by the decision in the *Sabbatino* case, and it was feared that the impact of that decision would have adverse effects upon overseas investment 'particularly in the less-developed countries.' And so the Rule of Law Committee felt that action by Congress was necessary in order to avoid this 'practical threat' to United States foreign investment. The Executive Branch through Nicholas deB Katzenbach, then Attorney General of the United States, testified against the bill in committee. He had argued the *Sabbatino* case on behalf of the Justice Department when it was heard by the Supreme Court and he presented a strong case for the act-of-state doctrine. His principal emphasis was on the difficulty of defining International Law on subjects such as nationalisation, and the consequent difficulty the courts would have in dealing with such ill-defined concepts in cases of great political, as well as legal, significance. His views were disregarded by the committee.

The bill was adopted almost without debate and certainly without public notice. There was a strong lobby in its favour and, in the spring of 1964, relations between the United States and Cuba had never been worse; there was not a single member of either House of Congress who was willing to say a word in opposition to the bill. The bill passed without dissent in the closing days of the 1964 session and became effective on 7 October 1964, by which time the District Court still had not entered final judgement. About five months had elapsed between introduction and passage, a surprisingly short period for an important bill in the (usually) controversial field of foreign affairs.

The language of the new law[10] is far from clear, and even the most meticulous reading will not clear up the ambiguities:

> Notwithstanding any other provision of law, no court in the United States shall decline on the ground of the federal act of state doctrine to make a determination on the merits giving effect to the principles of international law in a case in which a claim of title or other right is asserted by any party including a foreign state (or a party claiming through such a state) based upon (or traced through) a confiscation or

other taking after January 1, 1960, by an act of that state in violation of
the principles of international law, including the principles of compensation and the other standards set out in this subsection: Provided,
That this subparagraph shall not be applicable (1) in any case in which
an act of a foreign state is not contrary to international law or with
respect to a claim of title or other right acquired pursuant to an
irrevocable letter of credit of not more than 180 days duration issued in
good faith prior to the time of the confiscation or other taking, or (2) in
any case in which the President determines that the act of state doctrine
is required in that particular case by the foreign policy interests of the
United States and a suggestion to that effect is filed on his behalf in that
case with the court, or (3) in any case in which the proceedings are
commenced after January 1, 1966.

The law was originally enacted for one year, but was extended
indefinitely by the next Congress with only a trivial amendment, and it is
still in effect.[11]

Principal among the difficulties is the failure to define the operative term
'International Law', which appears three times in the statute and is
defined only by reference to 'the principles of compensation and other
standards set out in this subsection' although it is difficult to know what
'principles of compensation' are referred to. The failure to define
'International Law' was, of course, not a legislative oversight—it is
inherent in the nature of the problem.

However, the courts were confronted with a new law which must have
meant something, and which was obviously intended to change the law
as announced in the *Sabbatino* decision. It seemed strange that
Congress could pass a law which would retroactively affect a case already
decided by the highest court, and when the defendants moved in the
District Court for summary judgement in their favour, relying solely on the
Hickenlooper amendment, Banco Nacional argued that if the statute was
to be applicable to that case it was unconstitutional; so too, it argued, once
again, that Cuba's nationalisation laws did not violate customary
International Law. But neither the District Court, nor the Court of
Appeals, was prepared to challenge an act passed unanimously by
Congress; they both held the statute applicable and held that Cuba had
violated International Law.

The courts brushed off the argument that the statute was retroactive
and hence unconstitutional. In the District Court doubt was raised as to
whether Cuba was entitled to the protection of the due process clause of the
Constitution, the court taking the position that Banco Nacional and Cuba
were identical and that Cuba was not a 'person' in constitutional terms. I
held that the act-of-state doctrine was merely a procedural bar to the
consideration of the merits of the case and that Banco Nacional had no
secured any 'vested rights' as a result of the Supreme Court decision. The

Court of Appeals in essence agreed—*Banco Nacional* v. *Farr Whitlock*, 243 F. Supp. 957 (1965), aff'd 383 F.2d 166 (1967). The Supreme Court refused to review the case—390 U.S. 956 (1967).

The victory of Banco Nacional in the Supreme Court was thus aborted by Act of Congress. Not only the *Sabbatino* decision, but even the act-of-state doctrine seemed dead, and loud was the rejoicing of the large majority of the Sabbatino-watchers. But the rejoicing was premature; the doctrine proved to have a great deal of life.

During the long *Sabbatino* proceeding, the many Cuban cases still pending in the District Court in New York had marked time. Most of them involved the act-of-state doctrine in one form or another, and the District Court saw no reason to decide the cases while that issue was still undecided.

Principal among the act-of-state cases still pending were *Banco Nacional* v. *First National City Bank of New York* (known to friend and foe alike as 'Citibank') and *Banco Nacional* v. *Chase Manhattan Bank*. In the former case about two million dollars was involved and in *Chase*, about nine million dollars. And, pending in the Supreme Court of New York State (which the Sabbatino-watchers did not watch very carefully) was *French* v. *Banco Nacional*.

The first case to move forward was the *Citibank* case which arose under the following circumstances:

In 1958, a Cuban state agency borrowed fifteen million dollars from Citibank and deposited, as security, United States government bonds. After the revolution in 1960 Banco Nacional, by appropriate assignment, succeeded to the rights of the pre-revolutionary borrower. On 17 September 1960 the United States-owned banks in Cuba were national-ised pursuant to Law 851 of 6 July 1960. All the property of Citibank (as well as the property of the other United States banks) was accordingly taken over by the Cuban government. Citibank promptly declared its loan to Banco Nacional to be in default and sold the security. It realised almost two million dollars in excess of the amount of the loan. But when in late 1960 Banco Nacional sued for the funds, Citibank, admitting that it owed Banco Nacional the excess of two million dollars, counterclaimed for the value of its property which had been seized by the Republic of Cuba. The Citibank counterclaim was limited to the amount of Banco Nacional's claim, i.e. it agreed that no affirmative judgement in its favour was appropriate should the value of its property exceed the two million dollars it owed to Banco Nacional. Banco Nacional in reply argued: (a) the act-of-state doctrine barred the court from examining the validity of the nationalisation resolution; (b) in any event Citibank could not counter-claim against Banco Nacional for an obligation arising out of the action by the government of Cuba in nationalising the Citibank property, since Banco Nacional was, under Cuban law, an autonomous instrumentality of Cuba and it could not be held liable for the debts or liabilities of the government.

Years before, immediately after the District Court decision in *Sabbatino*, Citibank had made a motion for summary judgement, reading that decision as meaning that the act-of-state doctrine could not be invoked to support any of the Cuban nationalisation decrees. That motion lay undecided until the Supreme Court decision in *Sabbatino*, after which Banco Nacional moved for summary judgement, reading the *Sabbatino* opinion as meaning that the act-of-state doctrine could be invoked to support all of the Cuban nationalisation decrees. That motion, too, remained dormant until the Hickenlooper amendment had been enacted and the Supreme Court finally denied *certiorari* on the remand.

Then, in July 1967, the District Court decided the *Citibank* case. It read the Hickenlooper amendment as applicable, and hence held the act-of-state doctrine as not binding on the court. It likewise held that, for purposes of this litigation at least, Banco Nacional and the government of Cuba were identical. Judgement in favour of *Citibank* on its counterclaim was ordered, and Banco Nacional appealed.

In the meantime *French* v. *Banco Nacional* was making its way through the New York State courts. Plaintiff sued as assignee of a resident of Miami who held about $150,000 worth of ambiguously worded notes issued by the Cuban Currency Stabilization Fund prior to the revolution and guaranteed by Banco Nacional. Banco Nacional denied liability, challenging the plaintiff's interpretation of the notes themselves; it also pleaded act of state as a defence, in that payment on the notes had been prohibited by an order of the Cuban Currency Stabilization Board.

The New York State Supreme Court held the act-of-state doctrine not applicable because the order of the Currency Stabilization Board, on which defendant relied, was not sufficiently formal to be a genuine act of the state. Although the case was decided eight months after the passage of the Hickenlooper Amendment, that law went unmentioned, as neither party thought it applicable. The decision was affirmed by the Appellate Division by a three-to-two vote, the dissenting judges holding that the order of the Currency Stabilization Board qualified as an act of state. Again, the Hickenlooper Amendment was not brought to the attention of the court.

In the New York Court of Appeals, once again, the case was presented without reliance upon, or even mention of, the Hickenlooper Amendment. After argument, however, the court, *sua sponte*, ordered re-argument, and specifically ordered that the parties address themselves to the new law. This was a most unusual step, and what prompted the court to dig up an issue which neither of the parties had thought was involved is unknown. Possibly Judge Keating, a newly appointed member of the court, who had been in the Senate when the law was passed and who was an implacable foe of the revolutionary government of Cuba, called it to the attention of the court.

On the re-argument, both parties subjected the amendment and its legislative history to a searching inquiry. The result was a four-to-three

decision in favour of Banco Nacional—*French* v. *Banco Nacional*, 23 N.Y. 2d
46 (1968). The majority held that the Hickenlooper Amendment applied
only to a case in which one of the claimants relied on title to personal
property derived from a nationalisation decree made in violation of
International Law. No such situation was presented in the *French* case.
Further, the court held that the Currency Stabilization Fund order was
sufficiently formal to be an act of state; indeed, the court went much
further and held that mere failure or refusal of a state to pay a debt, without
more, was an act of state. Judge Keating, speaking for the minority of the
court, argued for a much broader reading of the Hickenlooper
Amendment.

The decision was totally inconsistent with the opinion of the United
States District Court in the *Citibank* case, and when the case was argued in
the United States Court of Appeals the next year, that court reversed the
District Court, unanimously holding for Banco Nacional in a decision
which relied in part on the French case – *Banco Nacional* v. *First National
City Bank*, 431 F. 2d 394 (1970). It held that the Hickenlooper Amendment
was not applicable to a case in which Citibank had, in effect, exercised its
self-help remedy in seizing the excess collateral and applying it against
Cuba's claim against it. The *Sabbatino* case was directly applicable; Cuba's
seizure of the bank was an act of state and it could not be challenged in the
courts of the United States. Citibank, of course, promptly filed a petition
for *certiorari* in the Supreme Court.

Just as Congress had nullified the *Sabbatino* decision in 1964 by its
adoption of the Hickenlooper Amendment, so now the Executive Branch
moved to nullify the Court of Appeals decision in the *Citibank* case. The
personnel of the Executive Branch had, of course, changed materially since
the *Sabbatino* decision. Richard Nixon, not Lyndon Johnson, was President. John Mitchell, not Robert Kennedy, was Attorney General. And
John Stevenson, foremost among the *Sabbatino*-watchers, was now legal
adviser to the State Department.

While Citibank's petition for review was pending before the Supreme
Court, Mr Stevenson addressed a letter to the court. He referred to the so-
called 'Bernstein exception' to the act-of-state doctrine and advised the
court that pursuant to that rule (which he termed 'clearly established') the
Executive Branch suggested to the court that the act-of-state doctrine
ought not to be applied

> when it is raised to bar adjudication of a counterclaim or set-off when (a)
> the foreign state's claim arises from a relationship between the parties
> existing when the act of state occurred; (b) the amount of the relief to be
> granted is limited to the amount of the foreign state's claim; and (c) the
> foreign policy interests of the United States do not require application of
> the doctrine.

Hence, he said, the act-of-state doctrine ought not to be applied to the *Citibank* case or 'like cases'.

The 'Bernstein exception' to the act-of-state doctrine was a reference to the decision of the United States Court of Appeals in *Bernstein* v. *N. V. Nederlandsche Amerikaansche*, etc., 210 F.2d 375 (1954), in which the court had refused to apply the doctrine to a pre-war seizure, by the Hitler government, of the property of a ship-owner of Jewish origin. The decision was prompted by a letter from the State Department suggesting that the doctrine ought not to be applied in that case. The *Bernstein* case was never reviewed by the Supreme Court, and the Justice Department, in its brief in the *Sabbatino* case, had raised some question as to the general applicability of such an exception to the general rule.

The Supreme Court granted *certiorari* and without hearing argument remanded the case to the Court of Appeals 'for reconsideration in light of the views of the Department of State expressed in its letter dated November 17, 1970'. On re-argument the Court of Appeals held firm, but this time by a two-to-one vote—442 F.2d 530 (1971). The majority denied the applicability of a 'Bernstein exception'; it stated that

the facts in *Bernstein* were most unusual, to say the least. . . . The acts of state there were performed by a German government with which this country had gone to war and which was no longer in existence at the time of the State Department's letter . . . Again . . . the State Department's letter in *Bernstein* was written during the aftermath of a great world war; and the Nazi government's actions, such as those of which Bernstein complained, had been condemned throughout the world as crimes against humanity.

The 'Bernstein letter' submitted by Mr Stevenson was of course seized upon by the Sabbatino-watchers who had opposed the act-of-state doctrine from the beginning. If, they argued, the principal reason for the act-of-state doctrine was to prevent embarrassment to the Executive Branch in carrying on its diplomatic negotiations, could not the Executive Branch waive its objections, as it had done in the *Bernstein* case, and did not such waiver free the court to decide the case on its merits? Much earlier in the *Sabbatino* controversy it had been suggested, by Justice White among others, that the act-of-state doctrine should be limited to those situations in which the Executive Branch asked for its application; here, however, the Executive Branch, in effect, was saying that there would be no embarrassment to it if the act-of-state doctrine were disregarded. In the words of Mr Stevenson, 'the foreign policy interests of the United States do not require the application of the act-of-state doctrine . . . in these circumstances.'

This argument, eagerly seized upon by Citibank, resulted in an important reformulation of the whole 'embarrassment issue', placing it on a much more realistic basis than had theretofore been the case. Justice

Harlan in the *Sabbatino* case had not discussed 'embarrassment' in those terms. He spoke instead of the doctrine of the separation of powers, arguing that the Constitution put the conduct of foreign affairs into the hands of the Executive Branch and that judicial interference might impede the proper conduct of foreign relations. When the *Citibank* case was argued before the Supreme Court, Banco Nacional in its brief developed the 'embarrassment' concept to answer Stevenson and the Bernstein exception. The embarrassment, it argued, was not only to the Executive Branch but, even more important, to the Judicial Branch of the government. Such embarrassment would arise whenever the Executive Branch and the Judicial disagreed on a proposition of International Law—a situation which might arise frequently. The courts would then be faced with the alternative of differing publicly with the Executive Branch on a matter which might be of grave public importance or compromising their integrity by accepting the Executive's view of the law. Indeed, the threat was not merely one of embarrassment—it was a threat, rather, to the independence of the Judiciary, a fundamental concept in the constitutional law of the United States.

The problem was not an imaginary one. In the famous Rose Mary decision, *Anglo Iranian Oil Co.* v. *Jaffrate* [1953] 1 Weekly L.R. 246; 1953 Int' l L.Rep. 316, the issue presented to the British court at Aden was the legality of the nationalisation by Iran of oil wells belonging to a British-owned company. The English government had taken a firm position in public that the Iranian decree was illegal, as a part of its effort to prevent the sale of Iranian oil in the world market. No English court could realistically have made a decision contrary to that policy position of the government, and the court was forced to agree with the British Foreign Office once it undertook to decide the case.

Again Citibank filed a petition for *certiorari* in the Supreme Court, and the court in October 1971 granted the writ.

Major changes in the personnel of the court had seriously eroded the eight-to-one majority in the *Sabbatino* case. Chief Justice Warren and Justices Clark and Goldberg had retired; Justices Harlan and Black had died; only three of the majority judges in the *Sabbatino* case were still on the bench, namely, Douglas, Brennan, and Stewart. Some of the replacements could not be counted on to give Banco Nacional a sympathetic hearing. Chief Justice Burger, while on the Court of Appeals in the District of Columbia, had, in 1960, dissented from an opinion by the court which had enforced the act-of-state doctrine in an early Cuban nationalisation case, and his views were apparent from that dissent. Justice Rehnquist was widely regarded as the spokesman for the Nixon administration, and it seemed most unlikely that he would support Banco Nacional in the face of the State Department position. Justice White had dissented in *Sabbatino*. Justices Powell and Blackmun were recent additions to the bench, and were unknown quantities.

The decision of the court was handed down in June 1972. It reversed the Court of Appeals by a five-to-four vote—406 U.S. 759. Justice Blackmun voted for affirmance but, surprisingly, Justice Douglas, one of the *Sabbatino* majority, voted for reversal. His vote was decisive.

The decision itself was most unsettling, so far as the law was concerned. Four separate opinions were written and none of them represented a majority of the court. Justice Rehnquist, writing for himself and for Chief Justice Burger and Justice White, had gone down the line with the Administration. While not purporting to overrule the *Sabbatino* case, they held that the State Department letter, in a case in which the act-of-state doctrine was being pleaded as a defence to a counterclaim, was decisive and the act-of-state doctrine would not be applied.

Mr Justice Powell wrote a decision in which he spoke for himself alone. He said he didn't like the act-of-state doctrine much and stated that he would consider application of the rule on a case-by-case basis. This was one of the cases in which he would not apply the doctrine. He did not state why and gave no guide to his future actions. The only points he did make clear were, first, that he was not at all influenced by the Stevenson letter, and second, that he was not at all influenced by the fact that the act-of-state doctrine was being pleaded as a defence to a counterclaim.

The opinion of Justice Douglas likewise took the position that the Stevenson letter was irrelevant. He was influenced only by the counter-claim point. In his opinion it was unfair for Banco Nacional to come into court and plead Cuba's act of state as a defence to a counterclaim when it was itself seeking the aid of the United States courts against Citibank. All of the majority judges and indeed even Mr Stevenson agreed that if the amount of the counterclaim was in excess of the amount of the claim, no affirmative judgement could be entered.

The dissent was written by Justice Brennan. It reaffirmed the basic approach of the *Sabbatino* decision. He denied the validity of the 'Bernstein exception' to the *Citibank* case, calling Justice Rehnquist's opinion 'mechanical and fallacious', being based on the erroneous premise that the act-of-state doctrine was designed primarily as an aid to the Executive Branch. The doctrine, he pointed out, had significance in that it related to the proper distribution of power between the various branches of the government of the United States. He likewise disagreed with the view of Justice Douglas, noting that the reasons for the act-of-state doctrine were equally valid whether the doctrine was pleaded as a defence to a counterclaim, or as a defence to a principal claim.

The result was an anomalous one. On every issue before the court, a majority agreed with Banco Nacional; yet a combination of minorities was sufficient to result in a reversal. Only three judges were influenced by the Stevenson letter; the other six expressly denied any 'Bernstein exception' to the act-of-state doctrine. Similarly, only four judges held that they would not apply the act-of-state doctrine where it was pleaded as a defence to a counterclaim. At least five judges reaffirmed their belief in the *Sabbatino* decision.

Situations in which decisions are made by a combination of minority opinions, each voting for the same result for different reasons, are not uncommon in the Supreme Court, and in some cases as many as nine separate opinions have been written,[12] often leaving the law in greater confusion than before the case was decided. This decision certainly left the law in a state of great uncertainty; it settled nothing—at least nothing that could not be upset in the next case or with the next change in the personnel of the Supreme Court.

Next on the agenda was *Banco Nacional* v. *Chase Manhattan Bank*. The facts in *Chase* were the same as in *Citibank*, except that the amount of the excess in *Citibank* was about two million dollars, while the amount in *Chase* was nine million dollars, a sum which, when interest was added, had almost doubled since 1960.

In the eyes of the District Court, the *Chase* case was governed by the *Citibank* decision, such as it was, and it proceeded on that assumption. And so the parties moved on to a new set of issues, and a new complex of legal problems, consequent upon the rejection of the act-of-state doctrine by the District Court. Assuming for District Court purposes that Cuba's action in nationalising the banks had been a violation of International Law, and that Chase was entitled to compensation for its Cuban property, how much compensation was it entitled to? And here the parties and the court ran into a series of problems which are inevitable once the salutory rule of *Sabbatino* is disregarded, and an effort is made to apply non-existent 'principles of International Law' to a litigated situation.

Had this been ordinary civil litigation, governed by conventional domestic law, it would have been passably difficult to determine the value of Chase's property in the rather unusual circumstances present here, but the federal courts handle more complicated questions every week, and the rules of domestic law governing the valuation of property are well-developed. There aren't many, if any, cases in which property was taken by a revolution, but there are hundreds of precedents decided under the prohibition in the United States Constitution against the taking of private property without compensation, and they offer a guide to any court called upon to consider such an issue.

But this was not ordinary civil litigation, to be decided under the rules of domestic law. It was clear from the Cuban cases already decided that the applicable law was *not* the law of the United States or of Cuba—it was 'International Law'. As both the Supreme Court and the Court of Appeals had pointed out in *Sabbatino*, there was not even any established International Law as to whether compensation should be paid for nationalised property; *a fortiori* there was no International Law as to *how much* compensation should be paid. And to make the situation worse, even that almost inexhaustible source of International Law, the academic commentators, offered no help at all. For this was an intensely practical matter. A judgement had to be made in the *Chase* case—not a judgement as to the applicable legal principles, but a different kind of judgement—one expressed in dollars and cents.

There are two major problems in the *Chase* case, and there is no precedent in International Law as to either. Not only are there no precedents; there are not even any ground rules, any signposts by which a court can find its way. The District Court is sailing on a totally uncharted and unmapped sea, but, unlike Columbus, it can not just continue sailing until it falls over the edge or reaches land. It has to make a decision.

The first of these problems is: how does a court calculate the *value* of a privately-owned bank which is seized in the course of a socialist revolution? Normally there are two alternative measures of value: (a) the amount the bank can earn in the future, i.e. its 'earning capacity'; or (b) the amount for which the net assets of the bank can be sold, i.e. its 'market value'. But a United States owned bank in Cuba in 1960 had no earning capacity at all, as the entire banking system of Cuba was being nationalised and banking was no longer to be a private function. And the bank likewise had little net asset value. The securities it held could, no doubt, be sold, and the small amount of cash on hand could be counted, but even its real estate had no 'market value' in a society in which private trading in commercial property was no more. The bank, of course, claimed large sums for 'future earnings', for 'good will', for 'going business value', based on what the bank would have been worth had there been no revolution, no Fidel Castro, or no threat to the pre-revolutionary dictatorship of Batista. But such a standard is based on fantasy, not on International Law.

The second problem was even more difficult: assuming that a value of Chase's property could be found, how much compensation is due to Chase for that value? Chase is not entitled to compensation for the full value of its property unless International Law says it is and there is no established custom or practice to such effect.

Neither of these problems arise when the usual international practice is followed. There have been three ways of disposing of such problems over the past half century:

(a) No compensation at all has been paid;
(b) The parties have reached an agreement after negotiation between them. In such circumstances, the parties bargain, taking into consideration all the relevant factors, the most relevant being that the owner of the nationalised property wants as much as it can get, that the nationalising state wants to pay as little as it can, and that both want to reach agreement. There have been, over the past fifty years, hundreds of such settlements. Generally the details and often the results have been kept secret; no-one has collected and made available the facts relating to such settlements;

(c) In about seventy-five instances, nationalisation disputes have been resolved by lump sum settlements between the nationalising country and the home state of the owner. In such cases, the nationalising country provides a lump sum, which is divided among claimants by the home state of those claimants. International custom and practice, at least as exemplified by the lump sum agreements, results in compensation to the owners of nationalised property of only a small fraction of full value. In the first place, the lump sum made available has never come near the value of the property nationalised. In the second place, the process takes a long time—often ten to twenty years—and no interest is available on claims handled in this way.[13]

The claims made by nationals of the United States against Cuba total $1,800,000,000. It is obvious that no such sum could possibly be made available by Cuba, even over a long period of time. If any settlement by way of a lump sum payment is made, it cannot result in anything more than a small percentage of the claimed loss, and even that amount will be paid more than fifteen years after the event.

So customary international practice shows a wide gap between the value of the property nationalised and the compensation paid for it. In the *Chase* case, therefore, Banco Nacional argued that, assuming compensation has to be paid at all, it should, under International Law, be far less than the claimed value, whatever that was found to be. Chase Bank made no effort at all to meet this argument. It proceeded to prove value as though it were a domestic bank that had been condemned by the government. Standard Fifth Amendment concepts of the evaluation of private property were called upon: the Cuban revolution was ignored. No reference at all was made to International Law;[14] it was assumed, without much argument, that 'value' meant value according to conventional capitalist standards, and that compensation was to be equal to value.[15]

The court took all of the arguments under advisement. The case was tried early in July 1974, and has not yet been decided. In the meantime, a new problem arose from an unanticipated quarter.

Perhaps the most complex of the Cuban cases was the litigation known as the tobacco cases. On 16 September 1960 Cuba intervened[16] all the Cuban-owned tobacco plantations and cigar factories. For many years prior thereto the Cuban cigar-makers had been shipping high-quality cigars to importers in New York, the most important of which were Faber, Coe & Gregg, and Dunhill & Co. The importers paid for these cigars on normal commercial credit terms, for the most part sixty or ninety days after delivery. After the decree of 16 September 1960, the importers continued to purchase cigars as theretofore, and to advertise and sell the cigars, all as if no intervention had taken place. The intervenor shipped the cigars ordered, and accepted payment for them.

In February 1961, the importers received communications from the former owners, claiming the right to the proceeds of the sale of cigars manufactured both before and after intervention by the intervened factories. The importers immediately stopped buying cigars and stopped paying for the cigars already received, which included most of the post-intervention purchases.

What followed was, in procedural terms, most complicated, and it would serve no useful purpose to detail all of the litigation here. In substance, the District Court held that, since the owners were Cuban nationals, there was no question of International Law arising out of the intervention decree, which, therefore, would not be questioned by a United States court under familiar act-of-state principles. The Cuban intervenor was therefore entitled to payment for all cigars shipped after intervention. This decision was affirmed on appeal—*Palicio* v. *Brush & Block*, 256 F. Supp. 481 (1966), aff'd 275 F.2d 1011 (1967).

The court then took up the matter of payment for pre-intervention shipments. It held that the former owners were entitled to such payments, and could have judgement against the importers; it further held that the importers had paid the intervenor by mistake, and were entitled to recover the sums so paid from the intervenor. Since the intervenor refused to repay the funds received by him, the District Court held that recovery by the importers from the intervenor could be effectuated by setting off the amounts due against the money owed by the importers to the intervenor for post-intervention shipments.

When the time came to add up various claims and counterclaims, it appeared that the intervenor was entitled to a net judgement in his favour against Faber, Coe & Gregg, since the value of post-intervention shipments was greater than the value of the pre-intervention purchases for which payment had erroneously been made by the intervenor. But the situation was different with respect to Dunhill. The intervenor's claim against Dunhill for post-intervention shipments turned out to be *less* than Dunhill's counterclaim by $53,000, and the court accordingly entered judgement in favour of Dunhill for that amount—*Menendez, Garcia & Co.* v. *Faber, Coe & Gregg*, 345 F.Supp. 527 (1972).

Everyone appealed from the decision of the District Court on every adverse ruling, and the Court of Appeals affirmed on every issue but one—*Menendez, Garcia & Co.* v. *Faber, Coe & Gregg*, 485 F.2d 1355 (1973). It held that the refusal of the intervenor to repay the money was an act of state. Under the ruling of the court in the *Citibank* case, the intervenor could not assert that defence against Dunhill's counterclaim, but under the same decision no affirmative judgement in favour of Dunhill was permissible. Hence, it set aside Dunhill's affirmative judgement against Cuba—*Menendez, Garcia & Co.* v. *Faber, Coe & Gregg*, 485 F.2d 1355 (1973). Dunhill promptly applied to the Supreme Court for a writ of *certiorari*.

The court granted the writ and heard argument in December 1974. A few months later, Justice Douglas, whose vote had been so important in the

Citibank case, suffered a stroke, which took him out of action for most of the rest of the Term. In November 1975, he resigned from the bench and, shortly after, Justice John P. Stevens was appointed in his place.

On 17 June 1975, just before adjournment time, the court ordered re-argument of the *Dunhill* case. It also instructed the parties to brief and argue the question of whether the holding of the *Sabbatino* case should be reconsidered: this was surprising. The *Sabbatino* case stood for the proposition that the act-of-state doctrine would be applied even if the act under consideration was a violation of International Law, and none of the litigants in the *Dunhill* litigation had ever argued that there was any International Law issue in the case. Clearly, some judge or combination of judges wanted an opportunity to put the *Sabbatino* decision and the act-of-state doctrine to another test in the Supreme Court. In view of the close division among the Justices in the *Citibank* case, this was ominous; the resignation of Justice Douglas and the appointment of a new Justice whose views were unknown, made the outcome even more uncertain.

In December 1975 after briefs on re-argument had been submitted, a brief *amicus curiae* was filed by the Solicitor General of the United States, accompanied by yet another letter from the legal advisor of the State Department, an office now held by long-time Sabbatino-watcher Monroe Leigh. This brief urged yet another position, namely, that the 'restrictive' theory of sovereign immunity should be applied to the act-of-state doctrine, and that that doctrine ought not to be given effect in 'commercial cases'.

Cuba, in a brief addressed to the Solicitor General's submission, opposed the extension of that doctrine to acts of state. It pointed out that while the principles of sovereign immunity and of act of state are related and are often confused, they are in fact quite different and serve different purposes.

Furthermore, Cuba argued, the restrictive theory of sovereign immunity had not been a success, and was difficult to apply—indeed it was often ignored even by the State Department, as in the *Bahia de Nipe* litigation.

All of this briefing and counterbriefing turned out to be irrelevant. At the argument before the Supreme Court all parties, including the Solicitor General, agreed that there was no genuine *Sabbatino* issue in the case, there being no International Law issue; hence there was no reason to reconsider that decision. The court, in an opinion handed down on 24 May 1976, held by a five-to-four vote that on the peculiar facts of the *Dunhill* case the intervenor had not established that his refusal to repay the money collected from the importers was an act of state and hence the *Dunhill* affirmative judgement was reinstated. This holding was set forth in an opinion written by Justice White and was concurred in by Chief Justice Burger and Justices Powell, Rehnquist, and Stevens. The minority were the same Justices who had constituted the minority in the *Citibank* case; this time Justice Marshall wrote the opinion.

In view of the decision of the court, it became unnecessary to pass upon the point raised by the Solicitor General; there being no act of state at all, the issue of whether this particular transaction could be properly defined as commercial was irrelevant. Nevertheless Justice White in his opinion argued that the act-of-state doctrine should not be applied to commercial cases. Here, however, he spoke only for four Justices, Justice Stevens abstaining on the issue since it was not necessary for a decision. On that important issue, therefore, the court now stands divided equally, with one abstention. The minority opinion signed by four Justices emphatically disagreed with any suggestion of a limitation of the act-of-state doctrine; the opinion by Justice Marshall was an extensive and thorough defence of the act-of-state doctrine.

The next Cuban case likely to reach the Court is that involving Chase Manhattan Bank, and that is probably two to three years in the future. We know of no other pending case likely to present the issue although, of course, such cases may arise at any time. Further changes in the personnel of the court and in the Office of the Legal Advisor to the State Department make the result of any future litigation totally unpredictable.

And so the *Sabbatino* decision and the act-of-state doctrine still prevail in United States law, though perhaps a bit precariously.

CONCLUSION

As the opinion by Justice Harlan in the *Sabbatino* case points out, the constitutional 'underpinnings' of the act-of-state doctrine arise from the fundamental principle, which every school child in the United States learns at a very early age, that the Constitution created a system in which the powers of government are divided between the Legislative, Judicial, and Executive branches. In theory, each of these branches is independent of the others and is yet tied to them by an elaborate set of 'checks and balances', many of which exist only on paper, but some of which are quite effective. Realistically speaking, of course, the three branches of government are far from equal and are not as independent of each other as the Constitution may have contemplated. However, the concept of an independent judiciary which can and frequently does invalidate laws of Congress and decrees of the President is very strong, especially on the appellate level. Similarly, the courts have always reserved the right to define their own jurisdiction and to decline to go outside it.

Justice Harlan was a fine, though conservative, constitutional lawyer for whom the concept of an independent judiciary was of the greatest importance. Obviously, he felt that to give the courts the task of deciding issues involving foreign affairs which were primarily political rather than legal might seriously compromise the judiciary. As the opinion in the *Sabbatino* case points out, the International Law governing nationalisation is a subject on which the community of nations is sharply divided; furthermore, that division is based not on superficial or ephemeral considerations but on basic economic and political ideology. For a national court to plunge into such a conflict of views seemed, to the court, to be most inadvisable as the issues presented were basically matters within the competency of the Executive Branch alone.

Time has shown the wisdom of the *Sabbatino* decision. A consensus is rapidly developing among most nations of the world on the law of nationalisation, but that consensus is sharply contrary to the position of the Executive Branch of the United States. The Assembly of the United Nations in adopting, in 1975, the Charter of Economic Rights and Duties of States, over the strong opposition of the United States and a few Western European nations, repudiated the 'prompt, adequate, and effective' compensation standard upon which the Executive Branch of the United States has traditionally based its policy. Absent the act-of-state doctrine the Judicial Branch might be required to choose between the International Law adopted by most of the nations of the world and the International Law advocated by the United States State Department. Such a situation would put an intolerable strain on the concept of an independent judiciary, and the *Sabbatino* decision was written to avoid this precise situation.

Paradoxically enough, as the wisdom of the act-of-state doctrine has become clearer, its standing in the courts of the United States has become weaker. As indicated above, changes in the personnel of the Supreme Court have brought to that court judges who, for one reason or another, do not accept the philosophy behind the act-of-state doctrine, or accept it only grudgingly. To attempt a prediction as to how the court will react to the next case which comes before it would be foolish. We can but watch with interest the progress of the pending cases and those others which may arise in the next few years in the likely event that the less-developed countries of the world continue a policy of nationalisation of alien-owned property.

NOTES

1 *Department of State Bulletin*, (29 June 1959) p. 958. Traditionally, the position of the United States has been that International Law requires 'prompt, adequate, and effective' compensation when the property of a United States citizen is nationalised by a foreign country. In practice this standard has never been applied except in polemics. The important article by Dawson and Weston, 'Prompt, Adequate and Effective: A Universal Standard Of Compensation?' 30 *Fordham Law Review*, 727 (1962), contains an analysis of international practice up to the date of its publication. In many subsequent instances of nationalisation, compensation has been stretched out over a period of several decades without protest from the United States Government.

2 Sugar has long been the foundation of Cuba's economy. Immediately prior to

the revolution it represented 81 per cent of Cuba's exports. Purchases by the United States amounted to about 70 per cent of Cuban sugar. Even under the best of circumstances Cuba's foreign exchange position was a precarious one, and any decrease in sugar sales had a disastrous effect on that economy.

3 The quota for the balance of the year 1960 amounted to 739, 752 short tons. The President's Proclamation cut that quota to 39,752 short tons.

4 The foregoing facts can be found in the record before the District Court in the *Sabbatino* case.

5 26 *Department of State Bulletin* 984 (1952). The doctrine of sovereign immunity and the act-of-state doctrine both arise out of the relationship between the courts of the United States and a foreign sovereign, and both involve an element of abstention by the courts. The two doctrines, however, are quite different in their intent and application and should not be confused.

The grant or denial of sovereign immunity relates only to whether a domestic court will accept jurisdiction of a case against a foreign sovereign, thus possibly incurring its ill-will to a greater or lesser extent. A grant or denial of immunity implies no finding one way or the other on the merits or even that the merits will be reached. The granting of immunity forecloses judicial consideration of the merits; its denial merely allows the suit to proceed on the merits of the claim including any defences the sovereign may have, such as the act-of-state doctrine.

The act-of-state doctrine, on the other hand, necessarily goes to the merits. Absent the doctrine, the courts would be required to pass judgement on the legality *vel non* of the acts of a foreign sovereign.

6 All of the relevant documents in the *Bahia de Nipe* litigation have been collected in Chayes, Erlich, and Lowenfeld, 1 *International Legal Process*, (1968) p. 87 – 144 as part of an in-depth discussion of the interrelation between the State Department and the courts in a case which is instructive as well as important.

7 See Leigh, '*The Supreme Court and the Sabbatino-Watchers: First National City Bank* v. *Banco Nacional de Cuba,*' 13 *Virginia Journal of International Law* 33 (1972).

8 See Friedmann, 'National Courts And The International Legal Order', 34 *George Washington Law Review* 443 (1966); Falk, *The Role of Domestic Courts in the International Legal Order* (1964); Reeves, 'Act Of State And The Rule Of Law–A Reply', 54 *American Journal of International Law* 141 (1960); Reeves, 'The Sabbatino Case: The Supreme Court of the United States Rejects a Proposed New Theory', 32 *Fordham Law Review* 631 (May 1964); Metzger, 'Act Of State Doctrine And Foreign Relations', 23 *University of Pittsburgh Law Review* 881 (1962).

9 See Hearings Before the House Committee on Foreign Affairs, 89th Congress, 1st Session on Draft Bill to Amend Further the Foreign Assistance Act of 1961, pp. 576 and 1033. So far as we know, the Rule of Law Committee had no existence other than as manifested in the testimony before the House Committee of Professors McDougall and Olmstead. Presumably the testimony given by those two witnesses represented the views of the Committee.

10 *Public Law,* 88–633, Section 301 (d) (4), 22 U.S.C. Section 2370(e) (2).

11 Care must be taken in connection with the nomenclature of two separate bills sponsored by the late Senator Hickenlooper. The earlier Hickenlooper Amendment, enacted in 1962, in general provided that the United States would withhold foreign aid from a country which expropriated American-

owned property in violation of International Law—22 U.S.C. Section 2370 (e) (1). This statute, only indirectly involved in the *Sabbatino* litigation, has been frequently used as a threat to countries which have threatened to nationalise United States-owned property, but it has rarely been actually applied except for very limited periods. The Hickenlooper Amendment to which we refer in the text (sometimes known as Hickenlooper II) is not addressed to the Executive Branch of the government; it is addressed rather to the courts. For reasons that will appear later in this recital, the statute has been utilised only in the sequel to the *Sabbatino* decision.

12 See: *Furman* v. *Georgia*, 408 U.S. 238 (1972).

13 The best sources on these settlements can be found in Lillich & Weston, *International Claims: Their Settlement By Lump Sum Agreements*, (University Press of Virginia, 1975). See also Lillich (ed.) *The Valuation of Nationalized Property in International Law*, (University Press of Virginia, 1972).

14 The attorneys for Chase Bank were, or at least presented a posture of being, totally oblivious of the International Law implications in the case, and throughout the litigation acted as though this were a case arising under the Fifth Amendment of the United States Constitution which prohibits the public taking of private property without just compensation. It was assumed that this principle of United States law was also a principle of universal law.

15 The problems raised by attempting to apply rules of International Law to a situation in which rules have not been well-formulated are manifest. All sorts of theoretical questions are raised: what is the substantive content of International Law? How is such law enacted? How is it enforced? How is it changed when changing conditions made the old law obsolete? Even after these questions are answered in theory—if they ever are—there are a host of practical problems: how do we reconcile the views of large industrial nations with those of developing nations? What role does the United Nations and its agencies play in making such law?

Insofar as International Law may be expressed in multilateral treaties, some stability may be achieved, but the task of finding and applying customary International Law is quite another matter. Discussion of that problem is outside the scope of this paper.

16 'Intervention' is a procedure which, in Cuban law, is a step similar to a receivership in United States law. For purposes of litigation, the courts in the United States have treated intervention to be the equivalent of nationalisation. When a company is intervened under Cuban law, the administrator of the enterprise is known as the 'intervenor'.

5 Law and Economic Coercion as Instruments of International Control: the Nationalisation of Chilean Copper

CARLOS FORTIN

1 INTRODUCTION

To the casual observer, the 1971 nationalisation of copper in Chile by the government of Salvador Allende and its aftermath may appear as a typical example of the power of multinational corporations to thwart the attempts at economic independence of nationalistic governments in underdeveloped countries. All the elements of the well-known drama were there: the attachment of Chilean copper in European ports by the expropriated American corporations; the intervention of the United States government both to block international financial support to Chile, and to provide direct covert assistance to opposition forces; the increasingly deteriorating economic position of the Allende government in 1972 and early 1973; the bloody military coup that put an end to the Allende experiment and to Chilean democracy in September 1973; and finally the rush of the new Chilean military rulers to settle the dispute with the American multinationals through agreement on the payment of satisfactory compensation.

On closer inspection, however, the situation appears to be more complex. A first distinction that needs introducing is between the retaliatory actions of the companies themselves and the actions of the American government. It can be shown that the former were on the whole unsuccessful. Kennecott, one of the nationalised corporations, set out to bring about a collapse in the market for Chilean copper in Europe through a series of *ex parte* attachments in various European countries, as well as through commercial pressures to buyers. This purpose was not achieved: with the exception of small sections of the French and Swedish markets, the sales of Chilean copper in Europe never ceased to proceed more or less normally. The other nationalised corporation, Anaconda, did not attempt to interfere with the sales of Chilean copper; while the proceedings it instituted in New York to collect compensation had the effect of blocking purchases of spare parts and inputs for the Chilean mines in or through New York, this had only a limited impact on production in Chile.

Different is the situation with respect to the pressures brought upon Allende by the actions of the U.S. government. Under the overt justification of the copper nationalisation (later combined with the 'credit-worthiness' issue) all bilateral aid to Chile was interrupted, the American government refused to re-negotiate its share of the Chilean foreign debt, and American pressure was instrumental in determining the interruption or drastic reduction of credit to Chile from the World Bank and the Inter American Development Bank. At the same time the U.S. government launched a sustained campaign of covert activities designed to prevent the consolidation of the Allende government and eventually to bring about its downfall. The combination of economic pressure and direct intervention was no doubt a major factor in creating the conditions for the overthrow of the Unidad Popular government, which in turn brought about a resolution to the conflict between Chile and the American copper multinationals.

Nevertheless, a number of questions still remain in connection with the actions of the American government vis-a-vis Allende. The first one is, to what extent was the copper nationalisation issue the decisive factor in determining U.S. government policy towards Allende? Though not without inconsistencies, the official American position was that the formal actions of economic retaliation of the U.S. government were a function of the Chilean stand on the copper compensation issue. How accurate is this explanation? Does it also apply to the covert action of the CIA and other U.S. government agencies? What was the role of the American copper corporations in the process of decision-making leading to the policies of economic blockade and support of subversion in Chile?

A second set of questions has to do with the effects of U.S. government intervention with respect to the Allende government. Did the actions of the U.S. government have any effect in Allende's policy towards the copper companies? More generally, how decisive was American economic pressure and direct intervention in the overthrow of the Allende government?

In what follows, an attempt will be made to take up the issues indicated above with a view to throwing some light on the question of formal and informal mechanisms of international control and domination in the relations between underdeveloped and dependent countries and multi-national corporations.[1] A description will first be offered of the development of the conflict with the companies and of its impact on the economic and political situation of Chile at the time. A similar description and assessment will then be attempted with regard to the intervention of the American government and the direct and indirect pressures exercised on the Allende administration. The questions suggested above will then be explored in that context. Finally, the chapter will present a brief account of the settlement of the compensation dispute by the military junta that succeeded Allende and a concluding section on some general propositions to be derived from the Chilean experience with respect to the question of the international viability of nationalisation attempts.

2. THE EVOLUTION OF THE INTERNATIONAL CONFLICT OF CHILEAN COPPER: THE CONFLICT WITH THE COMPANIES

On 21 December 1970—that is, less than two months after taking office—President Allende sent to Congress the bill of the constitutional amendment nationalising copper. The companies affected were those operating the mines of Chuquicamata and Salvador, in which The Anaconda Company was a 49 per cent shareholder; El Teniente, with a 49 per cent participation of Kennecott Copper Corporation; Exotica, with a 75 per cent interest of Anaconda; and the Andina company, 70 per cent of which belonged to Cerro Corporation. These companies had become joint ventures between the Chilean State and the American corporations following agreements signed by the Frei government in 1967–9. Together, they represented in 1970 80 per cent of the copper produced in Chile and 60 per cent of the total value of Chilean exports.

The bill approved by Congress after seven months of debates provided for compensation to be paid on the basis of the book value of the nationalised companies less certain deductions. In addition, it authorised the President to order the deduction of the whole or part of the excess profits derived by the nationalised companies or their predecessors since 1955. The determination of the final amount of compensation was entrusted to the Comptroller General of Chile, an independent official in charge of the control of the legality of the acts of the Executive power; and an appeal was established before a Special Tribunal composed of three higher court justices, the Governor of the Central Bank of Chile and the Director of the Internal Revenue Service.[2]

In September 1971, the President ordered the deduction from the compensation to be paid of all profits exceeding 12 per cent of the book value of the companies from year to year since 1955.[3] The result of this decision was that the companies operating Chuquicamata, Salvador, and

Teniente did not have a right to compensation over and above the indirect compensation involved in the government taking up the liabilities of the companies.[4] Up until that point there had already been signs of impending difficulties with both the companies and the American government, which reacted to the announcement of the content of the bill with indications of concern.[5] With the excess profits decision the conflict became open and started having expression in the judicial, the diplomatic, and the financial arenas.

Overtly, the conflict centred not around the principle of the national-isation[6] but around the question of compensation, and in particular the deduction of excess profits. Even though the companies often mentioned that the Allende government was violating the agreements entered into by the Frei administration in 1967 and 1969, which set up the joint ventures between the American corporations and the Chilean State, they did not place emphasis on the principle *pacta sunt servanda* in order to contest the validity of the nationalisation act in International Law.[7] They did, however, insist on the view that, in order to be valid according to International Law, the nationalisation had to be followed by prompt, adequate, and effective compensation.[8]

Faced with what they perceived as an act of confiscation, the companies set out to find redress by resort to both formal mechanisms (most notably, the legal challenge of the nationalisation measures in courts of the United States and Europe); and to informal instruments such as commercial and political pressures.

(a) THE FORMAL CONFLICT: JUDICIAL PROCEEDINGS IN THE U.S. AND EUROPE

The main component of the conflict with the companies was the judicial one. At first, it focused on the appeal before the Special Tribunal in Chile against the determination of the compensation done by the Comptroller General. This the companies had to do in order to exhaust local remedies, and therefore prepare the ground for possible actions in foreign or international courts. In the appeal the companies objected to the computation of the book values and of the specific deductions, and also appealed against the deduction for excess profits. The government took the position that the deduction for excess profits was a power vested solely in the President by the constitutional amendment, and that it was not therefore subject to judicial review. The companies then requested the tribunal to decide as a preliminary issue, whether it had or not jurisdiction to review the excess profits deduction.[9]

In September 1972, after almost a year of legal argument, the tribunal ruled in favour of the government, declaring that it had no jurisdiction to pass on the deduction for excess profits ordered by the President.[10] The very day in which the decision was announced Kennecott's President,

Frank R. Milliken issued a statement saying that Kennecott would withdraw from further legal proceedings in Chile and would 'pursue in other nations its remedies for the nationalised assets'.[11] A letter was also sent to customers of El Teniente copper advising them of Kennecott's continued rights of ownership in the copper.[12]

Concurrently with the proceedings in Chile, both Kennecott and Anaconda had initiated actions in the United States for claims derived from the 1967–9 sale of 51 per cent of the equity of their operations in Chile; these, they maintained, were totally separate from the proceedings resulting from the Allende nationalisation. In February 1972 Kennecott brought two suits in New York against the Chilean state for the payment of promissory notes that fell due in December 1971, for the amount of U.S.$5.8 million. These notes had been issued in 1967, at the time of the incorporation of the joint venture Sociedad Minera El Teniente, S.A., in which Chile had a 51 per cent share. It was agreed then that the value of the 51 per cent interest, which was paid in full by Chile, would be loaned back to the new company by Kennecott, to be repaid over a period of fifteen years beginning in 1972. The promissory notes in question represented the first of the instalments.

Since the constitutional amendment established that the state would assume the debts of the nationalised companies only if they had been usefully invested, the Allende government had decided to suspend payment pending an investigation as to whether the loan had in effect been usefully invested. The suit was brought against the Chilean state because the government in 1967 had unconditionally guaranteed the promissory notes signed by Sociedad Minera El Teniente, S.A.[13]

Kennecott was able to secure an *ex parte* attachment of property belonging to a number of Chilean state agencies operating in New York, including airplanes of the national airline; the order of attachment also included bank accounts of the Chilean Central Bank. Twenty days after the court granted the attachments, the Chilean government ordered the payment of the promissory notes, having decided that only a comparatively minor part of the loan had not been usefully invested. It is clear that the New York attachments were an important factor in bringing about a speedy response on the part of the Chilean government.[14]

Soon after this incident Anaconda decided to act also. Again, a set of promissory notes this time issued by the Copper Corporation of Chile, and guaranteed by the Chilean Development Corporation (but not by the Chilean state as such) had fallen due in December 1971. The amount was about U.S.$12 million. They corresponded to an instalment of the payment for the 51 per cent of Chuquicamata and Salvador purchased by Chile in 1969. Before the due date, the Chilean government requested the Special Tribunal to order the suspension of the payment until the question of compensation was resolved, since the constitutional amendment established that the compensation took the place of the obligations derived from the purchase of shares. Anaconda refused to be drawn on this issue, arguing that the notes were independent of any specific transaction, and hence outside the jurisdiction of the tribunal. The tribunal ruled in favour of Chile, and ordered the suspension of payment, while requiring that Chile deposited in the tribunal an amount in Chilean currency equivalent to the value of the notes in order to guarantee payment, were the tribunal in the end to decide in favour of Anaconda. At the end of February 1971 Anaconda requested and obtained a decree of attachment from the Court of the Second District of New York covering accounts and property of the Chilean Copper Corporation and the Chilean Development Corporation. The effect of this action was less spectacular than in the case of Kennecott because the Chilean state as such was not involved. Still, it meant that purchases of spare parts and inputs for the Chilean mines done in or through New York had to be stopped, since the goods could be subjected to attachment. Chile argued in court that the two Chilean agencies involved enjoyed sovereign immunity, as they were part of the Chilean state, but after a number of procedural delays, the defence was rejected in the first instance.[15] It was by then clear that Anaconda's strategy vis-a-vis Chile was concentrated in trying to obtain payment for the promissory notes representing the 51 per cent sold to Chile in 1969. As for the remaining 49 per cent, it chose to claim compensation from the Overseas Private Investment Corporation, a U.S. agency that insures American investment abroad against such risks as expropriation, with which Anaconda had in fact taken up insurance before the sale of the 51 per cent.

Kennecott, by contrast, decided to try and obtain compensation for its 49 per cent from Chile by claiming ownership of El Teniente copper in various countries where it was sold. This presented several legal difficulties. To start with, Kennecott had to establish that it had a property right over the copper deposits before the 1971 nationalisation. However, the Chilean Mining Code of 1932 was ambiguous on the question of the nature of mining rights, and one interpretation of its provisions was that the so-called 'mining property' is only a concessionary right to extract minerals, and involves no property right over the ore still in the ground.[16] Furthermore, Kennecott's subsidiary in Chile was only a 49 per cent shareholder in the nationalised company, and as such would only have in principle a credit for 49 per cent of the liquid value of the company, rather than any property right in the company's assets.

If Kennecott could overcome the preceding legal problems, it would then have to show that the Chilean nationalisation was null and void. For that it had to show that it violated either International Law or the public policy of the forum, and to convince the court that the violation entailed the nullity of the nationalisation, rather than some other effect (such as the obligation to indemnify the party injured by the violation).

Kennecott succeeded in three European countries in overcoming the preceding problems in order to obtain attachments of El Teniente copper or the proceeds of its sale. In all three, though, the attachment was short-lived, although legal problems remained afterwards; in two other countries the attempts were unsuccessful; in one country (Britain) no attempt was ever made.

The first action was in France. In September 1972 Kennecott appeared before the Court of Extended Jurisdiction of Paris to request that payment for two shipments of Teniente copper sold by Chile to French buyers, and due to arrive at the port of Le Havre shortly afterwards, be attached in the possession of the buyers until such time as the ownership of the copper be established, the attachment to be decreed without previous notification of the Chilean party, the Chilean Copper Corporation. The petition was granted on 30 September 1972. What was attached was, therefore, the money owed by the buyers to Chile, up to the value of the copper. The basis of the claim, however, was Kennecott's alleged right of ownership over the copper. To establish that, Kennecott argued that the national-isation of the assets of the El Teniente company and the actual takeover by the Chilean government meant that the company had lost all corporate purpose and was therefore dissolved; that according to French law the effect of dissolution is that the assets of the company dissolved become the undivided property of its members; and that therefore Braden as 49 per cent stockholder of the dissolved Sociedad Minera El Teniente, S.A., was the co-owner of the El Teniente mine deposit and of the ore extracted from it. Kennecott then proceeded to argue that the Chilean nationalisation was without any compensation and that it was consequently contrary to French public policy and hence the transfer of title to the Chilean state was not to be recognised in France.[17]

One reaction to the granting of the attachment in favour of Kennecott was a decision of the dockers' union at Le Havre to the effect that they should not unload the ship carrying the copper whose value had been attached. As a result, the charterers of the ship, a Peruvian company, rather than risking high port fees in Le Havre because of the dockers' decision diverted the ship to the port of Rotterdam. Wrongly believing that Chile was attempting to dispose of the copper elsewhere, Kennecott appeared before the President of the Rotterdam District Court to request the attachment of the copper. The petition was granted, whereupon the longshoremen of Rotterdam refused to unload the ship. This gave rise in quick succession to a number of legal moves from the charterers against both the union and Kennecott. At that point Kennecott realised that its position was being prejudiced by the fact that it had attached the value of the copper in Paris and then the copper itself in Rotterdam, and proceeded unilaterally to vacate the attachment.[18] The original presentation by Kennecott had been based on the same reasoning as in the Paris case, only that in Holland there was some reference to International Law, which was totally absent in the French presentation.

By a mixture of planning and coincidence, Kennecott had succeeded in a matter of twenty days to obtain attachments of Chilean copper in two European countries. The fact that the first request was made to a French court was, of course, no accident: due to the Algerian nationalisations of French property in the 1960s the French courts had in a number of cases decided that a nationalisation without compensation was contrary to French *ordre public*, although there were also some decisions in the opposite direction, both in Algerian cases and before. That Kennecott could have then attempted an action in Holland was sheer luck (though no doubt Kennecott was already prepared to act should the occasion arise). As it happens, Holland was the other major European country that, due to cases of expropriation of property in a former colony (in this case it was Indonesia), also had decisions requiring the payment of compensation as a requisite for the validity of nationalisation of foreign property.[19] In fact, it is arguable that Holland was the least favourable country for the Chilean legal position. On the other hand, the sales of Chilean copper in Holland were almost nil, although Rotterdam was used as a port to unload copper destined for Germany and Belgium.

In the French case, the Chilean Copper Corporation decided to fight the attachment and the subsequent ordinary proceedings on the basis of the claim of sovereign immunity for the corporation as an instrumentality of the Chilean State, although it also advanced several subsidiary arguments.[20]

In the decision on the Chilean appeal against the attachment, handed down on 29 November, the French court did not address all the arguments. In fact, the decision seems to be basically a stalling move, aimed at creating the least possible trouble while calling on the parties to attempt a negotiated settlement. In two important respects the decision is unfavourable to Chile: it rejects the plea of sovereign immunity of the Copper Corporation on the grounds of its being involved in ordinary trade as far as the copper is concerned; it further reaffirms that no legal effect is to be recognised in France to an expropriation by a foreign state without an equitable compensation. On the other hand, it lifts the attachment with only the rather peculiar condition that the Copper Corporation be prepared to produce the sums in the event of a final decision in Kennecott's favour in the ordinary proceedings. This is, of course, no more than the general obligation of any party to a suit involving the right to a sum of money to pay up if he loses; otherwise the Copper Corporation was not enjoined from using the sums in whichever way it thought fit, and in fact the sums were withdrawn from France afterwards. In addition it orders an investigation to determine whether: (a) the funds received by the Copper Corporation in the exercise of its commercial functions are nevertheless the property of the Chilean state, in which case the funds could benefit from immunity from execution; (b) whether there was an equitable compensation in the fact that the compensation to Braden was set-off against the excess profits; and (c) to gather all elements that could permit the global settlement of the dispute between the parties.[21]

The Copper Corporation then appealed the denial of the sovereign immunity plea, and refused to submit evidence to the official appointed by the court to conduct the investigation. The remainder of the proceedings looked long and complicated, and no clear prediction as to the outcome appeared possible at the time. In the meantime, the sales of Teniente Copper in France were interrupted, which was not a major problem for Chile as the French market for fire-refined copper (the type sold by El Teniente) amounted only to 16 thousand tons, out of total Chilean copper exports of over 600 thousand tons.

During the month of October, Kennecott attempted to obtain an attachment on Teniente copper or the proceeds of its sale in Sweden. The petition was denied by the District Court of Vasteras on the grounds of a technical defect of jurisdiction, but the Swedish buyer decided to pay the amount due to the Copper Corporation in the hands of the Provincial Council of Stockholm, which is entrusted by Swedish law to receive disputed payments; it also decided not to continue purchasing the comparatively small tonnages of Teniente copper it had contracted, for in 1971, due to the uncertainty introduced by Kennecott's action as well as to direct commercial pressures from Kennecott.[22]

By the end of 1972, Kennecott had achieved a limited degree of success in interfering with the sales of Teniente copper in Europe. The three largest customers by far, however, had not been affected, namely, Germany, Britain, and Italy, accounting for over 80 per cent of total Teniente sales. On 5 January 1973 Kennecott entered the German judicial arena by seeking the attachment of a load of 3,500 tons of blister copper, sent to Hamburg by the Copper Corporation in order to be refined at the Norddeutsche Affinerie and distributed later to various buyers. In order to secure standing as an ownership claimant, Kennecott used a judicial theory developed in Germany as a result of cases involving nationalisations in East Europe, and specifically in East Germany. This is the theory of the 'split' of 'residual' company, according to which if a company has been nationalised without compensation and there are assets of the company outside the territory of the nationalising state, the former owners can be regarded as a 'residual' company of the one that was nationalised for purposes of claiming the assets located in German territory. Kennecott obtained from a court in Hamburg the appointment of a curator for the split company Sociedad Minera El Teniente, S.A., that took the place in Germany of the dissolved Chilean company of the same name.[23] It then proceeded, through the curator, to claim ownership over the copper and to request its attachment. The presentation by Kennecott in Hamburg is by far the most comprehensive argument of its case of any of the similar ones elsewhere. It argues that the Chilean nationalisation is null and void according to both International Law and the German public policy, because of the absence of compensation that is 'prompt, effective, and reasonable'. The presentation also discusses the question of the nature of the mining rights of the Teniente company, maintaining that they were actual property rights; and includes a discussion of the famous case of the Indonesian tobacco, decided by the Court of Appeals of Bremen in 1959, which found in favour of Indonesia against the former Dutch owners of nationalised tobacco fields.[24] The presentation detailedly attempts to distinguish the Indonesian case from the Chilean case.[25]

The attachment in favour of Kennecott was granted on the same day, and Chile immediately filed an opposition to the attachment, which was also a most detailed exposition of the Chilean case. In addition to arguing the points raised in the French court, the presentation in Hamburg raised a number of points regarding Chilean legislation before the nationalisation that would invalidate Kennecott's claim to ownership, including both provisions of the Mining Code of 1932 and of the Civil Code of 1855.

In the oral arguments, Kennecott lawyers also maintained that the nationalisation had been discriminatory, as it had affected only American companies, and that there had been a denial of justice because the excess profits deduction was not subject to judicial review; they further claimed that the American companies had been required to pay enormous fees for the right to appear before the Special Tribunal. The Chilean lawyers rejected the discrimination accusation pointing to the fact that the nationalised companies represented 80 per cent of the copper production of Chile and had in fact been the subject of a special legal regime since 1955; they also pointed out that the fees payable for appearances were the ordinary ones in the Chilean judicial system, only that the very high sums being the subject of the litigation made for high fees. They finally reiterated the notion that the excess profits deduction was a discretionary administrative act.

Once again, the decision did not take up all the issues. However, the basic burden of it was clearly in favour of the Chilean position. To begin with, it rejected the claim that International Law calls for the nullification of a nationalisation that is contrary to its substantive rules. On the contrary, the court maintained that it was even more detrimental to international relations to introduce uncertainty in international commercial transactions, and therefore, while other remedies could be open to the injured party, the nationalisation should be recognised. It acknowledges, though, that a nationalisation that is completely abhorrent to Germany public policy—i.e. that violates the basic principles of German law—should not be recognised, and in fact suggests that that is the case with the Chilean nationalisation because of its being discriminatory (here the court did not have all the evidence in; whatever else the Chilean nationalisation was, it cannot be seriously suggested that it was discriminatory). Nevertheless, it finds that the connection of the copper with the German legal system is not sufficient to warrant an application of the public policy rule, as the copper was in Germany only for purposes of refining. After some inconclusive considerations about the issue of the nature of mining rights, it accepts a Chilean argument according to which this case is covered by a legal institution of the 1855 Civil Code named 'specification' whereby the person who, with raw material belonging to somebody else, makes something of much more value than the original material, becomes the owner of the product. It was declared that the blister copper was a product whose value was much higher than the original ore; hence Chile, even if the nationalisation were to be invalid, would be the owner. The court therefore vacated the attachment and ordered Kennecott to pay all legal costs involved.[26]

Although the decision left a number of issues unresolved, its gist, as was suggested above, was sufficiently in favour of the Chilean position to convince all buyers of Teniente copper in Germany to continue buying normally, with only a private guarantee from CODELCO that, should the final decision be in favour of Kennecott, CODELCO would indemnify the buyers for any damage they might suffer.

In Italy, Kennecott first tried to apply its general strategy of obtaining *ex parte* attachments, but having concluded that its chances of obtaining them were low it decided instead to institute ordinary proceedings against the Italian buyers of Teniente copper, demanding the surrender of the material. This was done in February and March 1973. The legal reasoning of the presentations followed the lines of the French writ.[27] The long-term prospects of the proceedings were clearly unfavourable to Kennecott, as there was a line of precedents stemming from the Iranian nationalisations of 1952 that established the principle of non-review of the acts of a foreign sovereign state in nationalisation cases.[28] In fact, one such case was decided precisely in February 1973 in the Civil Court of Syracuse, concerning the nationalisation of BP's oil concessions in Libya; even though the Libyan nationalisation was an explicit act of political retaliation against the British government, the Italian court decided in favour of the Libyan government on the grounds that according to Libyan mining law, the oil before extraction was the property of the state.[29] As in the case of Germany, this assessment of the legal prospects was sufficiently reassuring for the buyers of Teniente copper to continue purchasing the material on normal terms.

Finally, as suggested above, no attempt of any kind was ever made in Britain, no doubt because of the clearly established doctrine of British courts according to which an act of nationalisation of a foreign government concerning assets located in its territory is not to be reviewed by a British judge, irrespective of the nationality of the former owner or the presence or absence of compensation.[30]

(b) THE INFORMAL CONFLICT: ECONOMIC AND POLITICAL PRESSURES BY THE
   COMPANIES.

In addition to the legal moves, both companies attempted other forms of
pressure on Chile. Kennecott tried to get some buyers of Teniente copper
to stop dealing with Chile, threatening in some cases retaliation in the
American market if they did not oblige. With the exception of one firm in
Sweden, these pressures were not successful. Anaconda is reported to have
approached American suppliers of spare parts and machinery for the
Chilean mines to get them to stop the supplies. Although most suppliers did
harden their terms of sale (requesting, for instance, cash payment) there
was no instance of an American supplier refusing outright to sell to Chile.
   Both companies, of course, also did vigorous lobbying with the
American government. This was particularly the case with Anaconda,
whose Washington representative took the lead in organising in February
1971 an *ad hoc* Committee on Chile, composed of representatives of all
major American companies with interests in Chile. The chairmanship of
the committee was later taken over by the representative of ITT. The
committee had a meeting with the Secretary of State, William P. Rogers,
in which a hard line towards Allende was urged with a view to forcing him
to take a less harsh approach towards American companies. The meeting
was attended by Anaconda but not by Kennecott, whose involvement in
the committee was minimal. There was no suggestion in the meeting of any
covert activities against Allende, and in fact suggestions for an economic
blockade made by ITT had a mixed reception on the part of the other
business representatives.[31] Anaconda appeared to have favoured quite a
hard line, and did some strong direct lobbying in the State Department
and Congress.[32] The extent to which the lobbying by the copper
companies influenced the U.S. government position will be discussed
below.
   The companies also withdrew the American technical personnel from
the mines and in some cases made offers of employment elsewhere to highly
qualified Chilean technicians, who left as a result. There does not seem to
have been any demonstrable attempts at sabotage directly attributable to
the companies.

(c) THE IMPACT OF THE CONFLICT WITH THE COMPANIES: AN EVALUATION

In a number of respects, Chile was in an ideal position to nationalise
copper without fear of serious reprisals from the affected multinationals. At
the time of nationalisation the mines were manned basically by Chileans,
and the technology involved in the operation was well-known in the
country. As a result, the withdrawal of American technicians was not a
serious problem;[33] in fact, more serious was perhaps the continuous

presence of Chilean technicians who, for political reasons quite apart from the nationalisation, opposed the Allende government and in some cases sabotaged production. The companies furthermore had no control over processing or transportation of the copper, and the main international market was outside the U.S. and composed of companies with no direct links with the American companies. Chile moreover had already considerable experience in the international marketing of copper, as a result of the involvement of the Chilean Copper Corporation following the partial takeover of 1967–9. The most potentially dangerous area was doubtless that of the inputs for the mines, 95 per cent of which were of American origin (although none supplied by the nationalised corporations themselves).

In the circumstances, the basic instruments of pressure of the companies were the international legal ones and their ability to mobilise the U.S. government to exercise pressure on Chile. As for the legal weapons, as we have shown, they failed to produce a major disruption in either the market or the production of Chilean copper, and as such were basically unsuccessful. They did, to be sure, create some difficulties: small sections of the market of El Teniente copper in Europe were closed, specifically in France and in Sweden; the port of Rotterdam was abandoned for purposes of unloading copper for certain Belgian and German buyers, and costlier routes had to be introduced; and some negotiations on short-term lines of credit in Canada with the guarantee of the proceeds of copper sales were adversely affected.[34] All in all, however, Kennecott actions had more of a nuisance effect than of a serious impact on Chile.[35] Unlike what had been the case with the nationalisation of oil in Iran in 1952—when the sales of Iranian oil practically stopped—not a single ton of Chilean copper remained unsold because of the legal offensive of the American companies. The relatively minor changes in the distribution of markets for Chilean copper that took place between 1970 and 1973 were only marginally related to the attachments (Table 5·1). Kennecott's actions, far from forcing the Allende government to come to terms (as was undoubtedly the goal of Kennecott when undertaking them), in fact strengthened the will to resist of the Chilean government, and helped to rally support both from all Chilean political sectors and from other third-world countries. Thus, the Inter Governmental Council of Copper Exporting Countries (CIPEC), whose members were Chile, Peru, Zaire, and Zambia, held a special Conference of Ministers in Santiago in November 1972 in which a resolution was passed condemning the actions of Kennecott and pledging full support to the Chilean government.[36] Similar expressions of support took place in Latin American and U.N. forums.[37]

As suggested above, the Anaconda moves in New York created somewhat more difficult problems, because they effectively produced an interruption of the purchases of inputs for the mines in or through New York, and considerably reduced the purchasing operation in the United

States as a whole. Chile had to find substitutes in Europe, Canada, Australia, and Japan, and this was not always possible and almost always costlier. Still, by the end of 1972, approximately 50 per cent of all purchases were done in Canada and about 20 per cent in London.[38] Problems of supplies of spare parts and other inputs were not major, and the relatively small losses in production in 1971–2 (see Table 5.2), can be explained mostly by technical difficulties of the kind that require time to be solved (irrespective of the presence or absence of the American administration); by political difficulties with antigovernment Chilean personnel; and by labour discipline problems, the latter being a function of the disappearance of the system of rewards and penalties imposed by the American administration and the difficulties of introducing another system, based on workers' participation, which nevertheless maintained labour productivity.[39]

TABLE 5.1 Exports of Chilean copper by country 1970–3

| | % distribution | | | |
	1970	1971	1972	1973
West Germany	25·3	24·4	22·0	18·1
Great Britain	14·7	14·8	13·1	12·8
Italy	10·0	9·6	8·6	7·0
France	7·5	6·9	5·1	3·5
United States	15·2	7·6	10·7	8·9
Latin America	5·3	6·5	5·8	7·0
Japan	9·4	16·5	8·3	14·2

TABLE 5.2 Production of Gran Minería and Andina

| | thousands of metric tons | | | |
	1969	1970	1971	1972
Chuquicamata	283·4	263·0	250·2	234·6
Salvador	77·1	93·0	84·9	82·8
Teniente	179·9	176·6	147·3	190·6
Exótica	-	1·9	35·3	31·3
Andina	-	5·0	53·6	53·9
Total	495·4	540·5	571·4	593·2

Source: Copper Corporation of Chile.

3. THE CONFLICT WITH THE UNITED STATES GOVERNMENT

(a) THE ECONOMIC BLOCKADE

In his speech to the General Assembly of the United Nations of 4 December 1972, President Allende denounced the existence of a veritable economic and financial blockade against Chile inspired and managed by the United States government. The facts of the matter, clear enough at the time, became even clearer in the following nine months:

(a) All new bilateral aid from the American government to Chile was suspended in 1971. The only exception was military aid: a total of U.S.$15 million in low interest loans for the purchase of military equipment was extended between 1971 and 1973, the reason being the need for the U.S. government to remain in good terms with the Chilean military, which they viewed as potential allies against the Allende government. Even though disbursements on other existing loans continued, they were less than Chile's repayments;[40]

(b) In June 1971 the U.S. Export-Import Bank denied the Chilean government an already negotiated loan for U.S. $21 million to finance the purchase of three Boeing jet airplanes for the Chilean national airline, and in August Eximbank's president informed the Chilean Ambassador to Washington that Chile would not receive more loans until there was a satisfactory solution to the question of copper compensation.[41] Later Eximbank suspended its programme of guarantees and insurance of loans made to Chile by private American banks and suppliers, and in June 1972 it interrupted disbursements on existing loans;[42]

(c) The Inter American Development Bank only extended the Allende government two loans for a total amount of U.S.$11·6 million for university projects in 1971. Three substantial projects that were ready to be submitted to the Bank's Board were never submitted in the three years of the Allende administration. Although disbursements on existing loans continued, they amounted to only U.S.$10 million more than repayments in 1971–2;[43]

(d) The World Bank did not extend any new loans to Chile under Allende. Disbursements continued, but they were equal to repayments in 1972 and would have been less than repayments in the first half of 1973. The IADB and the World Bank together had lent Chile an average of U.S.$50 million a year between 1965 and 1970;[44]

(e) Short-term lines of credit of private American banks were reduced from U.S.$220 million in 1970 to U.S.$30 million in 1971–2;[45]

(f) Suppliers of inputs for the Chilean mines in the U.S. considerably

hardened their terms of sale: no credit was extended and in some cases payment with the purchase order was required;
(g) The American government refused to renegotiate Chile's foreign debt in 1971-3.

The official position of the American government was that, with the exception of the foreign debt point, all these developments were either independent of the United States government or due not to the copper issue but rather to the lack of credit-worthiness of the Chilean economy under Allende. Subsequent revelations have shown, however, that the United States government did have a decisive influence in bringing about those developments, although not necessarily that it acted motivated by the copper issue. The official U.S. position reflects a preference for what we have earlier called informal mechanisms of control, which in the international context of the time were regarded as more viable.[46] Thus the United States never voted against a loan for Chile in the Inter American Development Bank or the World Bank; through informal pressure on the staff and lobbying of other delegations it in fact helped prevent the loans being submitted to the banks' Boards at all.[47] Equally, the reduction in private lines of credit and suppliers credit to Chile is traceable to informal pressure on private business by the U.S. government.[48] The revelations, though, went further; they in fact showed that by the time of Allende's speech—and unknown to him—the American government had already embarked on a course of action designed to bring about the overthrow of the Unidad Popular government.

(b) U.S. COVERT ACTIVITY IN CHILE 1970-3

The revelations are of course those concerning the covert activity of the Central Intelligence Agency in Chile during the Allende government.[49] While no detailed account of them can be attempted in this chapter, the following points summarise the major aspects:

(a) Between March 1970 and the popular vote for President in Chile of 4 September, the CIA, under instructions of the so-called Forty Committee (an interdepartmental body in charge of overseeing the covert activities of the CIA) waged what was termed a 'spoiling' operation against the Allende candidacy. In all, about U.S.$1 million were spent for this purpose. The campaign included intensive pro-paganda efforts in Chilean and international media, funding of right-wing organisations and a 'scare' campaign equating Allende's victory with violence and Stalinist repression.
(b) On 4 September Allende won a plurality of the popular vote, but as he did not obtain a majority the Chilean Constitution called for an

election in Congress between the two highest pluralities, to be held on 24 October. The Forty Committee met on 8 and 14 September to discuss action to be taken by the CIA to prevent Allende from being elected. On 15 September—and seemingly unknown to the Forty Committee—Nixon summoned the CIA Director R. Helms and instructed him to organise a coup d'etat in Chile to prevent Allende's assumption. He further instructed him to orchestrate a total economic blockade against Chile should Allende be elected. (Helms wrote in his notes of the meeting: 'Make the economy scream'. A week later the American Ambassador in Santiago reportedly told President Frei that 'not a nut or bolt would be allowed to reach Chile under Allende').

(c) Between 15 September and 24 October the U.S. intervention in Chile proceeded along two tracks. One, decided by the Forty Committee on 14 September and reviewed on 29 September, implied the launching of a propaganda campaign designed to influence the Congressional election by means of emphasising the chaos that would ensue if Allende was elected; and the mounting of an economic offensive against Chile to create the conditions for a military coup before Allende's assumption. Both elements of the first track proceeded apace; the economic offensive included the cutting off of all credits, pressuring firms to curtail investment in Chile, and approaching other nations to cooperate in the venture.

The second track involved direct efforts at organising a military coup. To that effect, the CIA had contacts with key military officers in Chile, who were reassured of U.S. support should they decide to stage a coup. Weapons were also supplied to one group of conspirators. On 22 October one of the groups with which the CIA was in touch murdered the Commander-in-Chief of the Chilean Army in a last attempt to create chaos and provoke a military intervention. The reaction did not take place, and Allende was elected and inaugurated in November 1970. Track two was seemingly handled directly between the White House and the CIA, and was in addition known to Kissinger and Attorney General Mitchell. The 40 Committee was seemingly not informed of the activities of track two, although its own activities were explicitly directed towards creating the conditions for a military coup in Chile.

(d) During the period 1971–3, the intervention of the U.S. government continued to proceed along the two basic lines; namely, the economic blockade, and the direct support of subversion in Chile. The economic blockade was organised according to guidelines contained in National Security Discussion. Memorandum 93 of November 1970 which, in the words of the U.S. Senate Report on Intelligence Activities was to be implemented by several means: 'All new bilateral foreign assistance was to be stopped, although disbursements would continue under loans made previously. The U.S. would use its predominant position in international financial institutions to dry up the flow of new multilateral credit or other financial assistance. To the extent possible, financial assistance or guarantees to U.S. private investment in Chile would be ended, and U.S. business would be made aware of the government's concern and its restrictive policies'.[50] Simultaneously, the CIA spent about U.S.$7 million in 1971–3 to support right-wing opposition parties and media, as well as right-wing civilian groups, some of which were linked to paramilitary organisations or were involved in the organisation and implementation of the two major employers' strikes of 1972/73. It also maintained close contacts with the Chilean armed forces, and in particular with the group that appeared most likely to stage a successful coup. In particular, the CIA monitored the progress of the planning of the 11 September coup through the months of July, August, and September.

(c) THE IMPACT OF U.S. INTERVENTION ON THE ALLENDE GOVERNMENT

There could be little doubt that the combined effect of both lines of American intervention in Chile during the Allende period was the creation of major difficulties for the government, that interfered with its effectiveness, enormously complicated its task, and in the end eroded its viability and helped bring about the conditions for the military coup of September 1973. In particular, the economic blockade hit very sensitive aspects of the Chilean economy and its system of external relations.[51] At the time Allende took office Chile was crucially dependent on the United States in a number of important respects. About 40 per cent of total Chilean imports were of American origin, including as was suggested above over 90 per cent of the inputs for the copper mines; other areas of high dependence on American imports were that of motor-vehicles spares and oil, where over 60 per cent of imported crude was provided by American companies. All this trade took place on the basis of a financial network of lines of credit extended by private American banks and of suppliers credit, backed both by the guarantee of the U.S. Eximbank. United States or American dominated international institutions had furthermore been the main source of aid and loans to Chile for the preceding decade, and as a result over 50 per cent of Chile's massive foreign debt was owed to American public agencies. The Chilean balance of payments was, therefore, highly sensitive to American pressure, especially since the price of copper was low in 1971–2, and some of the economic policies of the Allende government—such as the redistribution of income in favour of the poorest sectors of the population—entailed also added pressures on imports.

By itself, however, the economic blockade did not represent an unsurmountable problem for the Allende government. By the first half of 1973 a vigorous campaign to find substitute sources of finance and trade undertaken by the Chilean government had begun to bear fruit in the form of increased trade and short-term finance from Europe and Japan, and especially from Latin America. The rise in the price of copper at the end of 1972 and the expected levels for the second half of 1973 would have further helped to ease balance of payment difficulties. No doubt the shortage of hard currency in 1972 had created disequilibria that could not be overcome quickly, and in addition had a politically destabilising effect; however, a process of political consolidation of the Allende government, coupled with the easier balance of payment position that was expected, would have opened a very real possibility of the American blockade becoming less and less relevant for the Chilean economy. It is possible that precisely this type of reasoning led the American government to step up direct covert intervention in 1973, especially following the Congressional election of March 1973 in Chile, in which the government coalition obtained 44 per cent of the vote, an increase of almost 25 per cent over the percentage that Allende received in the 1970 presidential election.

Considerations similar to the preceding also may help explain the fact that the American economic blockade had no impact on the policy of the Allende government towards the copper companies. To be sure, the blockade was a continuous source of difficulties for the government, and there was a point in early 1973 when an estimate of the Development Corporation of Chile indicated that sectors of industry were operating at no more than 70 per cent capacity because of the blockade. The pressure, however, was not perceived as decisive enough for the government seriously to consider giving way to the American pretensions in terms of copper compensation. This question will be dealt with in the next section.

The impact of the direct CIA intervention was, however, a different matter. There is no question that the basic dynamics of subversion in Chile under Allende had its roots in the internal class struggle and the reaction of the dominant sectors of society to the political project of Unidad Popular, which they perceived as fundamentally harmful to their interests. It is also clear, though, that the internal forces of subversion were decisively aided by the intervention of the CIA, which provided technical knowhow, finance, and political support to their activities. It can be said that the covert action of the CIA was a major factor in preventing the Allende government from consolidating a power position which, in the absence of such intervention, would have been a very real possibility—as the electoral results cited suggest—and would have allowed the government to face the economic difficulties partly stemming from the blockade in an effective manner. Thus, the economic blockade and the political subversion lines interacted, and their cumulative effect was to help render the Allende experiment unworkable.

(d) AMERICAN INTERVENTION AND THE COPPER ISSUE

With the background provided by the materials presented in the previous sections we can now come back to some of the questions raised in the Introduction regarding the real place of the copper issue in the relations between the American and the Chilean governments in the Allende period.

To begin with, it seems clear that American policy was not a response to the nationalisation of copper. The actions of the American government to undermine the Allende experiment preceded the nationalisation, and in fact preceded even the assumption of Allende to power. Furthermore, the confidential material revealed in the U.S. Senate investigation indicates that, while the question of the fate of the American companies in Chile was obviously a consideration, the basic reason of American hostility to Allende was a general political one: the success of the Unidad Popular experiment represented a threat to American hegemony in the continent.[52] It would also appear that the lobbying of the American copper corporations was not a decisive factor in defining the policy.[53]

Similarly, it seems clear that obtaining compensation for the American companies was not the fundamental objective of American policy. In broad terms, the aim of U.S. government intervention in Chile can be defined in terms of preventing the consolidation of the Allende government in order, at least, to impair its effectiveness in implementing the programme of Unidad Popular; the optimal aim being to bring about an early termination of the experiment, whether by constitutional means (impeachment, resignation) or by violent means. To achieve these goals, U.S. policy proceeded in what has been called a 'triad' of approaches.[54] Firstly it avoided taking public harsh measures of the kind employed against Cuba in the 1960s; the official position was described as 'cool but correct'. The reason for this first line was that the international situation and especially the Latin-American context made it potentially very costly for the U.S. government to appear overtly confronting the Allende regime; furthermore, Allende's foreign policy was successful in increasing the international political cost of a possible overt U.S. intervention[55], and in any case, the public posture allowed the U.S. to keep open certain options of accommodation should the rest of the strategy fail and Allende consolidate. Secondly, it implemented the economic blockade with the dual purpose of contributing to the political destabilisation of Allende, and also to influence specific areas of Chilean government policy; as we shall see in a moment, here is where the copper compensation issue came in. Finally, it launched the covert activities aimed at preventing consolidation and helping to bring about the failure of the experiment.

The copper compensation issue was, therefore, present at the inception of the policy, but in a secondary place; and as an objective it was also secondary to that of disrupting the Allende experience as a whole (although this was not always perceived by all Chilean decision-makers themselves). The economic blockade, in particular, was more closely linked to the question of compensation than the rest of the American strategy; as in time it became clear that Allende was not prepared to compromise on the issue of excess profits, the covert track of activities was stepped up.[56] The area in which the American government explicitly linked the copper issue to economic reprisals was that of the Chilean foreign debt. In November 1971 the Allende government requested a re-negotiation of the debt with foreign public institutions and suspended its payment. The re-negotiation took place in the so-called Paris Club composed of all fourteen major creditor countries of the Western World. In the negotiations the United States delegation introduced the question of compensation for nationalised foreign property as a prerequisite for an agreement on refinancing. Chile refused to commit itself to any specific agreement on compensation that could interfere with the proceedings under way with respect to the copper companies pursuant to the constitutional amendment. Through the mediation of some Western European countries a formula was agreed upon according to which 'the Chilean representatives confirmed their government's policies of re-cognition and of payment of all foreign debt and its acceptance of the principles of payment of just compensation for all nationalisation in accordance with Chilean and international law'[57] The formula was ambiguous in that according to Chilean law the companies had no claim, while according to the United States' interpretation of International Law they did, a contention also denied by the Chilean government. On this basis a general agreement was arrived at in April 1972 to postpone payment of 70 per cent of the services due by Chile between November 1971 and December 1972. The general agreement was to be followed by specific negotiations with each creditor country, and Chile was sub-sequently able to reach agreements with all of them except the United States. The American government made a condition of the re-negotiation that Chile agree on settlement of the compensation dispute by means other than the one established in the constitutional amendment. Notes were then exchanged in September and November 1972 and negotiations took place in December 1972 and in March, June, and August 1973. In the negotiations Chile proposed to resort to the Treaty for the Settlement of Controversies signed by both countries in 1914, which calls for the establishment of an Investigating Commission to review the issues and submit a report, upon which the governments are to attempt a direct settlement. If they are unable to do so, the dispute can be submitted to arbitration. According to Chile's proposal, the investigation should deal not only with the compensation issue but with the question of the extent to which U.S. policy in multilateral lending organisations was in violation of International Law.

The United States objected to the application of the Treaty because it did not lead to a binding decision and proposed instead a binding international arbitration solely on the question of the compensation to the copper companies. This same procedure could then be followed with respect to ITT.

This solution was not possible according to Chilean law as the copper nationalisation was done through a constitutional amendment that could not be modified by the decision of an international arbiter. To be binding, such a decision would have to be approved by the Chilean Congress in the same way as if it were another constitutional amendment; this the Chilean government was, of course, in no position to guarantee. Furthermore the American proposal meant to disregard the substantive criteria for compensation adopted by the constitutional amendment and to introduce new criteria based on purported international standards. While the Chilean government was prepared to discuss, within the framework of the 1914 Treaty, the criteria adopted with a view to arriving at a compromise, it was not prepared to accept the introduction of an altogether new set of criteria, particularly since it rejected the thesis that there are universally accepted criteria to judge the adequacy of compensation. Finally, Chile maintained that the activities of ITT to subvert the Chilean internal political process made it impossible to include its case in any general treatment of the question of compensation settlement.

Some new avenues of solution—including the joint application of the 1914 Treaty and presentations by the Chilean government to the Special Copper Tribunal set up by the constitutional amendment—were being explored by the two governments when the coup of 11 September 1973 took place.

By then, however, it is clear that not even a 'satisfactory' arrangement of the copper compensation question would have significantly altered the course of American policy towards Chile. A compromise earlier—at the expense of Allende's international and internal credibility—would have deprived the American government of the overt pretext for the economic blockade and therefore would have probably meant some easing of American pressure. It is our contention that it would not have meant a true *modus vivendi* with Allende; the latter required as an absolute precondition a consolidation of the Allende government in Chile, and the bulk of American intervention in the period was precisely directed towards preventing that consolidation.

One last point that deserves mentioning in this context is that the American economic blockade by itself proved also incapable of altering the course of Allende's policy towards the copper companies, and generally of disrupting the implementation of the nationalisation policies. The covert action of the CIA did have negative effects on the copper industry, both directly (support of disruptive action by antigovernment employees) and indirectly (transportation difficulties as a result of truck-owners' strikes). But they were by-products of the general destabilising activities of the U.S. in Chile. Paradoxical as it may sound, the Chilean case is one in which the pressures of both the American copper multinationals and those of the American government aimed specifically to change Allende's copper policy proved impotent to do so. It was necessary for the government to be overthrown—an event whose dynamics is of course much wider than the copper question alone—for the companies to obtain a satisfactory settlement of their claims.

(e) COPPER IN THE AFTERMATH OF THE MILITARY COUP

Shortly after the coup the new military rulers of Chile announced their intention to settle the compensation issue with the American companies. This was, of course, far from surprising, considering that the new regime placed itself firmly within the sphere of influence of the United States and international capital. The process, however, seemed to have been less than easy, and it would appear that the role of the American government was not only urging the Chilean junta to settle as quickly as possible, but also putting some pressure on the American companies to drop some of their most extreme claims. The result was an agreed compensation that, while being grossly in excess of what in the most favourable interpretation of the constitutional amendment of 1971 the companies could have hoped for, nevertheless falls short of the stated claims of the companies. The one exception to this statement is the case of Cerro, the smallest of the three corporations involved, which was on the verge of agreement with the Allende government on payment of compensation; in that case the agreement with the military was sufficiently more favourable to the company than the one negotiated with Allende to cover practically all their claims.

In the case of Anaconda, the military agreed to pay the full depreciated book value of the assets without any deduction for excess profits. This, coupled with other features of the agreement—such as the high proportion of cash payment—makes it very close to a full satisfaction of Anaconda's true expectations, although it falls short of the figure announced by the company in 1972 as the value of the write-off and insurance claims.

Where the discrepancy between the settlement and the pretensions of the company is most clear is in the case of Kennecott. In effect, the settlement amounts to about one-half of the figure put forward by Kennecott in 1971 as the minimum acceptable. It still is considerably more than it would have received according to the nationalisation bill even in the absence of excess profits deduction. The agreement with Kennecott took a full three months more to be completed than the Anaconda one, which may be an indicator of difficulties to get the company to accept the Chilean offer. If, as is likely, it is true that the American government did urge the company to lower its claim in order to settle quickly and help the consolidation of the new regime, this would be additional evidence that all along the U.S. government was less concerned with the fate of specific American companies and their interests in Chile than with safeguarding its overall politicoeconomic position in the continent, of which American business interests were one among other components.[58]

4. BY WAY OF CONCLUSION

It is undoubtedly difficult to extract any general conclusions from a case like the Chilean one, which in so many respects is unique, as the preceding pages should have shown. However, it appears that a summarisation of the main points presented above may be helpful at least to clarify some of the issues involved in the question of formal and informal mechanisms of international control in the relationship between multinational corporations and governments of underdeveloped countries which, for whatever internal reasons, decide on a course of conflict with international capital.

To begin with, the Chilean case seems to point to the limitations of formal mechanisms of control in connection with nationalisation experiences. As shown above, the legal efforts of the companies were by and large fruitless as far as disrupting the implementation of the nationalisation measures, creating difficulties for the Chilean economy or inducing changes in the policies of the Allende government. One point that merits emphasising is the relative lack of importance of International Law, as conventionally understood, to the strategy of the companies. As a review of the European proceedings instituted by Kennecott shows, the explicit basis of the company's claim of ownership to the copper and the subsequent decisions of European courts was not so much the violation of rules of International Law regarding minimum international standards in cases of expropriation, as the violation of the public policy of the forum. This no doubt reflects the fact that both the increasing presence of the third world in the international arena and the emergence of intercapitalist competition at the global level have eroded the basis for the former owner's claim to title under what are termed recognised principles of International Law. The clearest expression of the new situation—at least as far as natural resource industries are concerned—is resolution 1803 of the United Nations,[59] which in fact seems to establish the principle that a nationalisation of a natural resource is valid irrespective of the presence or absence of compensation, without prejudice to other remedies that the injured party may have in International Law.[60] This in practice means that the most effective legal instrument of pressure at the disposal of the former owner— that of claiming ownership of the material and pursuing it in whichever hands it may be—is denied him. This principle has been since reaffirmed by other U.N. resolutions,[61] and although the interpretation of them has in all cases been subject to considerable international debate—with the capital exporting countries generally reserving their position on the implication suggested above—the matter seems to have become sufficiently mooted to make a recourse to International Law a less than adequate pressure weapon for the nationalised corporations.

Although as far as the public policy of the forum is concerned the position is different, in that nullity of the nationalisation—and hence a reaffirmation of the former owner's property—is still possible, the European cases show the reluctance of the courts in developed countries to alienate third-world governments and the natural resources they control for the sake of preserving the alleged rights of multinational corporations based in other developed countries. Aside from purely 'legal' considerations, it is clear that this type of concern runs through all the decisions summarised above, again emphasising the effect on international decision-making of the growth of the third-world block and the erosion of the undisputed U.S. hegemony in the world capitalist system.

When it comes to discussing informal mechanisms of international control, the problem of deriving general non-spurious conclusions from the Chilean case is particularly serious, not only because of the many strong points that Chile had when it started the nationalisation process, but also because of the fact that the undoing of the nationalisation was not the primary objective of American pressure. With those caveats in mind, however, one can also suggest that the Chilean case points to some of the limitations of informal mechanisms of control for the protection of foreign investment in underdeveloped countries. The reasons seem to be pretty similar to the ones proposed above, to which one should add the presence of the socialist bloc, which in the Chilean case was a not negligible source of finance and technical support to Allende. In the event, the Allende government was basically able to withstand the American economic blockade without modifying its basic policies vis-a-vis American capital; the overthrow of the government was necessary to achieve a satisfactory settlement with the American companies; yet the overthrow clearly was not a function of the copper conflict. Whether Allende would have had to compromise had he remained in power is, of course, only a matter for conjecture now. We have suggested that a consolidation of Allende in power, through a more effective popular mobilisation and military policy, could have meant that the American government would have accepted the nationalisation of copper in Allende's terms, and decided to cut losses by agreeing to some *modus vivendi*. Which in the end may well point to the basic conclusion that without forgetting the fundamental external-internal dialectics of dependency situations, in the end the international viability of nationalisation experiences is a function of the degree of internal cohesion and political mobilisation that the nationalising government is able to generate.

NOTES

1 The distinction is, of course, one of degree rather than kind. By formal mechanisms we refer to processes that take place in more or less structured arenas, and in which the actions of the parties have a claim to legitimacy based on some recourse to generally accepted rules. The clearest example of formal instruments is international adjudication, whether done by international or national courts. The extreme case of informal instruments is the covert intervention of one government in the internal politics of another. In between there lies a vast array of possible mechanisms of control, including political and diplomatic actions and economic pressures, all of which may be formal or informal depending on the context. The importance of the distinction lies in that formal mechanisms contain an element of publicity or at least accountability that sets limits to the uses to which the mechanism can be put.

2 Law No. 17,450 of 16 July 1971, published in *Diario Oficial* (Chile) of that date. The full text in English translation is in 10, *International Legal Materials*, 1067 (1971).

3 Presidential Decree No. 92 (Ministry of Mining), of 28 September 1971 published in *Diario Oficial* (Chile), 29 September 1971. English text in 10 *International Legal Materials*, 1035 (1971).

4 Resolution No. 529 of the Comptroller General of Chile issued 11 October 1971, published in *Diario Oficial* (Chile), 13 October 1971. English version in 10 *International Legal Materials*, 1240 (1971).

5 Kennecott Copper Corporation, *Expropriation of El Teniente. The Largest Underground Copper Mine* (New York: 1971, hereinafter referred to as *Kennecott*); William D. Rogers; 'Preface', in Richard B. Lillich (ed.), *The Valuation of Nationalized Property in International Law* (Charlottesville, U.S.A.: The University Press of Virginia, 1972)

6 *Kennecott*, Supplement (1971), p. 1; Testimony of William Quigley, Vice Chairman of the Board of The Anaconda Co. in U.S. Senate, *Multinational Corporations and United States Foreign Policy*. Hearings before the Subcommittee on Multinational Corporations of the Committee on Foreign Relations on the International Telephone and Telegraph Company and Chile, 1970–1, 20, 21, 22, 28, 29 March and 2 April 1973 (Washington D.C.: U.S. Government Printing Office, 1973; hereinafter referred to as *ITT Hearings*), Part I, pp. 264–5.

7 See, for instance, Kennecott's submissions in Swedish and Italian courts, *Kennecott* Supplement No. 4 (May 1973), pp. 11 and 91 respectively, and compare with submissions to French and German courts, *Kennecott*, Supp. No. 3 (December 1972), pp. 54–8 and No. 4 (May 1973), pp. 34–56.

8 'Memorandum on Governing International Law Principles' by Covington and Burling, Washington D.C., 16 August 1971, in *Kennecott*, pp. 64–92.

9 For the proceedings in Chile, see Novoa, Eduardo, *La batalla por el cobre* (Santiago: Editorial Quimantu, 1972), pp. 297 ff. Kennecott's legal brief before the Tribunal appears in *Kennecott*, Supplement No. 2 (1972), pp. 9–56, where a translation of the Chilean government's briefs is also reproduced, pp. 57–82.

10 Decision of the Special Copper Tribunal of 11 August 1972, published in *Diario Oficial* (Chile) of 19 August 1972. English text in 11, *International Legal Materials*, 1013 (1972).

11 *Kennecott*, Supp. No. 3, pp. 49–50

12 *Ibid.*, p. 51

13 *Kennecott*, Supp. No. 2, pp. 83–95, and Supp. No. 3, pp. 1–7

14 Novoa, *op. cit.*, p. 324

15 *Ibid.*, pp. 330–9

16 Legal opinion of Guillermo Pumpin submitted by the Chilean Copper Corporation to the Hamburg court (unpublished); *contra*, affidavit of Antonio Ortuzar del Solar submitted by Kennecott to the Hamburg Court.

17 *Kennecott*, Supp. No. 3, pp. 54–60

18 *Ibid.*, pp. 61–3

19 See below, footnote 24

20 These were: (a) that the right of Sociedad Minera El Teniente, S.A., over the copper deposits was in the nature of a concession and not of a property right; (b) that Braden lacked standing to claim ownership since according to Chilean law the original Teniente company had not ceased to exist, and in any case the dissolution in Chilean law does not bring about a situation of undivided co-ownership, as alleged by Kennecott; (c) that what was at stake was the right to payment within a sale contract to which Braden acknowledgedly was no party; (d) that the credit claimed by Braden lacked the qualities of being certain, liquid and exigible, as required by the French Code of Procedure in connection with the type of attachment obtained by Kennecott (the *saisie-arrêt*, that applies to a credit as opposed to the *saisie-revendication* that applies to material assets, and would have required a stronger case for ownership on the part of Kennecott); and finally that the nationalisation was valid because it was the act of a sovereign foreign state, French public policy did not require its nullity even in the absence of compensation, and in any case compensation was being paid indirectly through the assumption of the debts of the nationalised company, and the remainder was being offset by the excess profits deduction, which was in the nature of a retroactive tax and as such not unacceptable to the French public policy. Transcript of oral argument of Maitre Cueff, on behalf of the Chilean Copper Corporation (unpublished).

21 An English translation of the decision appears in *Kennecott*, Supp. No. 3, pp. 63–6. Also in 12 *International Legal Materials* 182 (1973)

22 *Kennecott*, Supp. No. 4, pp. 5–25

23 *Ibid.*, pp. 26–33

24 N. V. Verenigde Deli-Maatschapijen and N. V. Senembah-Maatschappij v. Deutsch-Indonesische Tabak-Handelgesellschaft m.b.H. before the Hanseatic Court of Appeals (Oberlandesgericht) of Bremen, 21 August 1959. Previous decisions by Dutch courts had found in favour of the Dutch petitioners. A comment favourable to the Dutch decisions and critical of the German one is M. Domke, 'Indonesian Nationalisation Measures before Foreign Courts' *American Journal of International Law*, Vol. 54(1960), pp. 305–23. For the opposite viewpoint, Hans W. Baade, 'Indonesian Nationalization Measures before Foreign Courts – A Reply', *op. cit.*, pp. 801–35

25 *Kennecott*, Supp. No. 4, pp. 34–56

26 *Ibid.*, pp. 62–85. Also in 12, *International Legal Materials*, 251 (1973)

27 *Ibid.*, pp. 86–93

28 Anglo-Iranian Oil Co. v. Societa Unione Petrolifera Orientale, Civil Tribunal of Venice, March 11, 1953, reported in *American Journal of International Law*,

Vol. 47 (1953), pp. 509–510; Anglo-Iranian Oil Co. v. Societa S.U.P.O.R., Civil Tribunal of Rome, 14 July 1954, reported in *American Journal of International Law*, Vol. 49 (1955), pp. 259–61.

29 British Petroleum Exploration Co. (Libya) v. SINCAT Societa Industriale Catanese, Civil Tribunal of Syracuse, 15 February 1973. Reproduced in 13, *International Legal Materials*, 106 (1974).

30 *Luther v. Sagor* (1921) 3 K.B. 532; *Princess Paley v. Weisz*, (1929) 1 K.B. 718; *In re Helbert Wagg & Co. Ltd.* (1956) 1 Ch 323

31 *ITT Hearings*, Part I, pp. 43 ff. and 265 ff.; Part II, pp. 1083–92

32 *Ibid.*, Part II, pp. 1049 ff.

33 *Kennecott*, p. 14; M. Nolff, 'Los problemas basicos del cobre', in Gonzalo Martner (ed.), *El pensamiento economico del gobierno de Allende*, (Santiago: Editorial Universitaria, 1971), p. 176.

34 S. Allende, 'Exposicion del Presidente de la República ante la Asamblea General de las Naciones Unidas' (speech to the United Nations General Assembly, 4 December 1972), Santiago, 1972.

35 Orlando Millas, 'Exposicion sobre la politica economica del gobierno y el estado de la Hacienda Publica', 15 November 1972, in Banco Central de Chile, *Boletin Mensual*, No. 538, December 1972, p. 1421. The estimate of the Minister of Finance Millas at that time was that the direct cost of the French attachment to Chile was $140,500.

36 CIPEC, Extraordinary Conference of Ministers, Press Release, *Measures of Defence and Solidarity* (PR 118) 1 December 1972.

37 See discussions in the Trade and Development Board of UNCTAD in October 1972, in UN documents TD/B/SR 317–35

38 The purchasing office of the Chilean Copper Corporation in New York moved to Montreal late in 1972 and an agreement was signed with the Canadian Commercial Corporation, a state agency, whereby the latter was to act as a purchasing agent for the Chilean mines in the North American continent.

39 D. Silberman Opening Address to the First Seminar on Participation and Industrial and Social Development of the Chuquicamata Mine (21 March 1973). Reproduced in *El Siglo*, 31 March 1973, p. 8

40 ITT Hearings, Part II, p. 533

41 *The New York Times*, 14 August 1971; Elizabeth Farnsworth, 'More Than Admitted', *Foreign Policy*, No. 10, Fall 1974, p. 655

42 Paul E. Sigmund, 'The "Invisible Blockade" and the Overthrow of Allende', *Foreign Affairs*, vol 52, No 4 (January 1974), p. 565, and 'Less than Charged', *Foreign Policy*, No. 10, Fall 1974, p. 661.

43 *ITT Hearings*, Part II, p. 533; Inter-American Development Bank, 'Chile and the IADB during the Administration of Salvador Allende', in U.S. House of Representatives, *United States and Chile during the Allende Years*, Hearings before the Subcommittee on Inter-American Relations of the Committee on Foreign Affairs (Washington D.C.: U.S. Government Printing Office, 1975), pp. 440–1.

44 U.S. House of Representatives, *op. cit.*, p. 437

45 Millas, *op. cit.*, p. 1420

46 See below, note 55

47 Sigmund, 'The "Invisible Blockade". . .', p. 327 on IADB; on the World Bank, James F. Petras and Morris M. Morley, *How Allende Fell. A Study in U.S.-Chilean Relations* (Nottingham: Spokesman Books, 1974), p. 75

48 See below, note 49

49 U.S. Senate, *Hearings before the Select Committee to Study Government Operations with Respect to Intelligence Activities* (Washington D.C.: U.S. Government Printing Office, 1976), Vol. 7, Covert Action (hereinafter referred to as *CIA Hearings*).

50 *CIA Hearings*, p. 180

51 For the economic process in Chile under Allende and particularly its international aspects, see Sandro Sideri, and Ben Evers (eds.), *Chile: Structural Change in a Dependent Economy. Critical Studies of Allende's Economic Policies* (The Hague: Nijhoff, forthcoming).

52 *CIA Hearings*, p. 174

53 *Ibid.*, p. 43

54 *Ibid.*, pp. 175 and 193

55 Carlos Fortin, 'Principled Pragmatism in the Face of External Pressure: The Foreign Policy of the Allende Government', in Ronald G. Hellman and H. J. Rosenbaum, *Latin America: The Search for a New International Role* (New York: Halsted Press, 1975), pp. 217–45.

56 According to the New York Times, the participation of the CIA in the financing and preparation of anti-Allende activities was increased in October 1971, partly because of the September decision on excess profits. *The New York Times*, 24 September 1974.

57 Banco Central de Chile, *Economic News*, No. 19, 30 April 1972, p. 4

58 Carlos Fortin, 'Compensating the Multinationals: Chile and the United States Copper Companies', *IDS Bulletin*, Vol. 7, No. 1, April 1975, pp. 23–9

59 United Nations General Assembly Resolution 1803 (XVII) on Permanent Sovereignty over Natural Resources, 14 December 1962.

60 N.R. Doman, 'New Developments in the Field of Nationalization', *New York University Journal of International Law and Politics*, Vol. 3, 1970, p. 318; *contra*, P. J. O'Keefe, 'The United Nations and Permanent Sovereignty over Natural Resources', *Journal of World Trade Law*, Vol. 8, No. 3 (May/June 1974), p. 262. Brownlie leans towards the thesis that nationalisation of natural resources produces a valid title irrespective of compensation. Ian Brownlie, *Principles of Public International Law*, (Oxford: Clarendon Press, 1966), pp. 437–41.

61 Recent ones include the Declaration and Programme of Action on a New International Economic Order, U.N. General Assembly Resolutions 3201 (S-VI) and 3202 (S-VI), of 1 May 1974; and the Charter of Economic Rights and Duties of States, U.N. General Assembly Resolution 3281 (XXIX), of 12 December 1974.

6 The International Oil Industry and National Economy Development: The Case of Norway

PETTER NORE

1. INTRODUCTION

This chapter will analyse the role of the state in the international oil industry. The main focus will be a case study of Norway, but the chapter will also refer extensively to the present situation in the OPEC countries.

One question arises immediately within the context of this book. Why should the analysis concentrate on Norway which is a developed industrialised nation where oil is not even fully nationalised, when most internationally traded oil originates from the OPEC countries? The reason is that Norway and the OPEC countries despite their apparent differences, as oil producers have a number of common features. The influence of foreign capital in the form of the major oil companies is of great importance in both cases. Oil, furthermore, plays a crucial part in both Norway and the OPEC countries by drastically transforming their economic and social structures. Finally, and perhaps somewhat surprisingly, Norway can be classified as a 'half-peripheral' country and may therefore, as an example, have a wide relevance both for existing as well as for prospective oil-producing states.

An analysis of the oil industry in general, and the Norwegian case in particular, will also shed important light on the concept of nationalisation. It will show that nationalisation in the sense of state ownership of a natural resource is only one of many important aspects of a state's oil policy. Other questions such as the significance and consequence of state control of only one part of a vertically integrated industry, the possible spin-off effects of the oil-industry, and what such a policy may mean for the general economic and political development of a producer country, remain unanswered by analysing only state 'ownership'. In this sense the Norwegian case study is important both in making clear the possible alternatives to a strategy of nationalisation and by showing the limits of a social democratic oil policy.

Finally, the Norwegian case study is interesting in its own right. The oil sector will act as a catalyst for a new phase of Norwegian capitalism, here labelled for want of a better term 'state capitalism', in which the state is in the process of becoming the main 'carrier' of capital in the Norwegian social formation.

2 THE OIL INDUSTRY BACKGROUND

Oil production gives rise permanently to large financial surpluses in excess of 'average profits', which are called rent. Rent is the subject of conflict between the owners of the land where oil is produced (normally the state) and the oil companies that have leased the land for production.

The rent in the oil industry has a dual origin; differential and absolute rent. Differential rent exists because oil is of different qualities and is found under widely different conditions. Middle East production costs are ten cents per barrel, while North Sea costs vary between two and six dollars per barrel. This extra return earned by Middle East producers is differential rent.

But the return in excess of average profits can also take another form, and is known as absolute rent. Such rent exists when either the state as land-owner or the capitalist oil firm manages to extract rent for the marginal oil well. In the North Sea the marginal cost of extraction is a maximum of six dollars, while the present price earned by the producer for one barrel is almost fourteen dollars. This gives owners a possible absolute rent of eight dollars per barrel. Absolute rent then is a necessary part of costs for a capitalist working an oil field and will affect the final price of oil.

In the historically 'normal' case the rent from oil production has been divided between the state and the oil company.[1] As long as not all the rent is appropriated by the state, then the profit rates of the oil companies will tend to be higher than the average profit rate in the economy as a whole.

Profit in excess of average profits for the oil companies has its immediate origin in a price that is higher than both the marginal and the average production costs at an output necessary to satisfy the total world demand. This 'rent' is due to market restrictions in the form of oligopoly or monopoly in the oil industry.

Why then has the process of monopolisation been more effective in the oil industry than almost anywhere else in the world economy? The answer partly lies in the politically and economically special role that the oil companies have enjoyed as the suppliers of a strategic raw material. For example, BP was formed as a nationalised industry as early as 1914 at the initiative of the British Minister of the Navy, Winston Churchill, to ensure the security of supply for the Royal Navy which at that time was changing from coal to oil. But the monopolisation is also explained by the peculiarities of oil production. Ever since oil was first extracted commercially in 1859 it has been possible to produce additional oil either by using existing spare capacity or by rapidly finding new oil at a cost that was less than the average cost of extracting oil from known reserves. Such a situation meant that the industry was under constant threat of destabilisation. A new entrant to the industry producing in these low-cost areas could undercut the price that was charged and which was necessary for the companies already operating in the industry to earn an average profit in high-cost areas. Also in an industry with heavy capital investment and a relatively low cost of producing one additional barrel of oil, there is always a temptation for producers to unload additional oil on the market, as it would contribute positively to the company's cash flow. But the long run results of such behaviour for the stability of the industry would be catastrophic. Therefore to avoid such threats to the price structure, the companies set up a cartel system that both restricted entry into the industry and controlled production between the existing firms.

The modern oil industry can be interpreted as the fight for the breakdown or preservation of this kind of system. In this light OPEC becomes a necessary successor to the international oil cartel, as an organisation which tries to control both prices and production of oil, and which in the process guarantees large amounts of absolute rent.

A logical and necessary corollary of the control at the level of production has been control at all other levels of petroleum activity (refining, petrochemicals, retailing). This has historically led to an extensive vertical integration in the oil industry.

From the time Rockefeller set up Standard Oil in 1890, to the late 1950s, the oil industry was dominated by vertically integrated, internationally operating companies that controlled the market between them.[2] Only in a few cases did the official or unofficial cartel agreement between the major oil companies break down. This happened in the late 1920s in Europe and early 1930s in Texas, when the price per barrel for East Texan oil dropped by 90 per cent in one year; but both cases were quickly brought under control.[3]

The late 1950s saw the first concerted challenge to the dominance of the major oil companies, the so-called 'Seven Sisters'. A number of smaller U.S. companies, the 'independents', started to look for oil outside the United States, as a result of the U.S. import-quota system introduced in 1958. These companies were not under direct control by the 'majors', and together with some state companies (like the Italian ENI), they were willing to outbid the majors in the terms offered to the producer states in order to gain access to the exploration areas. This development, together with a sudden increase of cheap supplies from the Soviet Union to the West, had a profoundly disturbing effect on the stability of the industry and hence on the price structure of the oil market. All through the 1960s there was a downward pressure on prices in real terms. By 1970 oil was cheaper in real terms than at any time since the Second World War.

In 1960 OPEC was formed to counteract the consequences of the falling price of oil on the producer countries' share of the rent. OPEC also aimed to control the output of oil. Their fight for an increased share of the rent slowly paid off. Originally this share had been set at an extremely low level—in 1901 the King of Persia had leased half the country for a period of ninety-nine years to the Anglo-Iranian Oil Company in exchange for £30,000 and a small fee for each barrel produced. Just after the Second World War, Venezuela was the first country to secure a 50-50 profit-split agreement. But no dramatic changes took place in rent division until the late 1960s. Starting with the Libyan President Ghadaffi's demands for a larger government share of the rent, the relative strength of oil companies and producer states expressed in new forms of agreements began to change drastically from 1970 onwards. From initial agreements on government participation and higher prices, the development towards a greater state role gathered force, so that the oil industry is today (1977) officially nationalised in the major producing states, and decisions on price and output are taken by the OPEC governments themselves.

3 NORWAY AND ITS OIL INDUSTRY

Even a casual glance at the Norwegian oil industry shows that great changes have taken place in the relationship between the international companies and the Norwegian state over the last few years. When the first areas on the Norwegian Continental Shelf were offered to the oil companies in 1965, no government participation was asked for and the conditions were generally regarded as very favourable for the companies.

In contrast during the coming round of concessions both in the North Sea and off Northern Norway[4], the Norwegian state is reserving some blocks exclusively for the use of the state oil company, Statoil, or is in exceptional circumstances accepting minority participation by the majors. The Norwegian state has during this period also moved away from being a mere tax collector to active intervention in production using Statoil, as well as heavily engaging itself in downstream activities.

From the point of view of a traditional raw material producing country, Norway seems to have struck a very good bargain with the international oil industry.

There are many ways to approach an understanding of the overall development of Norwegian oil policies during this period. We will first look very briefly and schematically at Norway's historical development and its economic and political characteristics.

THE POLITICAL ECONOMY OF NORWAY[5]

Norway never went through a period of classical feudalism, possibly because the amount of extractible surplus was insufficient to support a feudal land-owning class. It was thus a country where small and independent farmers could become an important and relatively independent social class. This class played a significant political role from the beginning of the nineteenth century. It strongly supported the introduction of parliamentary democracy in the 1880s and was intimately linked to the fight for national independence, which culminated in Norway's separation from Sweden in 1905. This independence also heralded the start of an industrialisation process, a process that took place at a rapid pace and was virtually completed twenty years later. This period saw the birth of the Norwegian labour movement as a mass political force which significantly has maintained ever since its strong ties with the primary industries and especially with the small farmers and the fishermen. These factors go some way towards explaining the anti-centralist and antibureaucratic political tradition which is a major characteristic of Norwegian political tradition, not only on the left, but also permeating Norwegian politics in general. It also gives some insight as to why nationalism is such a powerful political force in Norway. The most recent expression of the strength of this sentiment was the 1973 referendum on entry to the EEC, where nationalist sentiments played a major role in the victory of the 'no' vote.

The Norwegian bourgeoisie is an historically weak class with the possible exception of the shipowners. Even though the class played an important part in the fight for independence from Sweden, it has historically been forced to rely on the Norwegian state to protect the accumulation process probably more than has been the case in any other Western capitalist country. This dependence was particularly clearly illustrated in 1951 when 'Lex Thagaard', a proposed set of policies advocating the continuation of the direct and strict post-war economic regulations, were never implemented. An alliance was formed between, on the one hand, leading sectors of the Norwegian bourgeoisie who sought an end to the very detailed intervention by the state and an opening up of the Norwegian economy; and on the other hand economic technocrats who at that time played a key role in the state apparatus and who, from the Bretton Woods Conference onwards, were committed to the principle of a more liberal and internationally oriented economy. This alliance in the end forced through a system of price controls which, compared with 'Lex Thagaard', gave the individual capitalists a much greater autonomy in decision-making and simultaneously started to lower tariff-barriers.

The key role of the Norwegian state and the Norwegian Labour Party (DNA) particularly in the post-1945 period is largely explained by the corresponding weakness of the Norwegian bourgeoisie. DNA's historical origins are very radical. It was for example the last Western Social Democratic Party to leave the Comintern (in 1923). The party has until recently totally dominated the labour movement. Having controlled the government almost continually since 1945, DNA has in effect acted as a 'guarantor' of the stability of the capitalist system in Norway. This has partly been done by building corporate structures into Norwegian political life, like the yearly centrally controlled wage negotiations between the Norwegian employers' association (NAF), the trade union organisation (LO), and the state. The immediate result of this has been a period of relative macro stability and growth, but at the expense of a tight political control from the top, leading to passivity and demobilisation at the grass-root levels of the labour movement. The most striking indication of this 'consensus' has been the yearly 30 per cent of GDP which on average has gone to investment in Norway in the post-1945 period, the second highest figure in the OECD countries next to Japan.[6]

But this development did not go unchallenged in the immediate post-war years. Sections of the working class, in many cases led by the Norwegian Communist Party which in the 1945 elections had obtained 12 per cent of the votes, fought the introduction of semicorporate political institutions and voiced their opposition to the cuts in the standard of living accompanying the high investment rate. These challenges to the social democratic policies were defeated with the advent of the cold war and as the first tangible results of the policy of sacrifice showed themselves.

The period between the late 40s and the EEC referendum was characterised by an unusual consensus in Norwegian political life. This is well expressed in the almost total absence of strikes in the period.[7] It is with this background that the EEC referendum takes on a great importance, which as we shall see also had repercussions on the oil policies. The outcome of the referendum represented a dramatic end of the 'consensus' period of Norwegian politics. The direct cooperation of the Labour Party with the Conservatives and the unprecedented popular mobilisation against entry and against a policy which was seen to reinforce already unacceptable tendencies in Norwegian capitalism shattered, at least temporarily, the political stability of the Norwegian post-war era.

These features of Norwegian history contribute to an understanding of the country's existing economic structure. Norway has been characterised by an uneven economic development, most clearly expressed in the dichotomy between Northern Norway and Southern Norway with the South as historically by far the richer region. This imbalance has also been reproduced in the relation between town and country in the state as a whole, despite attempts by the government to pursue regional policies to a much greater extent than, for example, in Sweden. Government policies can also go some way towards explaining why Norway has managed to maintain a fairly decentralised industrial structure (again in contrast to Sweden).

Norwegian industry operates in small units by international standards. While the country only has four million people, only 100 firms employ more than 500 workers. However the level of both industrial and geographical concentration increased rapidly during the 1960s.

Norway is a very 'open' economy. Today more than 60 per cent of the GDP is foreign trade. But until very recently the bulk of Norwegian exports consisted of raw materials or semiprocessed goods.[8]

Foreign capital has always played an important part in Norway, despite successive attempts to control its influence. The most notable example of these were the 1911 'Konsesjonslovene' that made it impossible for foreign capital to own Norwegian 'sources of power' (i.e. hydro-electric installations). But despite such efforts, by the late 60s, 32 per cent of total assets in Norwegian mining and industry was owned by foreign capital.[9] This was partly a result of a social democratic policy in the post-1945 period, when capital inflows from abroad helped to finance Norwegian investments; partly an expression of Norway's full integration into the Western economic and political system. The final characteristic of the Norwegian economic structure refers to the integration of industrial capital with finance capital. A rough indication of this integration is the share of industrial capital which originates outside the firm, normally from state and private financial institutions. In Norway 81 per cent of all capital is 'external' to the firm, the highest proportion in Western Europe.[10]

One noteworthy aspect of the Norwegian state's policies in the post-war period was the lack of nationalisations as an instrument of industrial policies. The number of industries taken over was small compared with other European countries[11] and the state has historically seemed to rely more on manpower policies as an alternative.[12]

It should by now be apparent that Norway does not conform to a standard description of an advanced country in the imperialist centre. As briefly suggested in the Introduction, many features of its situation give the country at least a 'semiperipheral' status in the world economy. A substantial amount of capital accumulation is covered by inflows from abroad, and a large part of its exports were until recently primary or semiprocessed goods. The country has a weak national bourgeoisie and the external inequalities are recreated on an internal scale both geographically and/or industrially.

These features of the Norwegian social formation explain the key role played by the Norwegian state both in facilitating the accumulation of capital and in legitimising the political system. While this framework has been used as a general way of analysing state behaviour in a number of countries,[13] it seems particularly suited to the Norwegian case due to the relative weakness of the Norwegian bourgeoisie and the political hegemony of the Norwegian Labour Party.

Norway may indeed be said to represent a particularly successful example of interaction between these two state functions. The Norwegian high rate of accumulation has in the long run facilitated the process of legitimisation and vice versa.

THE POLICY PACKAGES[14]

This section will give an overall description of the Norwegian oil policies from 1965 to 1976, while part four will analyse in more detail the key elements in this policy.

The first concessions on the Norwegian Continental Shelf (NCS) were granted to the oil companies in July 1965. The terms under which the companies were induced to start exploration were modelled on the ones put forward by the British government at approximately the same time. The companies were to pay a flat rate royalty of 10 per cent while they obtained special tax concessions. The standard rate of company tax was cut from 50·9 per cent to 41·9 per cent for oil companies engaged off-shore. The very favourable terms were at the time defended as being necessary to attract the companies at all. But one of the factors the British government took into account was the supposed effects of the terms in the North Sea on the attitude of the OPEC countries towards the two British and Anglo-Dutch majors, BP and Shell, arguing that tougher terms in the North Sea could induce the oil-exporting countries in turn to impose tougher terms and harming the British overseas oil interests. One can therefore deduce that the Norwegian state which had no such interests to consider could have pressed for stricter terms from the very start. Also the bargaining position of the Norwegian state remained consistently strong (as opposed to Britain's) because the country was in no permanent balance of payments difficulties, which in the British case were given as an excuse for the fastest possible rate of exploration (and which again served to justify the most lenient terms).

On the other hand, Norway had at that time a much less developed industrial structure than Britain, a factor which should have weakened the Norwegian bargaining position. If Norway wanted to initiate oil exploration it had no national alternatives to the international majors, for example in the form of a state oil corporation. Such an alternative was however never in the minds of the Norwegian policy makers. In this respect the policy package in 1965 was only a reflection of the world energy situation as a whole, in which the oil majors reigned supreme. It has been argued by defenders of the initial terms that the whole North Sea undertaking was a 'shot in the dark' as no-one knew whether there was oil in the North Sea at all. Therefore the governments (assumed to be risk-averters) opted for an arrangement that did not commit them to any spending. There is however subsequent evidence that the ignorance was not as widespread as originally thought, and that at best the oil companies had a fair idea about the very favourable geological structures in the North Sea.[15]

In other respects, however, the Norwegian state's oil policy was rather more positive. From the start it insisted on learning the maximum amount possible about the oil industry, so the Oil Council (Oljeraadet) which was the state's main advisory body in matters relating to oil made numerous study trips abroad. There were moves to get Norwegian industry more involved in the various spin-off industries. A 'gentlemen's agreement' was concluded between the government and the companies in 1965 which stipulated that Norwegian goods and services should be chosen if they were competitive.[16] It can be argued that this indication of state support for Norwegian industry, gave the national bourgeoisie confidence to undertake initial investments in the spin-off industry, and goes some way towards explaining the subsequent relative Norwegian success in this field. But with this small proviso, the initial set of government measures related to exploration of oil in the North Sea was extremely favourable to the companies.[17] An indication of the overall strength of the oil companies at that time was the ease with which they managed to dominate the Norwegian retail market for oil-products. By manipulating the transfer price of crude oil imports to Norway to their own advantage, the oil companies managed to circumvent Norwegian taxation laws. Despite the fact that this practise was 'common knowledge' as far as Norwegian policy makers were concerned, no action was taken and the companies paid no taxes on company profits to the Norwegian government all through the 1960s.[18] Norway was during this period regarded as one of the safest bastions for the major oil companies in all of Europe. By the time the second round of concessions was announced in 1969, the first traces of oil had been found in the Norwegian sector, and Norway started slowly to tighten the conditions of exploration. This was the beginning of a whole series of moves from the Government's point of view destined to get more control over the activities on the Norwegian Continental Shelf. Norway insisted in 1969 on government participation of up to 40 per cent on a 'carried interest' basis (although other agreements stipulated much lower levels of participation). This meant that the government had the option of taking a percentage ownership share once a discovery was made, in exchange for paying its share of the exploration costs incurred. The government also demanded a net profit share arrangement with the companies of the order of 10 – 17.5 per cent, another way of increasing the share of total rent going to the government. But the government remained a 'tax collector', (albeit a more efficient one than before), in the same way as the majority of the OPEC countries, because no state oil corporation was created. But as tax collectors go, the Norwegians certainly did better than their British counterparts who maintained unchanged the initial terms laid down in 1965 until after the 1974 Labour election victory. This tightening of terms was related to the growing awareness in Norwegian society of the potential importance of this new industry, spurred on by a realisation that the North Sea did contain oil. The oil companies also seemed increasingly

interested in the area as they started to look for 'safe' sources of supply
outside the Middle East. They partly feared that their long-run access to
the major oil deposits could be interrupted, but also anticipated a general
excess demand for crude developing during the next twenty years. Annual
growth in the world's oil consumption was at this time a staggering 8 per
cent. Therefore the strong demand of the companies for a new licence also
played an important role in the first tightening of terms.

A problem that was to be of ever-increasing significance in Norwegian
oil policies, control over volume of production, became important for the
first time. The number of concessions offered in 1969 were well below the
maximum number that could have been given, a situation which differed
dramatically from the British policies which at that time aimed to
maximise output at all costs. The exact form of Norwegian private and
public direct involvement in production and exploration also started to be
better thought out during this period. The Norwegian private sector had
attempted to participate as partners in the North Sea from the very
beginning, but had succeeded only partially. NOCO, a combination of
Norwegian industrial firms got a 15 per cent share in nine blocks, while
Pelican got 10 per cent in six blocks and 2·5 per cent in another eleven.
Hydro[19], which was at that time 47 per cent owned by the government,
actively cooperated from the very beginning with the French company
ELF, to form the operating consortium Petronord. But these individual
Norwegian groups were rather insignificant both in terms of their own
capital base and in the share they got in the different fields. In addition to
the Norwegian groups primarily linked to industrial capital, a number of
small oil companies modelled on the principle of 'People's capitalism' were
created, based on the savings of small investors eagerly waiting to
participate in the oil rush. These ventures had no success in gaining the
confidence either of the state or of the companies. But the first group of
Norwegian companies fulfilled an important function for the international companies which found that it was easier to get concessions if they
were in partnership with such Norwegian firms, while in return the
Norwegian firms in many cases were guaranteed an outlet for their
industrial goods to be used off-shore.

However, none of these Norwegian groups had any possiblity of
becoming an independent force from an exploration point of view. Their
resources were far too small. With this in mind the Norwegian state in 1972
cajoled the Norwegian private industrial groups already involved off-
shore, with the addition of some new ones, to form a single company—
SAGA Petroleum. The company today represents the ninety-one largest
Norwegian industrial groups, and also includes substantial sections of the
Norwegian shipowners. But despite the undoubted potential strength of
SAGA (which now operates in six countries), until 1975 its concessions in
the North Sea occupied only 2·5 per cent of the total leased area south of
the 62nd parallel. The only important Norwegian company, which

according to the state is capable of challenging the international majors in the North Sea is the state oil corporation, Statoil. Since its creation in 1972, it has become the main instrument of the state's oil policies on the Norwegian Continental Shelf. It has grown rapidly and by 1977 will have 400 highly qualified staff.

Philips Petroleum made the first commercial oil find in the North Sea on 23 December 1969. The field, Ekofisk, which was gigantic was described by the *Oil and Gas Journal* by the three words 'proximity, security, immensity'. Eight finds were then made within the following ten months, both in Norwegian and British waters. After the Ekofisk find the issuing of new blocks went extremely slowly. But even so, it soon became clear in which direction the development was heading. The farm-in agreements (for definition see note 27) concluded in 1971 and 1972 forced the companies to accept higher royalties and increased state participation. The new formal regulations of December 1972, which replaced the 1965 regulations, consequently represented a significant tightening which the companies had to accept. A flexible royalty rate from 8 – 16 per cent was introduced and the principle of government participation formalised, while the government's participation share was expected to increase drastically. But no concessions were issued on this new basis until November 1974, with the exception of the two 'Brent blocks' where the state obtained a 50 per cent share. But it was the formation of Statoil from 1 January 1973 which truly heralded a new phase in Norwegian oil policies. The state had actively entered the sphere of production.

Studying the 1972 package in more detail we see how it expresses the Norwegian state's continuous preoccupation with the fate of Norwegian industry. Instead of relying on a 'gentlemen's agreement' to ensure the maximum share for Norwegian private industry's involvement in the off-shore market, such conditions were now written into the agreements and thus formalised. While the Norwegian share in the off-shore market (including exports) had increased during this period, the new policy was a reaction to what the Norwegian state saw as an unsatisfactory response from the companies to the earlier initiatives to maximise the national share of the spin-offs.[20]

Once it was known that substantial reserves of oil existed in the North Sea, the additional question of further processing of the crude oil became an issue. Norway had already in 1965 stipulated that when possible, the oil from the NCS should be landed in Norway. But no definite steps had been taken by Norwegian authorities to ensure that Norway did not merely become an exporter of crude oil, but also captured part of the substantial increase in value added from further processing of the oil. Statoil became immediately involved in this problem. Together with Hydro and SAGA, it started to build a petrochemical complex in Bamble in Southern Norway based on hydrocarbons from the Ekofisk oilfield, shipped to Emden in West Germany by a pipeline, then to be exported back to Bamble. A second petrochemical complex is now planned on the West Coast based on gas from the Statfjord[21] field.

Once oil prices rose in 1973/74, the question of volume of production that had all the time been present in the Norwegian debate, came to the fore. The main reason for this was that the increased price of crude oil firstly implied a much larger quantitative indirect impact of oil on Norwegian society (see below). But increased government awareness of the political issues related to decentralisation and regional policies as a result of the EEC referendum, also played a part. The possible problems were clearly spelt out in Parliamentary Report No. 25 1973/74, which while promising the Norwegians a 'qualitatively better society', also put a heavy emphasis on the fundamental structural changes that oil production would stimulate for Norwegian society. Why then is control over volume a conflicting issue? Three factors explain the importance of control over volume for the Norwegian state.

The first relates to the deep-seated consequences for the industrial structure. It was initially estimated that the huge influx of earnings from oil will make at least 80,000 Norwegian workers, 5 per cent of the labour force, change their jobs in the period up to 1980. The main mechanism for this process is the strong exchange rate the Norwegian currency will command following the country's drastically improved external financial situation, thus pricing traditional Norwegian industrial products out of the world market. The consequences will be a major shift in jobs coupled with large movements of labour between regions. Given the peculiarities of the Norwegian social formation with its emphasis on decentralisation and regional balance, this is a development no Norwegian government can remain indifferent to. A particularly powerful element in the opposition to such induced structural changes is to be found among women, because a disproportionate number of the workers expected to change jobs due to the exchange effect of oil are women. When the textile and food-processing industries are expected to collapse, as they already are in the process of doing, it is the almost exclusively female labour force that will be thrown out of employment.[22]

Secondly, galloping inflation could follow from a decision to plough the proceeds from a high volume of production back into the economy. The reason is that the amount of money earned in the oil sector from a given amount of oil bears no relationship to the value of the capital and labour expended in its production due to the high level of prices paid for crude oil. To push more than 6 billion kr ($1·2 billion) in revenue into the economy would simply increase total demand without a corresponding increase in total supply. Any excess amount must be spent outside Norway. Since the Norwegian state is destined already at the given present estimates of an income of 15 billion kr per annum to spend 9 billion kr yearly outside Norway, one can with all justification ask why this sum should be increased. This is especially so if this capital only realised a rate of return on the international money market which is below the current rate of inflation.

Finally the dangers of an environmental catastrophe in the North Sea is an element that contributes to the opposition to a fast level of exploration. A full scale blowout of a well under winter conditions in the North Sea could take six months to control, by which time $1\frac{1}{2}$ million tons of oil may flow into the sea. For a number of exceptional reasons the April 1977 *Bravo* blowout did not develop into such a full scale disaster. The consequences of a blowout could be disastrous for the environment in general and the fishing industry in particular. The increased weight attributed to environmental and ecological aspects of Norwegian oil activities have also meant a general distrust towards a further industrialisation of Norway based on oil. This has for example led to a vigorous opposition to the establishment of new petrochemical industries in Norway. All three factors, i.e. structural changes, inflation, and safety reasons, have been instrumental in reducing the planned Norwegian output of oil wells below what it has been technically possible to produce, and also explain the continuous opposition to production of oil north of the 62nd parallel.

One should however be clear that the restriction in output was not an automatic and inevitable aspect of Norwegian policies but also a result of political struggles. Its success must partly be ascribed to popular attitudes following the EEC referendum. There were also important antagonisms within the Norwegian state apparatus on this question (for a further analysis of this see pp. 206–7).

The companies on their part want to increase their output on the Norwegian Continental Shelf. One of the basic attractions of the North Sea for both the oil companies and the West in general has been its location outside the control of OPEC. So partly in order to minimise production uncertainties due to political factors, and partly because the North Sea still offers the companies handsome profits in their upstream activities (see part four) the companies have consistently wanted to lift as much crude oil as possible from the North Sea.

The availability of large and secure amounts of oil which can ensure full utilisation of the oil companies' downstream activities situated near the main consumer markets also represents an added incentive for them to maximise their output from the North Sea. Given this background it can be seen why the Norwegian limit of ninety million tons oil equivalents of yearly production first announced in 1974 was greeted with little enthusiasm both from the oil companies and from the West in general.

The post-1973 situation also led to new perspectives with regard to government participation. The pressure for an increased government share stemmed both from a wish to capture an increased amount of rent, following the quadrupling of oil prices, as well as a response to an awakening of the nationalist awareness in Norway, following the EEC referendum and the simultaneous increase in oil nationalisation in the OPEC countries. The Norwegian bargaining strength also increased as it became clear that Statoil would be capable of initiating and leading oil exploration on the Shelf and that Norway was in no desperate hurry to increase its volume of extraction. So nine blocks allocated in 1974 stipulated 50–80 per cent government participation while another nine were set aside for Statoil. The government also increased its taxation in 1975 with regard to oil extraction in order to 'mop up' the increased rent in the post-1973 period. But the original plans drawn up by the Ministry of Finance which envisaged a rate of marginal taxation up to 95 per cent on fields like Ekofisk that were developed before the increase in costs from 1973 onwards, met with a howl of disapproval both from the industry and from the Ministry of Industry and were withdrawn in favour of a 25 per cent special profit tax (to be levied on top of the normal taxes.) The slow but relentless march towards a higher state involvement in the Norwegian oil industry is now continuing. In the fifth round of concessions due to be allocated in the autumn of 1977 (which now may be postponed due to the *Bravo* blow-out), Statoil has been exclusively reserved a number of blocks, the most promising of which are situated next to the Statfjord field.[23] Others are reserved as joint ventures between the three Norwegian companies Statoil, Hydro, and SAGA, while others again would give a minority role to the international companies. But in that case the Norwegians want to obtain the right to control the volume of production from any new finds. Meanwhile north of the 62nd parallel, much to the annoyance of the industry,[24] the Norwegian companies have been given a monopoly as operators, while the international companies again are allowed as minority partners mainly because of their technological knowledge.

The post-1973 period has also seen an increase in government involvement in retailing and the spin-off industries. The government bought BP's distribution network in late 1975 and for a period also controlled the most important concrete production platform builders in Norway (Høyer Ellefsen), a field in which Norway had acquired virtual world leadership. This involvement was a result of a state bail-out operation for the Norwegian shipping magnate Hilmar Reksten, who in exchange for state guarantees of his foreign loans had to part with his controlling equity share in Høyer Ellefsen. But significantly the state in 1976 sold back its share in the firm to other private Norwegian firms.

4 THE NATION STATE AND THE INTERNATIONAL COMPANIES

Part three described the increase of state involvement in the Norwegian oil industry. This section will analyse in detail and from a more quantitative point of view what this increase has meant for the relationship between the Norwegian state and the international companies. It will also make a parallel analysis of the increased role of the state in the OPEC countries with special emphasis on the effects of the recent nationalisations. We analyse in turn what we take to be the main points of confrontation between the companies and the nation-states: the upstream and down-stream division of rent, control over volume of production, and the backward spin-off effects of oil extraction.

(a) DIVISION OF RENT, UPSTREAM

Our method of assessing the division of rent will be a combination of 'government take', which simply gives total government income as a percentage of the total net income of the field; and 'internal rate of return', which is the rate of return on invested capital suitably discounted. The latter distinguishes between the worth of one dollar's income today as opposed to one dollar's income in ten years time. The reason for using both methods is that while it can be objected that 'government take' for a field is an undiscounted variable, when this concept is presented together with a computed internal rate of return for an investment we will know both the overall division of rent as well as what it means for the rate of profit of the company.

There are basically two ways in which governments can try to secure rent: either via taxation or from government participation. In the latter case the state pays a fixed percentage of development costs (normally not exploration costs which are borne completely by the companies) and gets an equivalent percentage of the total rents in return, thus diminishing the proportion of total rent which goes to the companies. But it is also up to the taxation policies to ensure that the rate of return on the companies' remaining share of the rent is not too high. This is necessary because it is possible for a company to earn a high rate of return on investment even if the amount of 'government take' is substantial. We therefore have to analyse the exact mix of these two policy instruments.

The 1965 Norwegian concession terms which did not include any state participation gave a 'government take' of 49 per cent.[25] What this would have meant for the internal rates of return for the companies is difficult to ascertain, because an assessment would have been based on expected as opposed to realised values of the key variables that determine profitability. No-one could, for example, determine in 1965 with much certainty the likely average size of an oil field in the North Sea which would influence both costs and revenues.

The first tightening of the terms in 1969 increased the 'government take', which now ranged between 41–75 per cent[26] depending upon the nature of the participation agreement. In one case (Shell) no new fiscal measures were announced. But as a consequence Shell was awarded two unpromising blocks in deep waters.

Again it was difficult to determine the likely rate of return on the companies' investment, but since prices and costs remained relatively stable and no new provisions which would affect the time profile of the companies' net income were introduced, we can conclude that the government's overall 'take' actually increased compared with the 1965 round.

The 1972 regulations would have given the state no dramatic increase in appropriation of rent. The introduction of a new flexible royalty rate meant only a slight increase for the largest fields compared with the 1969 terms. But the creation of Statoil in the same year gave the state a much better long-run possibility of controlling the declared amount of profits. This was (and is) important as long as the state appropriates some of the rent through taxation. The greater the state's insight into the workings of the oil industry (which normally would follow from the formation of a state oil corporation), the greater the potential efficiency of the taxation instrument.

It was not until a number of farm- in agreements[27] and the individually negotiated Statfjord agreement were signed in the post-1972 period that any sharp increase in the division of rent took place. Insisting on a 50 per cent government participation raised the amount of rent going to the state to give a government take from exploration of around 71 per cent,[28] a trend that was further stepped up in the 1974 round, which gave the state a sliding participation scale of 50–75 per cent, a policy which together with the excess profits tax will give a maximum government take of 85 per cent.[29]

In allocations where Statoil will be given total control over some blocks, 100 per cent of the rent will go to the Norwegian state. The only possible problem from the point of view of division of rent would be the production costs of Statoil. Only if these are above the average in the industry will such an arrangement mean a potential loss of rent for the Norwegian state.

The irreversible conclusion from the development of Norwegian oil policies is that the Norwegian state has slowly but surely gained a greater and greater percentage of the total amount of the rent which arises at the stage of extraction. This meant until 1973 a fairly stable rate of return for the companies, because no fundamental change had taken place with respect to the relative magnitude or timing of net receipts (which remained very favourable to the companies). Hence a comparison of 'government take' as an expression of government toughness remained valid. All this changed in 1973 in the aftermath of the quadrupling of the oil prices. Even the rapidly diminishing percentage of rent accuring to the companies nevertheless implied a very handsome internal rate of return for them because total rent had increased. Even following the attempts by the Norwegians by means of the 'excess profits tax' to capture an increased share of what was a much greater amount of rent, the computed internal rate of return of one Norwegian field (Ekofisk) reached a staggering 64 per cent,[30] which compared extremely favourably with an overall average rate of return for the majors of 12.5 per cent.[31] But in fields like Statfjord and Frigg which were developed mainly after the great increase in investment costs in 1974-5, the computed internal rate of return is closer to 20 per cent, with, in the case of Statfjord, a corresponding total Norwegian government take of around 75 per cent. However, this latter point notwithstanding, the history of the Norwegian policy shows how difficult it is even for a sophisticated state like Norway to appropriate all the rent by means of a taxation policy of 'fine tuning'.[32]

We shall now see that the trend towards greater state appropriation of rents at the level of extraction is general to the industry. Ever since the principle of state participation was first introduced in the 1960s and especially since it was accepted by the majors in the early 1970s, there has been a continuous development towards an increased state role at the level of extraction, with a corresponding increase in rent being appropriated by the state. But, in contrast to Norway, the OPEC countries have developed the power not only to expropriate a part of a given amount of rent, but also to increase the total amount of rent by charging higher prices.

Today the oil industry has already been or is in the process of being nationalised in a number of the most important exporting countries. Venezuela, Kuwait, Qatar, Iran, and Iraq have all completed this process which in principle should give all rent at the level of extraction to the producer states. Algeria, somewhat surprisingly, still accepts a minority role for some international companies for a strictly limited number of concessions. The great majority of the Algerian fields were however nationalised in 1971-2. Saudi Arabia has for a long time been in the process of signing the final nationalisation agreement with ARAMCO. On the other hand countries such as Nigeria, Gabon, and the United Arab Emirates have all said they will continue for the time being with a system of state majority participation.

One important difference between 'participation' and 'nationalisation' is that the former normally gives the oil company, by right, control over a certain percentage of the oil output called 'equity oil', which is acquired by the company at a substantial discount. In contrast it has to buy the government's share of the oil, 'participation oil', at full price. Nationalisation, on the other hand, gives the producer state full legal control over the whole output.

An indication of the development described above is provided by Table 6.1, which shows how the nation states have gained control of a higher and higher percentage of total production of crude.

Table 6.2 gives in a more concrete fashion both the net profit per barrel earned by the companies on oil from the Eastern hemisphere as well as the average 'take' per barrel by the producer states also in the Eastern hemisphere. It is clear from the table that the margin per barrel for the companies was squeezed as the government 'take' steadily increased.

TABLE 6.1 Production in % of output excluding communist world and North America

	1963	1968	1972	1974	1975 (first ½)
Majors	82·1	77·9	73·0	32·3	30·2
Governments	8·6	9·0	12·0	60·8	62·3
Others (mainly Independents)	9·3	13·1	15·0	6·9	7·3

Source: Shell

Table 6.3 shows the majors' return on net assets in the Eastern hemisphere, in the period 1957−71.

From 1 January 1975 OPEC introduced a completely new system of a fixed profit margin per barrel. This was because the companies under the then existing system of participation were earning a very handsome profit per barrel. The reason was that, as the price of crude oil increased, the margin on each barrel of 'equity oil' (which was specified in per cent of final price) increased correspondingly.

But even when a fixed margin of twenty-two cents per barrel was introduced for participation oil and a similar 'discount' given to the old concessionaires when fields were nationalised, this did not mean that rent at the level of extraction was decisively divided in favour of the producer states. The reason for this is that there is no unambiguous definition of nationalisation. The most important distinction is related to the existence of a state oil corporation. If the producer state has a state oil corporation which is capable of extracting the oil (like the Algerian 'Sonatrach'), then the situation is fundamentally different from the case where the state has to rely on the international industry to carry out this task. A situation of full legal nationalisation, where the producer state is forced to hire technology at monopoly prices from the industry, may therefore turn out to be less favourable in terms of rent division than for instance an arrangement like the Norwegian one with less than 100 per cent government participation, but where the producer state possesses an effective state oil corporation. The division of rent therefore depends upon the exact terms of the technological or service contracts which differ dramatically from case to case, as well as on the legal status of the oil industry.

For instance, Caltex, operator and purchaser of Indonesian crude oil, was paid up to two dollars per barrel for these services[33] just after 1973; in stark contrast, the new post-nationalisation agreements in Venezuela and Saudi Arabia envisage a 'service payment' of between fifteen and twenty cents per barrel for the lifting and refining of the crude oil. This

TABLE 6.2 Net profit per barrel in cents, 1957–72

	1957	1958	1959	1960	1961	1962	1963	1964	1965	1966	1967	1968	1969	1970	1971	1972
Government 'take'	78·1	75·7	76·5	70·8	70·0	70·9	75·1	75·2	76·4	77·0	79·7	82·8	83·9	86·0	126·4	1·34
Company profit**	77·1	60·3	58·4	56·5	54·3	53·1	56·3	43·2	41·8	41·1	36·9	39·9	35·6	33·0	33·5	28·0

** Relates to whole integrated operation
Source: 'Energy memo' First National City Bank, October 1969, January 1973, and January 1975

TABLE 6.3 Majors' return on net assets in Eastern hemisphere, 1957–71

1957	1958	1959	1960	1961	1962	1963	1964	1965	1966	1967	1968	1969	1970	1971
18·6	15·0	13·8	13·9	13·2	13·1	14·1	11·1	11·2	11·5	10·7	11·7	11·1	11·2	12·3

Source: 'Energy memo' First National City Bank July 1975

'technological fee' is to be paid to the companies in return for nothing except supply of often low-level technological knowledge, as under the new agreements the producer states themselves undertake and pay for all new investment.

Theoretically a nationalisation that brings about an increase in production costs per barrel through technological inefficiencies will also diminish the absolute amount of rent which accrues to the producer states. But to put such an argument into perspective, note that even if production costs doubled in the Middle East following a state takeover, e.g. from fifteen cents per barrel to thirty cents per barrel, this would only constitute 2·5 per cent of the final price. Once possible benefits related to national efforts to create a technological spin-off industry are taken into account such changes in costs may seem insignificant.

However, the present system of fixed profit margins is not operating effectively. The reported average profit margin on sales by the majors in the Rotterdam spot-market was in 1976 an average of $1.15 per barrel[34] which is a far cry from the twenty-two cents originally envisaged by the OPEC countries. Because most crude oil still goes through the integrated network of the majors, the spot-market could be said to be 'unre-presentative', but it is still an indication of the perennial problem that the producer countries have always encountered in assessing the down-stream situation of the companies. As long as the vertically integrated companies process a substantial amount of the crude oil through their own organisation it is virtually impossible to determine how much the crude oil is 'worth' to them.

The companies' slow recapture of upstream profits can be read directly from Shell's profitability structure. While 1975 saw 20 per cent of their profit at the level of extraction, in 1976 this figure had increased to 30 per cent.[35]

It therefore seems that formal nationalisation of the industry is not a sufficient condition for the state to capture the full amount of rent at the level of extraction, unless the state has a state oil corporation of average international efficiency which has access to and/or an extensive knowledge of the downstream markets.

But if nationalisation has not turned out to be any magic formula for the fulfilment of the aims of nation states, nevertheless state ownership is a necessary prerequisite for the maximum appropriation of rent. The only exception may interestingly be the low-cost producing countries of OPEC. Here the circumstances of production are so straightforward, the tech-nology so well-known and widely available that the instrument of taxation could in principle be sufficient to capture all rent at the level of extraction. But even in the Middle East one should note that the really aggressive taxation policies establishing the fixed profit margin per barrel were never implemented until the move towards full government participation had taken place, which suggests that the two are interrelated. This interrelation is even clearer when we analyse unilateral price setting as an instrument for increasing the total amount of rent. It is in effect impossible to run a cartel that fixes price levels, without having control over volume of production which in turn means full ownership of the oil fields.

We have described the increased role of the producer states in the oil industry at the level of extraction. But before we can make a definitive assessment of what this trend signifies, either for the North Sea or for the oil producers in general, limitations in our initial analysis which stem from the particular nature of the oil industry must be spelt out in more detail. The dramatic increase in rent following the oil-price increase in 1973 meant that the total amount of rent appropriated by the producer states may have increased without a corresponding decrease in the amount of rent going to the companies.

In the terms of game theory the confrontation between the producer states and the companies was not a zero-sum game, because it was the rest of the international economic system which paid for the increased rent in the oil industry. Therefore to establish in such a situation that one actor's part of the rent has increased dramatically (as happened to the producer states after 1973) does not necessarily prove that the nation states increased their power or control over the companies, nor that the companies lost economic power compared with other industrial groups. To underline this point Table 6·6 (p. 200) shows how the profits of the companies improved dramatically after the 1973 price increase, at the same time as the take of the producer states also increased.

But this qualification to our analysis is less important in the Norwegian case than for the oil producers in general because Norway as opposed to the OPEC countries is a price-taker which plays no role whatever in the setting of the oil price. If the price and therefore the amount of rent increases there is every reason to believe that the Norwegian state would wish to maximise its share of that new total of rent.

But a second limitation to the analysis presented above is of more consequence for the Norwegian case study. Because the capital requirements for developing oil in the North Sea are extremely heavy (see p. 193), it is only very few private firms even among the majors which have any possibility of raising the capital required internally. Therefore state participation of an 'appropriate' form can be the perfect vehicle for lessening the private sector's burden of finance. A government's 'sleeping' participation, like the early Norwegian agreements of 1969, which only provides a percentage of the capital so as to get the same percentage return of the profits, but which otherwise does not interfere with any decisions taken by the private company, may be the perfect solution for a company short of finance. If in addition the mere presence of the government in an operating committee means that funds can be borrowed on the money market at a discount, then the advantage to private industry of such an agreement becomes even clearer.

(b) CONTROL OVER VOLUME

We have already indicated the importance of volume control for the Norwegian case (pp. 172–3). The limit on total output from the Norwegian Continental Shelf is probably the single most important source of antagonism between Norway on one side and the Western countries and their oil companies on the other. For a full understanding of the significance of this confrontation, we must distinguish between two different forms of control. Control over the overall output from a geographic area ('macrocontrol') is different from regulation of the output of individual fields ('microcontrol'). For the companies 'macrocontrol' is less objectionable (although this does not mean they are indifferent to it).

Until recently Norway has used the 'macro' method of control simply by holding back the allocation of new blocks. It is only in the coming round of concessions in 1977 that Norway has contemplated using the second means of depletion control. Such an act, for instance 'lengthening' the life of a field from its microoptimal profit-maximising life, would directly interfere with the profitability of an investment, hence such regulation could lead to considerable company dissatisfaction.

What has been the effectiveness of the Norwegian policies? While it was initially thought that earlier stipulations in Norwegian concession agreements which referred to control over depletion for conservation reasons would be sufficient to cope with control of individual fields, the explicit mentioning of possible volume control in the coming fifth round of concessions belies such an interpretation.

Volume control has also been and today remains an important element in the confrontation between companies and the OPEC countries. According to one high OPEC official, historically, 'Disputes between petroleum companies and the host governments concerning the volume of production by the companies have probably been one of the most, if not the most important area of conflict'.[36] The present ability of the OPEC cartel to set prices and therefore maintain the cartel also critically depends upon the regulation of volume.

To use either form of depletion control the producer states need to overcome intense political pressures. In the Norwegian case this pressure mainly originates from the Western political system within which there is an eager search for new sources of energy supplies. The pressure for increased production is articulated by IEA (The International Energy Agreement) of which Norway is an associate member.[37] Norway's membership has sparked off a debate in Norway that has all the overtones of the extremely bitter campaign of the EEC referendum and centres on whether Norway can possibly pursue a 'national oil policy' while maintaining its links with the IEA.

The difference between the micro and macro form of control is that 'macroregulation' mainly involves withstanding these broad political pressures, while 'microcontrol' involves a more direct confrontation with the companies.

Putting the problem of depletion control within the context of state policies there seems to be no reason why direct state involvement should be important in deciding how many new licences should be granted, i.e. in 'macro control'.

It is with microregulation that the degree of direct state involvement becomes important. A state oil corporation can just be ordered to accept a change in its 'optimum' depletion rate, while experience has shown that this is an extremely difficult pressure to put on foreign multinational firms.[38] The special difficulty involved in using taxation to regulate production rates makes this point especially clear.

To use taxes for such a purpose they would have to be raised drastically to make marginal fields unprofitable, and thus control depletion rates. But such action would be conducive to the breakdown of a good relationship between companies and producer states because it involves a *de facto* rewriting of existing contracts. Consequently such a policy would be unsuitable to control depletion, especially for Norway which has consistently backed away from confrontation of this sort.

(c) THE DOWNSTREAM ACTIVITIES

By downstream activities we mean the petrochemical industry and the refining and retailing of petroleum products. The income from these activities in excess of normal profits we will label downstream monopoly profits. But as opposed to the upstream situation the main reason why producer states engage in downstream activities is not to capture this monopoly profit. (The average rate of return for companies engaging in only downstream activities has anyway historically been very low.[39]) The objective of engaging in downstream activities is to capture the maximum of the substantial value added that originates from this part of production.[40] Such a policy can contribute towards a balance of payments improvement for the producer state, increase employment, and in some cases lay the basis for a process of industrialisation (the Algerians call these industries 'industrialising industries'). Finally downstream facilities owned by a national oil corporation can for example in cases when there is an excess supply be said to be necessary for the realisation of upstream rents as they provide secure marketing outlets. As a shorthand notation for all these factors we will say that producer states seek to maximise downstream rents. (It must however be clear that this meaning of 'rent' differs from the one used for upstream activities.)

Most of the oil produced will be exported from Norway as crude oil, hence there is a limited amount of downstream rent to be appropriated by the Norwegian state. The reason why there are no major export refineries established in Norway is partly because of the strong environmental lobby and partly because processing in Norway does not suit the logistical operations of the companies.[41] Hence the refining capacity in Norway is mainly planned in relation to the internal market. It is only from the new petrochemical complex at Bamble that there will be extensive exports of petroleum products. There may also be some efforts by Hydro to market petroleum products on the Continent, but this is not expected to reach significant amounts. In this case crude oil would be exported to be refined abroad, but a percentage of the rent earned downstream would eventually filter back to the Norwegian state through its 51 per cent ownership in Hydro.

The Norwegian state controls directly only a part of the downstream activities that cater for the Norwegian internal market. Through the ownership share in the Mongstad refinery of its marketing corporation Norol, it will directly control 25 per cent of total refinery output;[42] the other two major refineries in the country are owned by Shell and Esso. In marketing Norol controls 24 per cent of total retailing of petrol in the country,[43] while in the petrochemical industry Statoil owns a 33 per cent share of the ethylene cracker and 33 per cent of other petrochemical activities, while Hydro owns 51 per cent and 33 per cent respectively. The remainder is owned by SAGA.

To the extent that the Norwegian state can tax the downstream profits of the companies, the amount of downstream rent going to the state has increased. But if these spin-off industries are located outside Norway it is impossible for the nation state to exert any jurisdiction over taxation, and hence part of the downstream rent remains 'lost'.

There has thus been an attempt by the state to take over parts of the internal and external downstream markets, but with the exception of petrochemicals this process has not been particularly threatening to the companies.

There are indeed many OPEC countries where the process of nationalising the domestic downstream activities has gone much further than in Norway, although in other countries such as Britain, there has been virtually no state involvement downstream. Yet even when the Norwegian state has become involved in downstream activities this was done with considerable ineptitude. The basis for Norol's activities was laid by the purchase of BP's Norwegian network which was essentially a classic bail-out operation for BP International. A number of the majors were at that time selling off unprofitable downstream subsidiaries.[44] It is thought that the Norwegian state bought BP's network which was in a bad state because 25 per cent of the share capital in the firm was Norwegian-owned. If the state had bought any other firm it would have had to compete with a partly owned Norwegian firm, a prospect which was not viewed favourably by the Norwegian policy makers.

The policy of the OPEC countries has been much more ambitious than

Norway's because they have tried to expand into the downstream export markets. In this process they have clashed directly with the companies which, in the wake of being excluded from direct upstream ownership since 1973, have increasingly been forced to rely on their downstream activities in order to make a profit. The companies, which historically earned the major part of their profits upstream, adjusted their product prices in such a way that profits to a much greater extent were earned downstream.[45] It is therefore crucial for the companies to maintain both their present ownership and control over downstream activities as well as securing stable long-run supplies of crude oil.

On present trends there should be little fear on the part of the companies that the exporting states will manage to displace their downstream hegemony. In both refining and retailing the movement towards state control has been very much slower than has been the case in extraction. Table 6.4 shows how the relative importance of the majors in refining has remained virtually unaffected by the recent waves of nationalisations.

TABLE 6.4 Refining*

	1963	*1968*	*1972*	*1974*	*1975 (first half)*
Majors	65·3	60·9	55·8	50·1	48·4
Governments	13·6	16·0	17·3	20·3	21·0
Others	21·1	23·1	26·9	29·7	30·6

* as a percentage of output (excluding communist countries and North America)
Source: Shell.

Table 6.5 likewise shows how the control of retailing still remains dominated by the majors. This is because it has been notoriously difficult for any company, let alone a state enterprise, to establish itself in the retail market for refined products.

TABLE 6.5 Marketing*

	1963	*1968*	*1972*	*1974*
Majors	62·6	55·6	53·8	45·4
Governments	10·6	13·6	15·4	19·2
Others	26·8	30·8	30·8	35·5

* as a percentage of output (excluding communist countries and North America)
Source: Shell.

One way that the oil-producing states could penetrate downstream markets could be through government-to-government deals which altogether bypass the majors. There have been some attempts at this, on a modest scale. Following an initial wave of 'panic deals' in 1973/74 the number of such deals has now stabilised. The Kuwait Oil Corporation has for example established direct government-to-government deals with Petrobras (Brazil), Hispanoil (Spain) and the Indian National Oil Corporation.[46] But this still only represents an insignificant part of the total international trading of oil. One obvious barrier to such a development becoming generalised is the lack of large state oil corporations in the major consumer countries.

An alternative strategy for the oil producers is to establish joint marketing with the majors. This is however being resisted quite successfully because there is, largely for ideological reasons, strong resistance by Western governments to third-world investments in profitable and strategic industries like the downstream industries. No such agreements have to date been concluded.

The final downstream activity which potentially can be taken over by the producer states is the petrochemical industry. Over the last decades this has been one of the world's fastest-growing industries with a present total world market of $100 billion. Western Europe and the United States today control 70 per cent of the total output of the industry, compared with 5 per cent for all third-world countries. Much of this output is controlled by the oil companies and their share is rapidly increasing.[47] In the U.S. alone the companies control 75 per cent of the basic, 50 per cent of the intermediate and 25 per cent of the final markets for petrochemical products.[48] In profitability terms this sector also pulls more than its relative share. As an example, the rate of return on the assets in Gulf Oil's chemical sector in 1976 was 15.3 per cent compared with an overall rate of return of 12.2 per cent.[49] This sector accounted in 1976 for 18.1 per cent of the group's total profit compared with 12.0 per cent in 1975.

Firm plans do indeed exist for the construction of petrochemical plants in oil-exporting countries, but their overall impact on the world market will be negligible for years to come. The estimates of the Arab region's market share ranges from 10 per cent of the *additional* world demand between 1980 and 1990,[50] to 10 per cent of the European market by 1990.[51] Furthermore, such plans might easily collapse if petrochemical products for protectionist reasons were excluded from the major consumer markets.

Given the importance of the downstream activities for the oil companies, we can better understand why guaranteed supply contracts have been negotiated in the wake of all major oil nationalisations. These contracts constitute the key element in all nationalisation agreements concluded so far, as they help the majors to maintain a stable flow of raw materials which ensures an optimal utilisation of their downstream activities in conditions of maximum predictability. Such supply contracts have been concluded between the oil companies and all the major producers who have nationalised their oil production, in some cases guaranteeing a market for as much as 90 per cent of a country's production.[52] These contracts represent nothing but a *de facto* continuation of the former vertical integration of the oil companies after the potential threat created by the nationalisations that this integration might be broken.

These supply contracts are also crucial for the producer states as long as they have no significant marketing outlets of their own. They guarantee a stable market and hence a stable income for the producer states. Such contracts furthermore prevent the different oil producers from being obliged to sell their own oil directly on the world market and thus potentially engage in a price war. Such a market would have to come into existence if no long-run supply contracts existed, but today one can hardly talk about a world market for oil.

On the basis of this section, we conclude that the producer states' juridical ownership and partial control over the extraction of oil, which is only one stage in a vertically integrated industry, clearly does not lead to a guarantee that all rent from oil production is captured by the producer states. And despite its short-run advantages, the present situation per-petuates the producers' long-run dependence on the companies' markets for downstream products. The price of such a dependence was something Iran found to its chagrin in 1953 when after nationalising the oil industry, the country managed to sell a mere 103,000 tons over a period of two years.[53] (This was the equivalent of one day's output before national-isation.) Control over markets is a condition for rent-maximisation which is unrelated to whether the industry at the level of extraction is nationalised or not. Therefore nationalisation is not a sufficient policy instrument for capturing the total rent which originates in oil production.

(d) SPIN-OFFS

Spin-offs in the oil industry can conceptually be divided into two: backward spin-offs—production of capital inputs for oil extraction like oil rigs, production platforms, and drilling equipment; and forward spin-offs—new industries not necessarily related to the oil production but financed by oil revenues. This section will concentrate on backward spin-offs as it is the category with most relevance for Norway. Also a full analysis of forward spin-offs would introduce at this point a number of completely new and for our purpose peripheral problems, such as the adequacy of access to capital for economic development.

In analysing more closely Norway's relative success in backward spin-offs three factors must be borne in mind. Firstly maximising spin-offs may clash with other aims of the Norwegian state, such as controlling the volume of production. Hence we must concentrate on maximisation not in an absolute sense, but maximisation of a fixed amount of possible spin-offs. Secondly exports of spin-off goods should be included. And thirdly the success of any country must be seen in relation to the capability it has of producing such goods. We have already outlined the different measures taken by the Norwegian state to increase the national share of the spin-off market. Especially in parts of the market where Norway could draw on earlier expertise Norwegian industry proved successful. Norway became a major constructor of deep-water drilling rigs. The H-3 design became the world's most successful drilling rig, and they were in many cases ordered by a new kind of Norwegian firm, the independent rig operator;[54] the modern equivalent of the independent tanker-owner. Norwegian engineers developed completely new concrete production platforms of the Condeep kind. But in other areas such as more sophisticated drilling equipment, barges, and steel tubes the companies very often continued to use their own traditional suppliers, and Norwegian industry did not manage to gain a foothold. While the French team which developed the Frigg field tended to use French suppliers,[55] the American Philips team at Ekofisk showed a definite 'bias' in favour of U.S. equipment. This is why the overall use of Norwegian equipment in the Norwegian sector of the North Sea on average was as low as 15 per cent as late as 1976.[56] But this figure masks the rapid change that has taken place recently, and especially following the creation and activation of Statoil. It is both because of Statoil's presence on the operating committee of the Statfjord field and because the major Norwegian off-shore suppliers have decided to cooperate more closely in *Norwegian Petroleum Consultants* (NPC), that Norwegian industry will supply between 60 and 70 per cent of the total worth of the Statfjord B platform.[57] As in the case of SAGA it was the Norwegian state in the shape of Statoil which was instrumental in bringing about the formation of NPC. There are however good reasons why the figure will never reach 100 per cent. A small country like Norway has only a limited amount of skilled manpower available, and to divert some of this into competing in fields like sophisticated drilling equipment, where very resourceful traditional companies reign, would seem non sensical from the Norwegian state's point of view.

On the other hand for a country to displace some of the traditional suppliers of the oil companies is to a large extent a political decision. If a country like Mexico, which has a relatively unsophisticated industrial structure, has managed to run its oil industry including off-shore drilling largely on Mexican equipment;[58] if Rumania is one of the world's most important producer of sophisticated drilling equipment; then there is a good *a priori* reason why there should be scope for states like Norway to continue to improve their spin-off position.

This last point is especially pertinent to the OPEC countries, the majority of which have an even worse chance 'objectively' than Norway of producing backward spin-offs. This is reflected in their almost total inability to date to enter the spin-off field with the one exception of shipping. But even here they are preferring joint ventures with the companies to independent tanker companies. The OPEC countries' share of the world's tanker fleet was 1 per cent in 1975, but is planned to increase to 7 per cent by the early 1980s.[59]

It therefore seems that an active state sector (not necessarily full nationalisation, but certainly one which includes an operating state oil corporation) is a necessary condition for expanding a nation state's share of spin-offs. In such countries it becomes easier to encourage the development of domestic sources of supply and/or to bring political pressure to bear on the companies to favour such sources, than if the operator is an international oil company with its traditional sources of supply. On the other hand there are countries in the world which simply will not within the foreseeable future possess any possibility of producing the sophisticated equipment necessary to extract oil, in which case no amount of national-isation with or without a state oil corporation will help.

5 AN ASSESSMENT

(a) THE REASONS FOR STATE INVOLVEMENT

Analytically there are two broad reasons for the described increase in the role of the Norwegian state in the oil industry, which largely operate independently from one another. The first, and most important, influence has been the historical peculiarities and special situation of the Norwegian state. The increase is, secondly, related to international developments in the industry. This influence operated directly on Norwegian policy makers as they tried to copy the policies of other oil-producing states. The situation in the rest of the industry was also indirectly important, as it set a limit to what the companies at any time were willing to accept or try to achieve.

(i) *The International Context*
In order to understand the nature of the confrontation between the Norwegian state and the companies we must analyse why there was a pressure for an increased state role in the OPEC countries. This must firstly be seen as a structural response to a distributional confrontation over the appropriation of a given amount of rent between the producer states and the oil companies. It was secondly also a confrontation at the level of production as the producer states, the companies, and the U.S. govern-ment struggled to increase the total amount of rent in the oil industry. Both of these objectives were achieved by what we choose to label a process of reorganisation of the industry in the shape of increased state involvement

and nationalisation. (We prefer this term to 'restructuring' which implies a change in the actual process of production.)

The exporting countries wanted a reorganisation of the industry because they felt their share of the rent was too low. Only 8 per cent[60] of the final cost to the consumer of a gallon of petrol in the late 1960s was made up of taxes received by the exporting countries. The desire by some producer states to increase their share of the rent became particularly clear around 1970. The countries which initially pushed hardest for nationalisations— Iraq, Algeria, and to some extent Libya—were also the ones which had the most urgent need for additional oil revenues.[61] These three countries were also the ones with the clearest 'developmentist' ruling classes. This 'instrumentalist' view of nationalisations goes against official OPEC statements which stressed that nationalisations did not take place for fiscal reasons, but rather for reasons of 'control'. But because 'control' often means nothing but control over volume of production, when profitability calculations are made based on net present value, the two objectives in effect amount to the same thing.

The oil-exporting countries also aimed to increase the total amount of surplus profit from the production of oil. This was most easily done by an increase in price.

But it was for the oil companies that such an increase was of primary importance, especially since they had seen their distributional share steadily diminish over time. This was partly as a result of a higher level of taxation by the oil-exporting countries, which it was difficult to pass on to the consumers in a situation which was characterised by a global excess supply. It was also due to a threefold challenge to the majors in the oil market: the rise of the 'independents' following the U.S. import quota system in 1958; the emergence of important state oil corporations in Europe like ENI, which tried to outbid the concessions offered by the majors; and the increase in Soviet oil exports to the West. The immediate expression of all these factors was a drop in the profit per barrel for the majors, which was only partly overcome by a sharp increase in total production.

Profit rates for U.S. direct foreign investment in the petroleum industry dropped from a 30 per cent return in 1955, to 14·7 per cent in 1963 to an all-time low of 11.1 per cent in 1969.[62] The overall average profitability of the majors also dropped to the beginning of the 1960s, but then stabilised at around 12 per cent in the period towards the beginning of the 1970s (see Table 6.3).[63] The shortcomings of these rates of return for the companies first became clear when oil exploration and production moved into high-cost areas (Alaska, North Sea, etc.) from the late 1960s. The industry was used to a very high degree of self-financing; but the profit rates earned at the time were insufficient to finance these new investments internally.[64]

As a result the companies had a clear interest in reorganizing the industry in such a way as to increase the price of oil from the early 1970s. (Why the companies were so opposed to price increases before 1970 is controversial. Rafai claims the companies changed their pricing strategy after 1970 at the instigation of the U.S. government.) They could increase their profitability either by increasing the final price of petroleum products by more than the original increase in crude-oil prices; or alternatively their volume of profit would increase as a result of a price increase if the companies could keep their share of the rent constant.

It is within this context that increased state involvement and national-isations can be seen to be a necessary byproduct of an increase in prices. The companies knew that if they raised prices on their own the reaction in the West would have been intolerable. The producer states therefore had to be seen to raise the price of crude oil. The companies were for this reason willing to accept higher state ownership, and in the process formalise a *de facto* change in the upstream fiscal structure if they could get higher prices, and in addition were guaranteed a stable business environment. The Teheran and Tripoli agreements of 1971–2 did exactly that.

As far as the companies were concerned the nationalisations were therefore partly a result of an already existing crisis in the oil industry. A director of Shell wrote later about this period that 'It was becoming clear that the role of government in oil matters must necessarily grow if crisis is to be avoided'.[65]

There was however also a more 'defensive' corporate strategy behind the actions of the companies. They understood that long-run stability of supply to feed their downstream activities and to provide a guaranteed outlet for their technological expertise might mean that they had to get out of direct ownership altogether. This strategy can be further corroborated by our observations on the energy corporations (see p. 200).

The third 'actor' with an interest in increasing prices was the U.S. government. From 1970 onwards the U.S. clearly pressed for an increase in the general price level of crude oil. Oppenheim[66] shows how the U.S. government's actions were interpreted by the oil-producers as a desire for higher prices; a point of view that has also been forcefully put by Chevalier[67] and Rafai.[68] Such a rise would make a number of indigenous production wells in the U.S. commercially viable and therefore help the U.S. to achieve a higher degree of self-sufficiency in oil, as well as in a direct way help the profitability of the U.S. oil companies.

The push towards higher prices was also related to inter-imperialist rivalries. The U.S. government saw how an increase in crude-oil prices would deliver a serious blow to its industrial competitors in Western Europe and Japan. The problem for the U.S. was that prices finally increased far more than originally anticipated, but this can to some extent be ascribed to exogenous events, notably the Yom-Kippur war.

This interpretation of the rise in the state roles in the rest of industry goes some way towards explaining why the companies operating on the Norwegian Continental Shelf gracefully gave in to the demands for state participation.

(ii) *Norwegian Peculiarities*

We must now show how the general framework described in part three can pave the way for an explanation of the increased state role in the Norwegian oil industry.

Because of the peculiarities of the Norwegian state structure the concept of 'control' has a very different meaning in Norway than in other oil-producing countries. This means more concretely that depletion control becomes of special importance in a way which is unique in oil-producing states. Once the Norwegian state realised what importance oil would have on the economy as a whole, and especially the threat it posed to the non-oil-related sectors of the economy, the state was forced to act by restricting output. While the restriction on the granting of new licences until 1973 was more part of the bargaining with the companies over control of technology (a slow rate of exploration would give the Norwegians time to 'catch up' technologically); after the price rise in 1973 it became clear how oil production would affect the industrial structure in general. The corresponding restructuring of Norwegian industry would not be accepted by large sectors of the Norwegian national bourgeoisie, who owned the industries that were likely to be most seriously affected, neither would it be accepted by the workers in the same industries. The state then intervened to try to control volume.

This action is only understandable if it is accepted that the state intervenes on behalf of the capitalist class as a whole in its attempts to induce a balanced process of capital accumulation, and does not represent or directly articulate the interests of only one fraction of this class or one industry. The control over volume is furthermore specifically related to the important legitimising role of the state, given the particular political situation in Norway in 1973. The Labour government and the traditional Norwegian political machine had just been defeated in the EEC referendum, and was seeking measures to counteract the growing left-wing drift in Norway in order to legitimise its own position. The stipulated production ceiling of 90 million tons oil equivalents a year (however arbitrarily the exact amount was originally fixed) was such a measure. And it was thought that such an aim was more likely to be fulfilled by direct state intervention.

But within a framework that primarily sees the state as representing the capitalist class as a whole, we do not claim that the more traditional functions of the state have been dispensed with. The state's role as coordinator and guarantor of private capital accumulation has been maintained within this framework. The success of the Norwegian private drilling and platform construction firms, as well as of the other spin-off industries, would have been unthinkable without the active intervention of the state.

The second reason why there was an increase in state involvement in the Norwegian oil industry is related to the increasing socialisation of the process of production. The demands for capital necessary both to explore and to construct the fields in the North Sea and maintain a process of capital accumulation have been far in excess of anything that could be undertaken by any Norwegian private capitalists, especially because oil-in-the-ground could not originally be used by private firms as collateral to obtain finance. (This provision was changed in 1972). The yearly amount of investment in the Norwegian sector of the North Sea is today in the order of $1·5 billion, compared with $2·9 billion of total net private investment in Norway.[69]

But we must take this argument one step further once it is realised that the international companies had access to enough capital to carry out an investment programme in the North Sea. (This is not to claim they had enough capital to carry out such heavy investment programmes everywhere). Why then did the Norwegian state overcome its traditional attitude of non-involvement in productive industries and intervene directly if indeed there was enough finance available? The reason is that the Norwegian state is first and foremost directly a national state. This feature clearly expressed itself in the choice between whether accumulation of capital should be undertaken by the Norwegian state or by international capital, once it was clear that Norwegian national private capital was not able to undertake the task itself. In this situation Norway opted for a state oil corporation after first having rejected a plan to make Hydro into the main instrument of Norwegian oil policies. This latter solution was firmly resisted because Norway would not accept substantial foreign (French) share-holding in its state oil corporation.

To what extent can the increase in the state's involvement be said to be a result of a crisis in the Norwegian oil industry and the subsequent need for a reorganisation of the industry? This line of argument, which has frequently been employed as an explanation for state intervention in nationalised industries, at first glance seems irrelevant, because there initially was no Norwegian extractive oil industry. But if we see the trend towards increased Norwegian state intervention purely as a response to developments in the international oil industry, and that this development was brought about by a crisis at the world level of the industry (see pp. 189 – 91), then we can argue such a case.

Alternatively, if the need for a reorganisation of the oil industry was in response to a wider crisis of Norwegian capitalism, then such a starting-point will also gain credence. One way to argue such a case is to claim that heavier state involvement was a result of the threatened structural dislocations springing from the higher oil prices. (This we have already argued, see pp. 172 – 3). Another way is to argue that increased state intervention and ownership was a solution to a 'fiscal crisis' of the Norwegian state. Both because Norway is the country in the Western world where total taxation, reaching 47 per cent of GDP, is among the highest,[70] and because increased state ownership and control is the only foolproof way of appropriating the total amount of rent from the North Sea, such an explanation seems appealing. But it can be objected that if the Norwegian state's main aim was to maximise its total rent, the state would presumably have wanted to maximise its production. And this has clearly not been the case. But this seeming paradox is explained by the fact that an intensified rate of extraction would mean a more than proportional increase in state expenditure, due to the whole range of externalities which would result from an increased rate of production.

Given the crucial importance that oil has for the functioning of modern capitalism both because of its widespread use, but also because of its non-substitutability both in the short and the medium run, it is tempting to classify oil as a 'general condition of production'. In this way it would feature alongside other basic inputs into the production process like roads, canals, and railroads as well as steel, electricity, and gas which all traditionally have been publicly owned. An increased state involvement and control of the oil industry would in this way represent no great novelty, but simply be a 'lagged' response to a basic and historically verified trend within modern capitalism. But one immediate objection arises. Because most of the Norwegian oil will be exported there would be no need for state intervention on a large scale to ensure the functioning of the *Norwegian* system; hence to classify oil as a general condition of production becomes immediately difficult. Also, there is little in Marxist writings to support such a classification of oil. Marx concentrates the bulk of his discussion of 'general conditions of production' on commodities whose value it is difficult to realise on the market.[71] Oil is clearly not such a commodity. Altvater's[72] analysis of the problem is written within a methodological framework, where the state is (incorrectly in my view) described as being by necessity 'non-capitalist'. He not only touches on the material characteristics of the commodity, but also looks at the inability of the system to supply such goods because of the low rate of profit to be earned in their production. This seems a much more fruitful approach than Marx's, but unfortunately it will not settle the issue because the definition of 'general conditions of production' is too broad. Clearly not any industry should be classified as supplying a 'general condition of production' because its profitability is too low. It therefore seems that we have reached a negative conclusion that the concept of a 'general condition of production' in its present shape gives little insight as to why the state has so heavily intervened in the Norwegian oil industry.

(b) LIMITS TO STATE DOMINANCE IN THE OIL INDUSTRY

We have tried above to analyse the reasons behind the increase of state involvement in the oil industry. We will now examine in more detail the limits to this process. The conclusion will be that, in the foreseeable future, on presents trends, we will not see an industry which will be dominated by the producer states and their state oil corporations. The reason is that there still will be a definite, and at times even dominating role for the private oil companies to play, both in the traditional producer countries and in Norway.

The basic shortcomings and limitations for the producer states of operating within the present economic system are perhaps best perceived if we outline the worst possible scenario for the oil companies in the post-nationalisation world. We will then immediately realise how far removed from such a situation the industry today finds itself. The worst situation would not only mean that the companies lost ownership over crude oil, but also that they were pushed out of the steady, secure, and ample access to the raw material that the oil companies today maintain in the form of their long-run supply contracts. It would also mean losing ownership of their downstream activities, either to the producer countries integrating downstream or to national oil companies of the main consumer countries. Furthermore, if the present number of direct government-to-government deals increased and became a generalised phenomenon, they would constitute a further threat to the hegemony of the oil companies. If finally the technological dominance of the majors continued to be undermined, their last rational claim to a presence in the oil industry would disappear.

Fortunately for the companies this grim scenario is not being realised. As made clear in part four, for nationalisations to be successful they should be accompanied by a number of other policies: these are in many producer states not fulfilled. In a preface to Shell's 1976 Annual Report, Chairman Sir Frank McFadzean made the point that the group's 17 per cent return on average net assets was 'a further indication of the ability of Shell companies to adapt to the fundamental changes imposed on the industry in recent years'. The healthy state of the oil companies is corroborated by our factual analysis in part four, which described the present upstream/downstream 'division of labour' between the companies and the producer states. The producer states may have dramatically increased their upstream 'take', but there is no indication that this has been at the expense of the majors, for the now familiar reason that total rent increased in the wake of the quadrupling of the oil prices. It is the rest of the economic system which has paid for the increase in rent going to the producer states and not the companies.

Norway is an important starting-point of analysis because it represents a maximalist social democratic policy in the field of energy. The Norwegian case study shows the limits of how far a producer state can go without breaking any of the 'ground rules' of the industry. The difference between the Norwegian and other North Sea producer states' policies during the first ten years of exploration supports such a characterisation of Norwegian policies. Norway consistently moved against the companies to try to get as good a bargain as possible, while Denmark and Britain pursued extremely weak and passive policies in relation to the oil companies. As noted before, the British terms remained virtually unchanged from 1965 until 1974, while in the early 1960s Denmark gave the Danish Underground Consortium headed by the Danish shipowner, A. P. Müller, an exclusive fifty-year concession for the whole Danish Continental Shelf. What then are the limits to the Norwegian energy policy?

Firstly, on the present trend there are no plans for the Norwegians to dispense with the services of the companies completely. They are viewed as being important in the foreseeable future, mainly as providers of the more sophisticated technology needed in the exploration of increasingly deeper waters of the Continental Shelf.[73] In exchange, the companies will gain access to secure supplies of high-quality oil close to the major markets in a geographic area outside the control of the OPEC cartel. As long as there are to be joint ventures between Statoil and the international companies, the aim of the Norwegians remains to squeeze the companies so that they accept what for them is a 'normal' rate of return on investment. Norwegian policy makers in the early 1970s assessed this rate to be on average 20 per cent with a special rate of 17 per cent for companies that either were 'crude-short' or which (like the German Denimex) were in effect state entities trying to secure long-run supplies from 'safe' sources, partly for reasons of national security.[74] That Norway in the new concessions has managed to squeeze the return on investment down to a 'normal' rate conceals that this return must reflect the world-wide returns of a monopolistic firm. It does not reflect the supposedly high amount of 'risk' which is the industry's standard justification for a high rate of return. The main quantifiable risk in the industry is the cost of drilling dry holes, a negligible expense compared with total development costs in the North Sea. The actual risk of dry holes has also been vastly exaggerated. In areas of the North Sea like East of Shetland traces of oil and gas have been found in one hole out of three,[75] significantly above the world average, which is one in twenty.[76] As long as the international oil industry shows a rate of return on its investment comparable to that of other industries, there is no way one can say that the Norwegian government has fundamentally threatened the existence of private capital in the oil sector. All it has done is restrict its expansion. This basic limitation of Norwegian policies is also readily seen in the question of re-negotiation. Norway has scrupulously refused to change existing concessions, but has just imposed tougher and tougher terms for each additional round of licences. The only exception was the introduction of the 'excess profits tax' in 1975. But from a legal point of view there is little doubt that Norway was entitled to change the tax rate, even under the existing concessions. This aspect of Norwegian policies is clearly appreciated by the international oil companies, which on several occasions have favourably compared the Norwegian policies with for instance the British efforts (however feeble) to suddenly 'catch up' with existing terms for concessions.[77]

Similarly there is every reason to believe that the major oil companies will retain a foothold in the Middle East and other major oil-producing areas.

The extensive use of joint ventures between the majors and the producer states is an indication of how closely linked the two really are, and provides a clear expression of the producer states' continued dependence on the companies. These joint ventures are not only restricted to activities in oil. The nationalisation agreement in Saudi Arabia also foresees the company becoming a consultant and partner in the Saudi Arabian development plan.[78]

More specifically there are three possible reasons why the producer states may or may not continue to depend on the companies. We will examine each of these factors in turn, both with respect to Norway and the traditional oil-producing states.

(i) *Marketing*

In relation to distribution of oil there is little indication that even a totally nationalised oil sector in Norway would find difficulties in selling its oil. The supply of energy has now become a policy issue which is increasingly supervised and controlled directly by nation states which are mainly interested in 'security of supply'. There are strong suggestions that IEA is less interested in what kind of company is lifting the Norwegian oil, as long as it is forthcoming in adequate quantities. So were Norway, for example, to fully nationalise its oil industry there would probably be no difficulties similar to the ones which confronted Mossadeq at the beginning of the 1950s.

But what may be the case for Norway may not hold for all oil exporters as a whole. While we have seen that the state oil corporations undertake some direct sales themselves, most of the crude oil is still sold directly to the major integrated companies for them to market. The most serious obstacle to direct government-to-government sales becoming a generalised trend arises from the nature of the oil business, where the major companies have a logistical advantage over the state companies. Because of the majors' geographically diversified sources of supply, they can at any time change the blend of different crudes (acting as input to the refining process) in response to a change in demand patterns. A correct mixture is difficult to achieve for a state oil corporation, which often only disposes of one specific kind of crude oil or has guarantees for the purchase of fixed quantities of one particular kind of oil. The only solution open to the producer states would be to increase their cooperation and thus, on a joint basis, be able to offer a number of crudes. This requires a much greater amount of cooperation than exists at the moment between OPEC countries.

(ii) *Technology*

In the field of oil technology it is, and will always be, objectively impossible for the Norwegians to be fully independent of external sources of supply. This may not even be desirable given the limited amount of skilled manpower Norway commands in key fields. The best possible strategy for the Norwegians would be to import as much technology as possible under Statoil's own direction (a development which is already under way in bilateral negotiations between Norway and Sweden)[79] and try to ensure that they were not charged monopoly prices for the technology.

However, as pointed out above the conquering of technological obstacles is also a political problem. So even states which have 'objectively' a much worse chance of overcoming technological bottlenecks than Norway may in the long run find themselves in a more favourable position than Norway. Yet one should not underestimate the extent to which there exist real technological barriers to oil exploration in parts of the world, such as deep off-shore waters. It is the extent to which the companies manage to maintain their present hegemony in such areas that will help to determine their long-run rate of survival. Mandel[80] sees such control over technology as the main basis for the power and influence of the transnational companies in the coming years.[81]

(iii) *Foreign Policy*

The main external limit for Norwegian social democratic policies would become clear, if there was a threat that a fully integrated Norwegian state sector would cut its production. (Given the Norwegian political situation this might at some point be a likely scenario.) In such a situation IEA would exert even more pressure on Norway to increase its production than exists at the moment. Such pressures would transmit themselves through all the traditional channels that bind Norway to the Western capitalist world, be they of an economic or of a more political nature.

But to recognise such pressure with respect to overall volume of production is not to underestimate the direct political pressure which, for example, the U.S. government could exert bilaterally against Norway, were all the major U.S. companies forced to withdraw or be barred from future participation on the Norwegian Shelf. This kind of pressure would exist and be of maximum efficiency as long as Norway remained a member of NATO. Finally the companies themselves can bring some pressure to bear on the Norwegian state. Because the companies have traditionally been the main charterers of Norwegian oil tankers on the world market, they possessed a strong bargaining card in their dealings with the Norwegian state. The threat to stop using Norwegian tankers constituted, as Norwegian policy makers were well aware,[82] a powerful last argument for the companies in any confrontation. But with the decreasing dominance of the shipping industry in the Norwegian economy from the early 1970s onwards this bargaining card has quickly been losing some of its former force. On the other hand, to generalise about the political dominance that the West exerts over the traditional oil-producing countries is difficult. There seems in this case to be a clear case for differentiating among the oil-producing countries. For instance the shift in strength towards countries like Algeria, which has a distinct history of anti-imperialist struggle, does have a number of political consequences for the relationship between the imperialist centre and the dependent capitalist countries of the periphery. Simply to classify Algeria and other countries in a similar situation (Iraq) as representing the ideal solution for 'capital in general', just because they represent 'stable' countries (for a further discussion see pp. 202 – 3) is a clear oversimplification from a political point of view. On the other hand, any process of development towards political autonomy of the oil-exporting countries is seriously impaired by the political allegiances and class background of the rulers of the majority of these countries. Their intimate historical reliance upon, and continuous cooperation with imperialism, as well as their own repressive states, put clear limits to any challenge to the existing international political and economic order.

The analysis points to technology and marketing outlets as being the main international underpinnings of a future strategy of survival of the oil corporations, in addition to the political backing they might receive from their mother countries. Therefore as long as a producer state operates within the present Western-dominated political and economic world system there seem to be clear limits to the full effectiveness of state ownership of the oil industry. These limits seem to operate both for Norway as well as for the more traditional oil-producing countries, albeit the two are faced with different problems.

But one should not presume that such a dominance would last for ever. As a number of the oil-producing states develop in a state-capitalist fashion, and become part of the expanding capitalist system, there is good reason to believe that even these new forms of domination will come under strain. There are for instance very few *a priori* reasons why a developing strata of state-technocrats which such a development inevitably would produce, should not try to master the (in most instances low-level) technology of oil production.

The argument is largely similar for Norway, except that we are not analysing a country's full integration into the international capitalist system, of which Norway has been an integral member for half a century. Also when we are talking about the necessity of company controlled technology in Norway this refers to the new frontiers of technology, while it is clear that Statoil today is fully capable on its own of undertaking production at least in the more shallow parts of the North Sea.

Faced with these pessimistic long-run perspectives, it may be no surprise that the oil companies are changing from being pure oil corporations to become energy corporations. This strategy is also pursued partly in anticipation of an end to the world's oil reserves by the turn of the century. The purchase by the oil companies of other energy sources, like coal, atomic energy, and oil shales, will ensure them future access to sources of energy. A number of these resources are to be found in politically 'secure' areas, which could yet again provide the companies with the prospect of controlling the whole integrated production structure. For instance 60 per cent of all present U.S. coal reserves are owned by the U.S. oil industry.[83] The purchase of such new interests requires substantial amounts of internal finance, which may explain the time pattern of the oil companies' rent maximisation. A short-run maximisation of rent in present activities may signify a wish to get out of crude-oil production with a maximum amount of money to finance new investments.

(c) CONSEQUENCES FOR STATE ROLES

The most significant consequence of the present reorganisation of the oil industry has been an increase in the power and influence of the states in the producer countries. The most immediate expression of this trend is the huge increase in state revenues from oil. In Norway the income of the state will reach 15 billion Kr ($2·9 billion) by the early 1980s or equivalent to 7 per cent of GDP.[84] The situation in the OPEC countries is summarised in Table 6.6.

TABLE 6.6 Division of Oil Rent (in $ billion)

	1970	1972	1974	1975
OPEC revenue (net)	7·9	15·2	110·72	115·76
Net income thirty largest oil companies (including U.S.)	6·5	7·0	16·4	11·5

Source: Petroleum Encyclopedia, 1975, and Chase Manhattan Bank: 'Financial Analysis of group of petroleum companies'

Even if one need not go as far as Mandel,[85] who as a result of the increase in government revenue predicts the emergence of a new stratum of Arab financial capitalists, the key long-run feature of the present situation is nevertheless that producer states have gained control over a larger slice of the world's total surplus value than at any time before. There has been a dramatic change in the geographical distribution of surplus value on the world scale. What has this redistribution meant for the capitalist system as a whole? The term 'oil crisis' has become an integral part of the vocabulary of the West. But to what extent was there a genuine crisis for the capitalist system as a result of the increase in the price of oil and the corresponding wave of nationalisations?

One reason for making a distinction between the fate of the international oil companies (which has been our main preoccupation until now) and the capitalist system is because what may hurt the individual capitalist can even strengthen the system as a whole. The analogy with the process of competition is tempting. In competition, someone always 'suffers', but this 'suffering' is a prerequisite for the functioning of the system. As long as the basic 'ground rules' are adhered to, no threats can be said to exist to the system as a whole. In the case of oil nationalisations these rules were strictly adhered to as compensation has been paid in all cases. To insist on compensation for nationalised property, no matter how small, is therefore important as it reaffirms the sanctity of private property. (But this is of course scant consolation for the individual firms whose assets have been seized.)

But to answer the question of whether the capitalist system faced a crisis, the analysis must now proceed beyond the question of 'ground rules'. We will first analyse the extent to which this redistribution has laid the basis for a process of capital accumulation in the producer countries, and thus helped or hampered the expansion of the world capitalist system. We will then turn in more detail to the case of Norway and trace the impact of oil on the Norwegian state and the different form that capital accumulation subsequently takes.

We have so far implicitly assumed that the individual oil-producing state in a theoretical sense represents the landowners who have seen a transfer of surplus value in the form of rent in their favour. But it can be argued that if all rent is captured by a landlord there is the danger that capital accumulation will not take place at a maximum rate. The reason is that there will be no continuous inducement for oil companies to look for the most productive sources of a raw material, if all they will be left with at the end of the day is a 'normal' rate of profit. Our task is now to determine whether this framework can adequately deal with any contradictions that spring from the present reorganisation of the oil industry.

If we use a historical parallel from the nineteenth century, the existence of a strong social class whose income was based on rent constituted an impediment to the development of the capitalist forces of production because rent did not enter the circuit of self-expanding capital. It was only by breaking down the obstacles related to the existence of rent that capital would be able to expand. Marx described this process exclusively in relation to developments within the nation state.[86] What is new in our case is that the international companies face nation states which, while they may formally be seen as landlords, in the last analysis, represent the hegemonic class within their own social formation; be they a weak national bourgeoisie (Norway), a feudal royalty (Saudi Arabia), or a bonapartist petty bourgeois stratum (Algeria). So while capital in historical terms needed to break down the forces related to rent, the very same forces now reassert themselves, albeit on an international level and in the guise of nation states. One can make out a fairly straightforward case why this is so. While capital had to deal with obstacles to capital accumulation on a national scale, such obstacles now tend to reassert themselves internationally, partly as a result of the uneven development of modern capitalism.

On the assumption that all surplus profit is initially transformed into rent, one further potential barrier to accumulation of total social capital can be postulated. Accumulation comes to a halt when the rent is neither used internally nor externally as investments in productive industries.

To clarify the importance of this potential barrier to accumulation we must first of all distinguish between different OPEC countries. Countries like Saudi Arabia and Kuwait use a large percentage of their oil revenues either on luxury imports or arms or on investments in property and treasury bonds in the West, all of which will in no direct way increase total social capital. This use of the oil rent is a reflection of the development of the productive forces, as well as of the composition of the ruling classes in these countries. For instance the reluctance of the Kuwaiti ruling class fully to industrialise reflects their fear of the political consequences of such a process. The need to import labour, which especially in the skilled sectors is Palestinian labour, could in the long run upset their own political power. That this policy is not merely related to the reserve and absorption characteristics of the producer states (both Kuwait and Saudi Arabia are 'excess supply' countries) is clearly shown by T. Turner in the case of Nigeria.[87]

Iraq and Algeria are the most typical representatives of another set of countries for which the oil revenues will almost totally be invested in development projects. This will tend to increase the amount of social capital on a world scale. This 'developmentalist' policy, which expresses itself through an industrialisation process undertaken almost exclusively by state enterprises, is again a reflection of the correlation of political forces within such countries, and in particular the aspirations and the aims, of the ruling elites.

Whether the present situation constitutes a barrier to capital accumulation therefore firstly depends on the division of oil revenues between these different state types. But we should note that a process of accumulation is even taking place in the most feudal and backward of the oil-producing states. Abu Dhabi, for instance, is presently engaged in the construction of huge aluminium smelters and building petrochemical plants.

So far we have restricted ourselves to outlining the conditions for the accumulation of 'capital in general' on a worldwide scale. As it stands, this is a necessary, but not a sufficient exercise. It is also too mechanistic an exercise, which needs a more political perspective. Petras[88] partly falls into the same mechanistic mistake of disregarding the political when he claims that U.S. imperialism today is redefining its own position in the world, and that stable long-run agreements which for instance include guarantees of no nationalisations for U.S. corporations operating in countries like North Vietnam, Angola, and Algeria, may in some sense be an 'optimum' long-run solution from the point of view of imperialism. But he does not spell out the serious political consequences of such arrangements. Most importantly there is no reason to believe that the Western corporations could wield a similar political influence within such 'stable' countries as they now exert within countries which economically and politically are treaty linked to the West. Petras' argument furthermore must assume that the basis on which multinational companies were to gain access to such countries would be their technological expertise. But in that case we cannot postulate such a policy as a long-run solution for imperialism. This is because there is ample evidence to suggest that such countries would not renew these contracts once they had acquired the required technological knowledge themselves. For instance, there is no reason to assume that the North Vietnamese will let the Western oil companies which are now drilling off their coast on 'service contracts' gain a permanent foothold once the Vietnamese have acquired the basic technology them-selves.[89]

It nevertheless seems clear that within a traditional Marxist framework of analysis, no immediate barriers to accumulation are discernable in the wake of the present reorganisation of the oil industry. This conclusion is reinforced by the fact that within the Western financial system the technical problems relating to the recycling of the petrodollars largely seem to have been overcome.

Extrapolating into the future, let us now regard the state not as a rent-receiver, but rather as an entity acting as an individual capitalist. The basis for this assumption is the emergence of numerous state oil corporations in producing countries. Consequently the confrontation in the oil industry is no longer mainly between capitalist and landlord, as we so far have assumed, but rather between state and private capital.

If these state oil corporations are allowed to operate as if they were private units of capital (the Brazilian state oil corporation Petrobras which is diversifying internationally being one example), then capital accumulation would not be affected. The only novel element in such a situation might be that the rent remains within the nation state and in this way would support a process of 'modernisation' either directly by positively discriminating in favour of national supplies of 'spin-off' or indirectly by the use of oil revenues for the purpose of industrialisation.

If on the other hand severe restrictions were put on the operations of such state companies, either by limiting their access to capital or by forbidding them to operate internationally, then barriers to accumulation would result.

The final outcome of such a choice would again in each case depend upon the specific historic circumstances of each producer state and in particular on the strength of a technical-administrative sector in the state apparatus, which might gain from the existence of an unconstrained state oil corporation. An unconstrained state oil sector would then both be a vehicle of political influence for this technical-administrative sector and at the same time represent an optimum condition for the accumulation of capital.

Two qualifications must at this stage be added. We are only witnessing the beginning of an important trend, which has so far by no means been generalised. While countries like Mexico and Algeria now have state oil corporations which are fully capable of developing and extracting oil on their own, this is not the case in countries like Gabon, Ecuador, Nigeria, Saudi Arabia, or the Emirates.

Secondly, while the state may play an increasing role in the oil industry, the interests of the state and private interests in a number of oil-exporting countries are extremely difficult to separate from one another. Our assertion that there is an increasing productive state role in the industry may therefore lose some of its force in cases like Saudi Arabia or the Emirates, where to all intents and purposes the income earned by the state oil corporations tends to get directly appropriated by private individuals. This situation is drastically different, e.g. from the situation in countries like Norway where, given the nature of the state, no such direct appropriation is possible.

(d) NORWAY AND STATE CAPITALISM

Part four showed how the Norwegian state will be the principal controller of the rent coming from the oil fields in the North Sea. This control is not mainly exercised by means of taxation, but is increasingly a result of the state's involvement in the process of production. The state has made a number of traditional mistakes in this process; the amount of rent appropriated by the state may not have been as large as could have been the case. But the state will nevertheless be the main accumulator of surplus value both in the oil sector as well as within the Norwegian capitalist system as a whole. The conditions of accumulation are therefore rapidly changing in the Norwegian social formation. We will now argue that as a result of this development Norway is entering a new phase of capitalism, where the state is becoming the main 'carrier' of capital. We must first briefly say why it is permissible at all to talk about different phases of capitalism.

The increased importance of the state has until recently mainly been characterised by the appropriation of surplus value in the form of taxation, the proceeds from which then has been redistributed both to the company and to the personal private sector.

By establishing that surplus value in Norway in the future will increasingly be extracted by state productive enterprises, we can legitimately claim that Norway has entered a new phase of the capitalist Mode of Production. But to complete the argument we must furthermore show that only a small part of the surplus value extracted by the state will be spent as revenue and thus be removed from the circuit of capital (as opposed to being reinjected and serve as a basis for a further expansion of the same circuit). To definitely determine the question of a new phase we will therefore in the last analysis have to look more closely at the composition of state expenditure. State productive enterprises are therefore merely a necessary condition for such a new phase.

The level of class struggle corresponding to this state capitalist phase tends not be restricted to one specific sector at a time, but takes place at a more generalised level and therefore cuts across different industries and social groups.

What are the general limits and perspectives for the development of Norwegian state capitalism? This question is tightly interrelated with the question of oil. In 1975 the Norwegian state bought a controlling interest in Alcan Aluminium at a price of Kr 600 million. The ready availability of the money was clearly a reflection of the country's expected future oil incomes. A distinguishing feature of the Norwegian situation is that buying up foreign enterprises in Norway and thus expanding the state productive sector appears as an entirely rational way of spending the expected oil income, given the Norwegian domestic economy's limited ability to absorb all future income. It is therefore theoretically possible to see the Norwegian state buying out all foreign industry in the country. The political and economic limit for such a development becoming generalised to the whole economy is that no Norwegian private firm would be bought out in the same way. The state may move against private foreign capital; but only in exceptional cases will it take over Norwegian national capital. The resale of Høyer-Ellefsen (see p. 174) strongly supports such a view of future trends.

But while the 'objective' conditions for the expansion of the state's productive sector at the expense of foreign firms exist, there has not been any corresponding political will by the Labour Party to take full advantage of this possibility. On the contrary, the key government White Paper about the future of Norwegian industry stated: 'Even if state productive industries play an important role in Norwegian industry, the majority (hovedtyngden) of industrial production will still be carried out by private firms . . .'[90] A leading Labour Party politician was more explicit when he stated: 'We will continue to have a mixed economy. But the present mix is unsatisfactory. A new one with more socialist elements will push itself forward.'[91]

There is also every reason to believe that while the Norwegian bourgeoisie is a relatively weak social class it would also oppose such a wholesale purchase of foreign industry. This is partly because Norwegian industry has significant joint ventures with foreign capital operating in Norway. Indeed Norwegian industry has become increasingly internationalised as a result of the oil activities.[92] This class is also opposed to such a policy because it suspects (however misguidedly) that it would be the next in line to be bought out by the Norwegian state.

So there are clear limits to the likely expansion of state ownership in Norwegian productive industries. The total amount of state productive ownership will probably increase only slowly from the present figure of 45 per cent of total equity shares in Norwegian industry,[93] while not representing in the short run any fundamental challenge to the capitalist mode of production.

The present limits of the threat of Norwegian state capitalism towards the capitalist system as a whole is further underlined by the fact that the productive state sector in oil as well as in other industries is largely run according to capitalist criteria. This is the main reason why Statoil was initially accepted by the Norwegian bourgeoisie without any significant political opposition. It was created by a unanimous vote of the Storting (the Norwegian Parliament) in 1972. The urge by such state industries to succumb to the imperatives of the market is seen most clearly in the pressures that Statoil is exhibiting towards expanding its operations. This pressure is almost inevitable given the kind of competition Statoil is faced with. The continuous pressure by the personnel in Statoil to bring a pipeline from Statfjord ashore on the Norwegian Western coast south of Bergen under the company's guidance is merely one expression of such an 'imperative'.[94]

But there are also important contradictions within a development towards Norwegian state capitalism. The state sector in oil is subject to stricter control by the Storting than is the case of most other state enterprises in Western Europe. Its budget is presented to the Storting one year in advance, and Statoil has until now not been allowed to expand its operations outside of Norway. While being totally inadequate as a control mechanism, these provisions nevertheless tend to counteract the most unfettered tendencies towards expansion referred to above.

Also a gradual increase in the role of the state means a relative displacement of the major international companies (with all the ifs and buts discussed until now), as well as a continuous shrinking of the 'accumulation base' of private Norwegian industry in favour of state capital.

Finally there have been important divisions within the Norwegian state apparatus as a result of recent developments in the oil sector. The Ministry of Finance, which was instrumental in producing Parliamentary Report No. 25, 1973/74 advocating strict regulations of the industry with a dominant role for Statoil, has on numerous occasions clashed with representatives of the Ministry of Industry which wished to give the private companies a much freer hand. The most celebrated clash came over the introduction of the special profits tax in 1975 (p. 174), while there is reason to believe that the Ministry of Industry leaked the original proposals, which were eventually rejected, to the press. This was done to embarrass the Ministry of Finance which originally had drawn up the proposals, and also to give 'public opinion' time to mobilise against the proposals. Thus this tendency towards state capitalism is by no means free of all contradictions.

NOTES

1 In most countries (outside the U.S.) the right of landowners to reserve mineral rights to themselves was successfully opposed by other classes, and the rent from subsoil activities was in principle appropriated by the state—see e.g. the Mexican Constitutional Provisions after the Mexican Revolution.

2 The first was solved by a market-sharing agreement concluded in 1928 known as the 'as is' or Achnacarry agreement; the second by the setting up of an official production regulating body, The Texas Railroad Commission, which still controls Texan production.

3 Exploration off Northern Norway was meant to start in the summer of 1978, but will yet again be postponed until 1979 due to the *Bravo* blowout in the North Sea in 1977.

4 For a good radical summary of the early history of the oil industry see Harvey O'Connor, *The Empire of Oil* (New York: 1955), and *World Crisis in Oil* (London: 1963). For a more traditional approach which covers the period until 1970, see N.H. Jacoby, *Multinational Oil*, (New York: Macmillan, 1974)

5 Unfortunately there is no single text in English which adequately summarises the relevant aspects of Norwegian history. An analysis of the key economic developments in the post-war period can be found in Statistisk Sentralbyrå (SSB), *Norges Økonomi etter Krigen*, (The Norwegian Statistical Office, *The Norwegian Post-war Economy*), (Oslo: SØS no. 14, 1965). For a fair description of the political developments, see Stein Rokkan, 'Numerical Democracy and Corporate Pluralism', in Robert A. Dahl, *Political Oppositions in Western Democracies* (New Haven, Yale U.P. 1966)

6 For the period until 1958 Norway had the highest investment rate of any industrialised country. Gross fixed investment reached 32 per cent of GDP in 1958. The period 1967–71 shows Norway with an average investment rate of 28·2 per cent of GDP, second to Japan with 37·8 per cent. (SSB, 1965 *op.cit*, p. 123, and OECD, *Economic Survey, Norway*, March 1974.) Another feature of the rate of investment is that a much higher percentage of total savings in Norway originates from the government than in other countries. In the period 1958–61 government saving as a percentage of total saving reached between 48 and 50 per cent (SSB, 1965, *op.cit*. p. 138). Because the government's share of total investments was much lower, there was therefore an important transfer of investment funds from the government to the private sector.

7 The average number of strikes in Norway during the period 1945–62 was twenty-three, with a total loss per annum of 136,000 working days (*ibid*, p. 113).

8 Norway exported in 1970 18 million tons of raw materials and semiprocessed goods, while it imported 25 million tons of the same. This relation between exports and imports is drastically different from other Western capitalist countries, where the volume of imports normally is many times the volume of exports: A.S. Svendsen, 'Verdensproduksjon og Verdenshandelen med Råvarer,' *Norges Industri*, (June 1974) p. 29.

9 This figure contrasts with 23 per cent in the economy as a whole. See J. Einarsen, 'Foreign Investment in Norway', in I.A. Litvak and C.J. Maule (eds), *Foreign Investment: The Experience of Host Countries* (New York: Praeger, 1970). On this background it is interesting to note the comment in Stortingsmelding (St. meld.) (Parliamentary Report) no. 39, 1967/68 which stated, 'There is probably little that can be done on Norway's part to meet this development' (i.e. foreign investment).

10 The corresponding figure for Britain was 40 per cent. If we look at new investment in the period 1962–6 the Norwegian figure increases to 87 per cent. *Innstillingen om obligasjons og aksjemarkedet i Norge* (A Report on the financial and equity markets in Norway), 6 February 1968.

11 As late as the early 1970s only twelve industrial firms had a majority state share (*The Economist*, 15 November 1976, Survey: Norway, p. 19). See also footnote 90.

12 One indication of this very 'Scandinavian' feature of modern capitalism is the extent of retraining of the labour force. Ten times the percentage of the labour force is yearly retrained in Sweden compared with Britain (*The Economist* 21 May, 1975).

13 James O'Connor, *The Fiscal Crisis of the State*, (New York: St. Martin Press, 1973) tries to apply this framework to a case study of the U.S.

14 For an overall view of the different Norwegian policy packages until 1974, see *Parliamentary Report (Parl. Rep.) no. 30, 1973/74* (English Translation). For a comparable British overview, see *First Report from the Committee of Public Accounts, 1972/73*.

15 Two AMOCO geologists wrote in 1965 that 'the seismic maps (of the North Sea, PN) do show the presence of a number of very large structural traps . . . Furthermore the size of the as yet nearly virgin area to be explored is a great attraction. Not many like it, almost untested, are left in the free world. Statistics concerning discovery ratios alone suggest that a number of fields should be found'. Sander and Humphrey, *Why Look for Oil and Gas in the North Sea?*, Paper given to conference of gas engineers, Solihull, May 1965, p. 11.

16 The contrast with British policies pursued at the same time is telling. The British rejected, largely for ideological reasons, any kind of policies related to the spin-off industries which had 'protectionist' overtones. When there finally was a change in British policies in the mid 1970s this was largely due to pressure from British Civil servants, and not from industry: Michael Jenkins, *The British Offshore Supply Industry*, (Ph.D. Dept. of Government, Manchester University, 1977).

17 The 1965 law was later described by J. Fox Thomas Director of Philips Petroleum as 'a hell of a good law' (*Guardian*, 21 March 1973).

18 Atle Seierstad, *Norge og Oljen* (Oslo: Pax, 1972), Chapter 3 assesses the loss of

the Norwegian balance of payments to Kr 340 million in 1970 as a result of the manipulation of transfer prices, while quoting a report from the Tax Council (Riksskattestyret) which assessed the loss in 1967 to be Kr 200 million. The Head of the Norwegian Central Bank is quoted in 1965 as pointing to the activities of the oil companies as the prime example of how transfer prices could be used to shift profits out of countries with a high taxation rate (*Ibid*, p. 30)

19 Norsk Hydro was at the time Norway's second largest industrial firm, specialising in the production of heavy chemicals and light metals. The government share increased in March 1971 to 50.2 per cent. According to Petroleum Press Service (PPS) 'The move was made in order to cooperate closely with Norsk Hydro in North Sea exploration and in the development of petrochemicals,' March 1971, p. 113.

20 Director of the Ministry of Industry, Nils Gulnes, defended the stricter conditions by saying that 'the government has . . . not been statisfied with the oil companies use of Norwegian goods and services so far' (Financial Times, *North Sea Oil Conference*, London, December 1972).

21 Statfjord, found in 1974, is the largest existing field in the North Sea with recoverable reserves of more than 400 million tons, or forty times the present annual Norwegian consumption. This makes it among the ten-to-twenty largest oilfields in the whole world. The Norwegian state has a 50 per cent share in the field.

22 Production estimates have been revised downwards since the publication of Parliamentary Report No. 25. According to the latest estimates by the Norwegian Petroleum Directorate, production will reach 69 million tons oil equivalents (mtoe) by the early 1980s (*Noroil*, no. 11 (1976) p. 87). On the other hand the experience in the British sector suggests that peak output of a field is normally reached earlier than previously announced. This may be connected to the bargaining strategies of the companies which wish to downgrade the expected rate of production in order to extract a maximum amount of concessions from the producer states.

23 *Noroil* (No. 11 (1976) pp. 33–6) in a major review of the geological prospects of twenty blocks on the Norwegian Shelf claimed there was an 80 per cent chance of a commercial find in block 34–7, north east of Statfjord. This block is nicknamed 'The Crown Jewels'.

24 'To declare the principle of a monopoly on operator status (north of 62°PN) today is thus neither understandable nor acceptable', *Noroil*, No. 4 (1977), p. 19

25 All results related to the division of rent are based on a cashflow model which incorporates different participation-scenarios, developed by the author in connection with work on his Ph.D. To facilitate comparisons between different policies all results refer to a hypothetical 700 million-barrel field where cost and revenue-conditions change with time.

26 The majority of the participation agreements would have yielded a division of rent towards the bottom end of this range. For example, a 17.5 per cent net profit agreement would have given the state 41.5 per cent of the rent. The results also indicate that none of the 1969 participation-scenarios would affect the companies' internal rate of return in anything but a marginal way.

27 At times there are companies that either want to sell or exchange their acreage in the North Sea. For this they need the government's permission, which they will only obtain, in many cases, in exchange for further concessions like higher

rates of government participation.

28 One novel feature of the Statfjord agreement was that Statoil had the right to sit on the operating committee from the very start of exploration instead of only being admitted when a field was declared commercial.

29 Note that in such instances the Norwegian state would be responsible for finding very large investment funds.

30 Calculations made by the Scottish stockbroker firm Wood McKenzie, quoted in *Petroleum Economist* (hereinafter *PE*), (December 1975).

31 The 1976 return on equity capital for the seven majors. This compared with 18·3 per cent in 1975. *PE* (May 1977) p. 177.

32 Alexander Kemp, 'Taxation and the Profitability of North Sea Oil', *The Fraser of Allander Institute Research Monograph no. 4*, (1976) shows how the British policy of taxation in the North Sea leaves the companies with a disproportionate amount of rent and often has the exactly opposite of the intended effects, e.g. in relation to marginal fields.

33 *PE* (April 1977) p. 143

34 Peter Odell & K. Rosing, *The North Sea Oil Province* (London 1975)

35 According to a Wood McKenzie report on Shell, quoted in *PE* (May 1977)

36 R.F. Miksell (ed.) *Foreign Investment in the Petroleum and Mineral Industries* (Baltimore: 1970), p. 46

37 IEA was perceived as a threat to a 'national' oil policy in general and to the question of the rate of depletion in particular when the agreement was first ratified by the Storting in April 1975. Ms Berit Ås, leader of the Socialist Electoral Alliance (SV) criticised the IEA as the product 'of an American move to create a new, US dominated organisation similar to previously established organisations like the World Bank, the IMF and NATO'. Former Prime Minister Per Borten (Centre Party) called for reassurance that Norway would have the right itself to define Norwegian reserve production capacity for oil in case of an emergency as well as to define when an emergency had arisen. *Financial Times* (hereinafter *F.T.*) (1 May 1975).

38 A moments reflection should make it clear that it is only by pure chance that the optimum volume lifted by an international company which attempts to maximise profits from its global network should coincide with the optimum volume of production by a producer state. The dissatisfaction with this state of affairs was one of the main reasons behind the demand of more 'national control' from the early 70s.

39 A study of twenty-five Western European downstream companies showed that for the period of 1962–72 their average return on invested capital never moved above 6 per cent and at times even fell below 2 per cent. First National City Bank, *Energy Memo*, (October 1973).

40 There was in 1975 a difference of $52/tonne between the value of crude and refined products like naphta; $232/tonne when compared with basic petrochemical inputs like ethylene; while crude transformed to textiles gives a value added of up to sixty times.

41 This potential discongruity of interests was clearly shown in a statement by J. Fox Thomas, Director of the Philips Groups, immediately after the discovery of Ekofisk to the effect that, 'no new refineries would be built in Norway because the Philips group already had a big refinery in Britain' *Petroleum Times* (hereinafter *P.T.*), (19 June 1970) p. 38.

42 *Stortings proposisjon* (Parliamentary Proposition) no. 20, 1975/76.

43 *Ibid.*

44 According to *F.T.* (10 June 1975) BP was very eager to settle the deal. The discussed price seemed 'rather attraetive in view of the present market conditions'. *Business Week* (December 1975) reported that BP was raising capital to finance new exploration by selling subsidiaries all over the world. A Special committee had been formed to recommend which subsidiaries to sell.

45 Dillar Spriggs, Executive Vice-President of Baker Weeks & Co. Inc, declared to the U.S. Senate 'Hearings before the Committee on Multinationals' (The Church Committee) that the oil companies had shifted their profits downstream between 1971 and 1973 in anticipation of producer state ownership. While profit margins per barrel of final products was thirty cents on average in 1971, this had been increased to ninety cents in the spring of 1973. (Hearings, 30, January 1974, pp. 56–61, part 4).

   Shell's downstream profit was ten cents/barrel in 1971, nil in 1972, but shot up to sixty-nine cents per barrel by 1976. (Wood McKenzie, *op. cit.*)

46 Despite such efforts total sales to third parties (a number of which are not even state oil corporations), only account for 455,000 barrels per day out of a total of 2·5 million barrels per day *P.E.*, (July 1975) p. 255.

47 *P.E.* (June 1977) p. 234.

48 Unpublished paper by Professor Stobaugh to seminar on *Integration and Disintegration in the Oil Industry*, Oxford, (10 February 1976).

49 *P.E.* (May 1977) p. 177.

50 Dr Abdul Karim Hilmi of the Industrial Development Centre for Arab States at the Second Arab Conference on Petrochemicals, 1976, Quoted in *P.E.* (August 1976) p. 302.

51 *P.E.* (April 1977) p. 125.

52 Up to 90 per cent of Saudi Arabian production will even after a total state takeover continue to flow to the four members of Aramco in 'secure . . . well-defined . . . and hopefully long-run' contracts. (*F.T.*, 12 January 1976). As late as the beginning of 1976, direct sales from the state oil company Petromin accounted for a mere 200 000 barrels per day out of a total production of 8·5 million barrels per day. (*ibid*).

53 Ragnar Johnsen, *Oljeindustriens rolle i Irans økonomi*, Samfunnsøkonomisk seminar, Norges Handelshøyskole, Bergen, 1968, p. 25.

54 The first H-3 platform from Aker Shipbuilding was contracted in 1971 and delivered in early 1974. Twenty-five H-3's have since been ordered either to be built in Norway or on licence abroad. By 1 November 1974 Norwegian capital had a full or part ownership in sixty-seven offshore drilling rigs, representing a total investment of between Kr 11 and Kr 12 billion, SSB, *Økonomisk Utsyn*, (Oslo: 1975).

55 The French company Elf is operator on the Frigg field. Of the six platforms needed, three were built in France. This is a far higher percentage of French-produced components than is normal in the North Sea.

56 Reidar Engell Olsen (Undersecretary of the Dept. of Industry) in a speech to Scandinavian industrialists, quoted in *Norsk Industri*, no. 19, (1975) p. 25. Engell Olsen stated that the Norwegian overall share was expected to reach 40 per cent by the late 1970s, and that Norwegian industry had supplied 50 per cent of all drilling rigs and supply ships used in the Norwegian sector in 1974–5.

212 Nationalisation of Multinationals

57 Statoil's purchase manager, Dåstøl, in an intervention at *Offshore North Sea*, Stavanger 976. (ONS). NPC is set up by the ten largest Norwegian engineering and supply firms to carry out multidiscipline work on major integrated petroleum projects. NPC and Brown & Root have jointly been awarded the main engineering contract for Statfjord B and the majority of the work will be done in Norway.

58 Ever since the nationalisation of the Mexican oil fields in 1938, the state oil company, PEMEX, has had a monopoly of production and distribution of oil. In a very limited number of cases it has let foreign companies drill on entrepreneur contracts.

59 Unpublished paper by Walter L. Newton (Petroléum Economics Limited) *Integration in the Tanker Industry*, delivered at Oxford seminar *op.cit*, (17 February 1976).

60 OPEC-*Bulletin*, (September/October 1969).

61 Especially in the case of Algeria the nationalisation of oil was part of a strategy for financing the very large investments under the first five year plan. For a good background to the Algerian and Libyan cases see: Henri Madelin, *Oil and Politics*, (Farnborough: Saxon House, 1975)

62 Jacoby, *op. cit.*, p. 248.

63 Against this evidence there is a number of studies which have computed a much higher rate of return on the companies' Middle East (as opposed to overall Eastern Hemisphere which includes all downstream activities in Europe) investments. There is however reason to believe that these studies are unrepresentative because the companies had an incentive to transfer their profits upstream as the total amount of tax which was paid to exporting countries could be subtracted from profits made in consumer countries. This concession (which made the oil industry one of the lowest taxed industries especially in the U.S.; Exxon paid an effective 11·2 per cent of their net earnings to the U.S. tax authorities in 1973 (Church Committee, *op. cit.*, p. 13)), was made partly in order to avoid double taxation, but was also used as a method by the U.S. government to increase its aid in an indirect manner to the Arab countries in the 1950s. (Church Committee, *op. cit.* Introduction, p. 2)

64 The companies just assumed that the future investment in the industry would be provided from retained earnings. Hence it followed almost automatically that the industry wanted higher profits (and therefore higher prices) once it was expected that production costs would drastically increase. According to *PPS* (Petroleum Press Service), August 1971, p. 212, higher prices were inevitable to produce 'the enormous quantities of oil needed to satisfy demand in the 70s and 80s . . . (which) would have to be sought for and developed in more and more difficult places.' . . . 'the rise in prices will have to be greater than the rise in costs, because of the need for larger earnings.'

65 Geoffrey Chandler, *Oil, Prices and Profits* (Discussion Paper no. 13, Foundation of Business Responsibilities, London: 1974) p. 4.

66 V. H. Oppenheim, 'The Past: We Pushed Them', *Foreign Policy*, (Fall) 1976.

67 J. M. Chevalier, *The New Oil Stakes*, (London: Allen & Unwin, 1976).

68 Taki Rafai, *The Pricing of Crude Oil*, (New York: Praeger, 1974).

69 Total net private investment in Norway in 1974 totalled Kr 15·4 billion compared with a total yearly expected investment on the Norwegian Continental Shelf of Kr 8·25 billion ($1·5 billion). Extrapolated from H. E.

Anonsen, Manager, Den Norske Croditbank, *Financing the Norwegian North Sea*, ONS 1976, E-II/6, p. 2.

70 *Parl. Rep.* no. 1 (1976/77) Table 16.

71 K. Marx, *Grundrisse* (Harmondsworth: Penguin, 1973) p. 526.

72 Elmer Altvater, 'Notes on Some Problems of State Interventionism', *Kapitalis-tate* 1 & 2 (1973).

73 *Parl. Rep.* no. 91, (1975/76) justifies the state's changed position which would allow foreign companies to hold an equity share north of 62° by reference to the technical expertise and financial strength of the international companies.

74 Personal information given to the author by a Norwegian civil servant.

75 *F.T.*, 30 April 1976.

76 Up to October 1975 142 wells had been drilled on the Norwegian Continental Shelf with 14 expected commercial finds. (*P.E.* January 1976, p. 33). When disregarding the delineation wells this gives a success ratio significantly below 1:10.

77 See interview with Dr Jesse Wyllie, Executive Vice-President of Gulf Oil, *The Banker*, (December 1974) p. 1484.

78 According to *P.E.* (June 1975) one key Saudi Arabian objective was for 'Aramco to play a major role in the country's massive industrial development programme'. Aramco is already involved in the Eastern Provinces electricity supply system. (*F.T.*, December 1976)

79 An inter-government committee was formed in the winter of 1976 to study the possibilities of an increased coordination between the two countries' petroleum industries. Final recommendations will however await the decisions on the future of the Swedish nuclear programme. *P.E.*, (April 1976) p. 152.

80 E. Mandel, *Late Capitalism*, (London: New Left Books, 1975). See especially Chapter 6.

81 The practice of the companies of charging all the costs of the development of new technology to their present activities, so that for instance all research and development related to the North Sea is deductable from profits made in the same area, constitutes an indirect subsidy to the future earning-power of the companies in other off-shore areas from the Norwegian and British taxpayers.

82 The Oil Council headed by the present Minister of Maritime Law, Jens Evensen, argued in a letter to the Norwegian Ministry of Industry of 27 February 1968 against the notion of a direct Norwegian state involvement in the oil industry among other reasons because of 'problems of foreign policy like regard to our tanker fleet'. *Parl. Rep.* no. 11, (1968–9), p. 6.

83 United States coal reserves are estimated to be in the order of one trillion six hundred billion tons or equalent to twelve times total proven world-wide oil reserves. See *Petroleum, Raw Materials and Development*, Algerian Memorandum to the UN General Assembly 1974, (Switzerland: 1974) p. 160, 163.

84 Estimates by Den Norske Creditbank, quoted in Anonsen *op. cit.* p. 8.

85 E. Mandel, 'L'emergence d'un nouveau capital financier Arabe et Iranian,' *Critiques de l'economie politique*, no. 22.

86 *Capital*, III, part 6.

87 In 'The Political Economy of Nigerian Oil', *Development and Change*, (October 1976) she argues that this is due to the class domination within the Nigerian state of a strata of commercial middlemen who have nothing to gain from such a development. The important element in Turner's work is how she relates oil

politics to the internal class relations of a producer country.

88 J. Petras and R. Rhodes, 'The Reconsolidation of US hegemony', *New Left Review*, 97.

89 The Vietnamese first invited bids for off-shore permits on 6 August 1975. Interest has since been expressed by a number of companies (Elf, ENI, BP, and a Norwegian composite offer from different firms), but no final agreement has yet been reached: *P.T.*, (17 September 1976), p. 6.

90 *Parl. Rep.* no. 67, (1974–5) p. 24.

91 Guttorm Hansen, quoted in *Kontrast* (Oslo), no. 66, p. 24.

92 No comprehensive analysis has as yet been undertaken concerning this trend in Norwegian capitalism, but even a casual glance strongly suggests such a trend. SAGA operated in 1974 in six countries; U.K., Holland, Italy, Peru, Guatemala, and Ireland, while Hydro saw an equal expansion as a producer in the U.S., Abu Dhabi and off-shore Italy. The realisation by the international companies that their chance of obtaining concessions were proportional to the degree of participation by Norwegian firms in their operating consortia also helped to tie Norwegian firms closer to international capital. This tendency is also clearly seen in the mechanical industry, (cf. the creation of NPC and the many bilateral production agreements between Norwegian and foreign firms, e.g. Aker's cooperation with Brown & Root, De Grooth Offshore Contractors, and Moran Bros. Inc., just to mention a few).

93 During 1975, the state increased its equity holding in Norwegian industry by Kr 2.3 billion which increased its share of total industrial shares to between 40 per cent and 45 per cent. The Ministry of Industry directly controls 36 per cent, compared with 15 per cent in 1970 and 21 per cent in 1974. *Norges Industri*, no. 22, (1975) p. 5.

94 Such a project will give the personnel of Statoil an opportunity to take responsibility for and carry out one major (and very demanding) task of engineering.

7 Firm and State in the World Economy

SOL PICCIOTTO

On the face of it, the notion of 'nationalisation' would seem to be quite straightforward: it must mean simply the takeover of a private firm (company or corporation) by the state. Together with this apparently simple notion there are often associated some equally crude ideological conceptions: that such state takeovers are acts of 'socialism' and anti-capitalist in nature; that nationalised business or nationalised industries are, or by state control can be made to be, more socially responsible or accountable than private firms; or that 'national' control through the state of the economy is more beneficial than foreign ownership. Such ideas have only to be stated for it to be apparent that the question of nationalisation is much more complex than this, and that many of the views held about it, even only subconsciously, contain only a small grain of truth. In order to understand the processes involved in nationalisation, it is necessary first to look behind the institutional or legal forms involved. The aim of this paper is to try to establish some sort of theoretical perspective, based on a Marxist approach, to help us understand what is behind the changing relations of the state and private business all round the world.

I THE FIRM, THE ECONOMIC SPHERE, AND THE STATE

Increasingly, a major preoccupation in all parts of the world is the degree and form of state 'intervention' in the running of 'private' firms or enterprise. In many ways the boundaries between public institutions and private enterprise are becoming unclear. Even in countries where 'private enterprise' is a political and even moral philosophy the degree of state intervention, taking many different forms, has reached the point where talk of the 'mixed economy' or the 'managed economy' has been overtaken by new labels such as the New Industrial State or the Corporate State. This reflects not only state intervention but also the immense scale of enterprise that now dominate economic activity and social life. It is hard to see in what sense a firm such as General Motors is a 'private' concern if its gross revenues are equivalent to about one-eighth of the total receipts of the U.S. federal government[1], and would put G.M. just above Switzerland and behind Argentina in a table of states ranked by GNP[2].

It is under capitalism that the 'private' firm (from the workshop to the factory to the multinational, multiplant corporation) has become the primary unit of economic production[3]. Economic production consists dominantly of the exploitation of wage labour in combination with capital to produce goods for sale at a profit. All the external relationships of each firm take the form of market transactions: purchases of raw materials, instruments of labour and labour power itself, plus borrowings of money capital if needed; and sales of the commodities that result from the combination within the firm of these factors of production. Whatever the method of organisation of work within the firm may be, its ultimate aim must be the optimisation of profit, as measured by the difference between the cost of purchased inputs and the price obtained for output. From the development of double entry bookkeeping up to the most modern elaborations of managerial sciences (including, most importantly, 'man-management'—the extraction of the maximum amount of productive labour time from living labour) the actions of the firm have been subjected in ever more sophisticated ways to value as translated by the market and quantified in prices.

It is important to stress, however, that this characteristic organisation of the direct process of production in separate 'private' units, whose interrelationship is through economic competition, is not the cause or precondition but the result of the spread of the capitalist mode of production. The central characteristic of capitalism as a mode of production is the separation of the workers from control of the means of production, leaving them with no means of subsistence except the sale of their labour power. From this basic feature can be derived the characteristics of the forms of social relations, including the private firm and the economic system. However, this process of derivation is not simply a logical exercise, but involves grasping the development and transformation of those forms as part of the actual historical process of growth of capitalism[4]. Thus, as we will see, the nature of the private firm and of the economic system have undergone significant changes, as part of the struggles over and the transformation of general relations of production.

The separation of the worker from the means of production results not only in the organisation of work in separate private units within the economic system, but also in the separation of 'work' and of the economic sphere from the rest of social life. The worker's fragmented existence as wage labourer within the economic sphere and as a private individual within society is reflected in the separation of the economic from the political sphere, in which each individual is recognised as a citizen equal to all others regardless of their economic positions. This separation is established and maintained by the development as a particular form of the capitalist state—a form of power apparently separated from society. The main characteristic of the capitalist state is its apparent neutrality. Although the state involves the legitimation of or the application of coercion to social relations, the fragmentation of those relations between economics and politics means that there is no direct correlation between economic and political power. Within the economic sphere individuals appear as owners of different sources of income (land, capital, or labour power), but their political status is unrelated to the nature or quantity of this income source. Within the individual unit of production (the firm), where capital directly confronts labour, there is no immediate political relationship (of legitimation or of coercion); the worker is not a slave or serf subject to forced labour, but a free citizen who exchanges a certain amount of labour time for a wage. It is only in terms of the totality of social relations, in which social production as a whole proceeds, that class relations become clear. It is in these general social relations seen as relations of production that we see the fundamental split between those who control the means of production and those who are compelled to sell their labour power in order to live. It is also by analysing the changing nature of these essential relations of production that we can understand the changes in the social forms of appearance in which they are expressed. It is in this way that we will try to analyse the changing nature of the firm as the individual economic unit, as well as the changes in the interrelationship of firms through competition and in the role of the state and its 'interventions' in the economic sphere.

2 THE CHANGING NATURE AND RELATIONSHIPS OF FIRM AND STATE

As we have seen, a basic characteristic and aim of capital is the separation of the organisation of material production from the reproduction of social relations, the former being carried out by individual units of capital, while the latter takes the form of the public sphere, dominated by the state. The idealisation of this separation is celebrated by the ideologies of liberal capitalism: based generally on the premise that the development both of material production and of harmonious social relations are best achieved by the free play of market forces in the economy, the maximum freedom of choice for the individual in social life, and the minimum interference by the state in either. However, this ultimate development of capitalism is rendered impossible by its own internal contradictions, and no actual society approaching these liberal ideals has ever existed, or could ever exist. With the development of capitalism and with the changing forms of class struggle, which is its dynamic, the nature of social forms has undergone a continual transformation. In order to give a perspective on the current conflicts about the nature and relationships of firm and state, it is useful to sketch out their historical transformations.

The 'corporation' was initially a political as much as an economic body, from the mediaeval to the mercantile period in Europe: an association of persons linked by a common purpose and status in an institution through which they regulated themselves and their relations to the rest of feudal society. In England there were ecclesiastical, municipal, trading, or charitable corporations. It was with the development of trade, through the growth of capital in its first form of merchant capital, that the economic and political purposes came to be separated. This occured first in the separation of the merchant gild and the municipal borough, then in the fragmentation of gilds for the various productive crafts, and later in the disintegration of the gilds and the domination by the merchant companies of the domestic and rural-based craft production of the journeymen[5]. As part of the same process, the corporation as an institution with jurisdiction (in a sense that was neither political nor economic as such), was merged into the company with an economic franchise over trade, a monopoly granted by the political power, the central state.

Yet the merchant trading companies were far from the industrial capitalist firm. Merchant capital does not directly employ labour in production, but aims simply to 'buy cheap in order to sell dear': the company was not a framework for the organisation of the exploitation of labour by capital, but an association of merchants, initially operating individual accounts. Incorporation by royal charter was sought in order to grant them a public status: a political guarantee of their economic privilege or monopoly. In the case of the increasingly powerful foreign trading companies, such as the East India companies, state-backing meant the grant of a part of state sovereignty, state support in their assertion of governmental/trading power over foreign territories: the chartered companies accepted the quasi-feudal suzerainty of their monarchs and they themselves frequently granted away fiefs[6]. At the same time, they were far from purely 'private' ventures independent of the state: in many cases monarchs personally initiated the formation of such companies, and they and layers of the nobility both lent their status to the enterprises as well as participating in them financially.

In effect, the alliance between a growing merchant capital and the European absolutist monarchical states was the key to the development both of a world economy based on trade and of the international state system, in transition from the absolutist to the mercantile period from the sixteenth to the eighteenth centuries. Both internally and internationally state power was used very directly to foster the development of commerce. In fact, the very development of centralised state power in the form of the absolutist monarchies involved the abstraction of political power from the hierarchical feudal estates by monetising vassalage obligations and fostering commerce, in order to provide a financial base (through excise taxes, customs dues, etc.) for a state power that was therefore autonomised. Commerce was by no means free and equal exchange, but the ruthless fight for trade advantages, backed by military force if necessary.

However, the mercantile state did not seek territorial empires in the old sense, by the extension of its boundaries to include new lands over which its administration would levy tribute. Its aim was rather to establish and control the terms of exchange: thus commerce included all sorts of piracy, looting, and slavery. Within the European states, especially England, the growth of merchant capital in alliance with royal power meant the dissolution of production relations of a feudal character, and the fostering of capitalist production. This did not occur through the autonomous development of economic relations, but by means of the direct application of force through the state: by the transformation of the feudal system of land-holding and the development of private property in land; the dispossession of small producers and the wholesale expropriation of the agricultural population from the soil, as well as the welding of the masses of surplus population thus created into labour forces by means of forced labour, slavery, deportation, vagabondage legislation, and houses of correction. The mercantile state was therefore the state of the propertied classes through which commerce was fostered and production controlled in very direct ways.

It was with the rise of industrial capital in western Europe and north America, beginning in England at the end of the eighteenth century, that there was a strong movement directed towards the overthrowing of the monopoly-trading philosophies and regulatory structures of the mercantile state, of which the growth of liberal ideologies in political economy and political philosophy formed an important part. During the mercantile period, industrial production, previously carried on in the form of handicraft, was in Europe increasingly subjected to capitalist production in the form of manufacture. However, manufacture, whether on the basis of the workshop or of domestic industry (e.g. the various forms of 'putting out' jobs to home-based workers) was generally dominated by merchant capital. The merchant, who controlled the supply of raw materials and the marketing of the product, dominated the terms and conditions of production. The revolutionising of production by the introduction of machinery was the impetus for the growth of industrial capital. But, although the period of the industrial revolution was the era that came closest to the ideal of business firms accumulating unrestrainedly through a free market, it was the age not of the company or corporation, not even of the individual entrepreneur, but of the partnership or family business[7]. Furthermore, although the growth of industrial capital led to the further separation of the economic sphere ruled by the blind competition of individual firms trying to maximise profits, the laissez-faire ideal of the state was never achieved (nor indeed was it ever unambiguously advocated by the leading ideologists). The reason is plain: despite its form of appearance under capitalism as an economic relation separated from politics, the relation of production, the capital labour relation, is in fact a relation of exploitation in social and political as well as economic terms; capitalist accumulation seen as a total social process is itself the form taken by class struggle under capitalism. The liberal principles of freedom and equality are the reflection of the extent of the dominance of the capitalist mode of production, in which rapid accumulation seems best served by the unrestricted circulation of all commodities including labour power on the basis of equal exchange. In other words, classical liberalism assumes that social relations can be regulated purely as distributional relations. However, the wage labourer is not 'free', but is obliged to sell his labour power in order to live; and he does not obtain an equivalent in the exchange, since the capitalist (to whom he is obliged to sell his labour power) must, in order to accumulate, extract both necessary and surplus labour time from the labour he buys. Hence, the liberal state is engaged in a continual process of upholding the principles of freedom and equality, while constantly modifying their application in practice, in order to overcome the contradictions continually created by the inequality at the heart of relations of production. Or, put another way, since capitalist accumulation proceeds as a crisis-ridden process of class struggle, it results in the constant restructuring of the state as part of the process of recomposition of the whole complex of social relations.

The reproduction of social relations in a period of industrialisation, or liberal accumulation of capital, is most directly concerned with the reproduction of the labour force. During the first industrial revolution in Europe, capital sought to make unlimited use of the labour power available to it by the ruthless extension of the working day and the subjection of men, women, and children to unbearable conditions of work. In purely economic terms it is hard to see how it could have been otherwise, since the competitive pressures on each firm must force it to exploit its labour to the uttermost. But the resulting sharp revolts and class conflicts, throughout the main industrialising centres of Europe, created a 'public' concern for the welfare of the labouring population, which eventually produced measures throughout the state for the regulation of the general conditions of reproduction of the labour force: in England the Poor Law, the Factory Acts, the Education Acts, etc[8]. The struggle to impose the control by capital of the conditions of reproduction of social relations involved the defeat of the working-class movements of the 1830s and 1840s in Europe, and the integration of that class, on new terms, within the social relations of capitalism. The characteristic ideology of liberalism and forms of liberal state resulted from this process of struggle and integration, with variations caused in different industrialising states by the specific characteristics of each. The important point for our present purposes is that even the purest liberal state is forced to accept some state 'intervention' in the economy. It is the characteristic of liberal economic intervention that it avoids the intrusion of politics into the direct process of production, which is left to the individual firm; the state seeks to regulate the economy in terms of circulation, by establishing and guaranteeing the equivalence of exchange.

The capitalist firm, as we have seen, is driven by the impetus to accumulate, to reinvest revenue in the replacement and extension of machines and raw material, and the employment of more labour power. Since there are natural (and social) limits to the amount of surplus that can be extracted from labour by the more intensive or extensive use of labour power on the basis of unchanged conditions of production, there is an impetus to improve productivity by changing those conditions, so that the same amount of labour power can produce more goods. For the individual firm such improvements are seen as increasing the competitiveness of its products, so that it can underprice rivals yet still achieve higher profits; but as such improvements become generalised among competing firms, the general effect of improvement in productivity is to cheapen commodities. The drive to improve productivity is therefore relentless. It also involves a relative increase in the rate of exploitation of labour, rather than easing the lot of the worker: 'hand in hand with the increasing productivity of labour goes . . . the cheapening of the labourer, therefore a higher rate of surplus-value, even when the real wages are rising. The latter never rise proportionately to the productive power of labour.'[9] Thus the expansionary drive of capital takes two forms: (a) to find effective markets for the sale of the increasing mass of commodities produced by increased productivity, and (b) to find fields of investment which can yield a higher rate of profit. What this means is that capital is impelled to seek ever more social relations which can be turned into commodity relations. At the same time, the improvement in the social productivity of labour undermines capitalism as a mode of production, since the effect of the cheapening of commodities is to create a constant threat to the rate of profit. 'The progressive tendency of the general rate of profit to fall is therefore, just an expression peculiar to the capitalist mode of production of the progressive development of the social productivity of labour'.[10] This tendency is the source of the crisis-ridden development of late capitalism, in which periods of expansion are followed by periods of crisis which involve the re-organisation of the 'historical complex of general social conditions of production and relations of exploitation'.[11]

An important aspect of the struggle to maintain the rate of profit is the drive to combine capital on an increasingly social scale in order to economise on the means of production and the deployment of labour power.[12] However, under capitalism this does not take the form of the rational social organisation of production, but of the competitive concentration and centralisation of production through bankruptcies, mergers, and takeovers of firms. Thus, following the initial period of development of industrial capital in Europe based on small firms in the

period from approximately 1820 to 1870, this process meant the rapid
growth in the size of the individual enterprise after 1870, so that bursting
the bounds of the family firm or partnership it became fully fledged in the
corporate form. In England, although limited liability had been available
from the middle of the nineteenth century, it was not until the end of that
century that the large firms developed which took advantage of this form to
concentrate within one enterprise money capital beyond the resources of a
few individuals.[13] Marx's famous comment on this development was: 'The
capital, which in itself rests upon a social mode of production and pre
supposes a social concentration of means of production and labour-power,
is here directly endowed with the form of social capital (capital of directly
associated individuals) as distinct from private capital, and its undertakings assume the form of social undertakings as distinct from private
undertaking. It is the abolition of capital as private property within the
framework of capitalist production itself.'[14]

In these and other similar comments on the implications of joint-stock
capital, Marx anticipated many of the 'discoveries' of modern commentators on managerial or corporate capitalism. However, he was far
from saying that it entailed the abolition of private property within society,
still less the advent of a classless society or the abolition of wage labour.
The important point is that the immense scale of capital combined within
the firm directly, rather than through the market, enables the firm itself to
be considered as social capital. Concentration makes possible economies in
constant capital (i.e. fixed capital such as buildings and machinery, plus
raw materials) and enables the large firm to include as its own provision
facilities that must otherwise be socially provided by the state. The firm
that is able to integrate extensive production processes, and thus wield
large masses of capital, benefits from exploiting the social power of
labour.[15] Hence corporate capital can become welfare capital. As Mr
Gladstone remarked when opening a new men's dining-room and
recreation hall at Port Sunlight built for the soap firm Lever Bros: 'In this
hall I have found a living proof that cash payment is not the only nexus
between man and man'.[16]

Nevertheless, the increasingly social scale of production brought about
by the development of means of production is only partly accommodated
by the concentration of capital in the large firm. However large the mass of
capital involved, and however long therefore its time horizon, the
individual firm still aims ultimately to make a profit from sales, even
though the nature of this profit changes as the structure of the economic
system and of competition change. Within the public sphere the increasingly social nature of production appears as the problem of ensuring the
existence and development of the general conditions of production. These
are 'generally useful works, which appear at the same time as *general*
conditions of production, and hence not as *particular* conditions for one
capitalist or another'.[17] An item becomes part of the general material

conditions of production if it is used by more than one firm as part of its means of production, such as a road, a telephone exchange, or a computer. As can be seen from these examples, it is not possible to specify categories of objects which necessarily become general material conditions of production, although it may be possible from the analysis of the production process to identify activities which tend to be social aspects of production (most notably, means of communication and transport, or sources of energy). However, under capitalism what is important is the conditions under which these 'useful works' may be produced as commodities, since this will certainly affect whether they enter into the production process as particular or general conditions of production. Commodities which, on the basis of the specific historical development of capitalism in a particular society, are in general terms part of the general conditions of production may be produced or operated entirely by private firms, or by the state, or produced by the former and operated by the latter. Here again, the parameters of possible outcomes are established by the historically developed conditions in that society under which such items may be produced as commodities. This is particularly problematic for the general conditions of production, since they tend to require a large and indivisible capital outlay which is embodied in items of fixed capital with a long life-span, creating severe turnover problems. Hence the frequent arrangement whereby such items are produced by private capital but purchased by the state, which must then devise a means of relating use to payment, or operate the facility as free-access, financed from revenue.[18]

The analysis of general conditions of production enables us to see the way in which the question of direct intervention in production by the state is posed under capitalism. The general tendency is, with the increased socialisation of production and complexity of the social reproduction process, for evermore all-inclusive general material conditions of production to become necessary. This tendency provides a further material basis for the struggle to achieve the direct social organisation of production by the associated producers. This struggle is countered by being channelled into pressure-group conflicts over which industry or which firm should be state-run or receive state support, and by limiting direct state involvement to the functions which, through such pressure-group politics, are determined to be necessary general conditions of capitalist production. It is also important to analyse the way in which this problem is posed in order to grasp the nature of struggles over the forms of direct state intervention in production. So long as the general system of production remains production for profit by individual firms, the effect of public control over some sectors of production by the state remains in economic terms simply an intervention in the process of equalisation of the rate of profit through the price system. Thus the state control or subsidisation of some sectors of production does not withdraw those sectors from the operation of the general laws of capitalist accumulation: on the contrary, it attempts to ensure the continued operation of those laws by maintaining the necessary proportionality between sectors. This is done in the last analysis through financial mechanisms, so that the state-controlled sector is subjected more or less indirectly to the same pressures which the market exerts on the firm. At the same time, as we have seen, state intervention is resisted and restricted as narrowly as possible to firms or sectors needed for the production process of other firms, and whose continued production on purely capitalist terms is endangered. The state must therefore attempt a reorganisation of those firms and of their relationships with the economy in general, a restructuring of the social and economic relations of capital, on a shorter or longer term basis. The direct intervention by the state in production is always an uneasy matter under capitalism, a continual tension between guaranteeing and carrying out an activity as a social necessity, while at the same time applying the laws of capitalism by financial and institutional mechanisms which ensure 'public accountability'. Hence the wide variety of forms of 'public enterprise', which are continually changed to produce a new balance between social provision and financial accountability.

The growing involvement of the state in ensuring the provision of the general conditions of production is only one aspect of increased state 'interventionism', or the reformulation of the forms and relations of firm and state, during this century. In general, the state apparatus becomes no longer concerned mainly with the sphere of circulation and with the reproduction of labour power, but increasingly with the direct reproduction of capital itself. This means that the state apparatus must increasingly enter into relations with individual firms, that it must discriminate, that the individual measures of the bureaucracy come to replace the general laws of Parliament and the rule of law.[19] The growth of oligopolistic firms means that relations between firms are decreasingly open and equal; this is reflected in new, closed channels for the expression of the interests of firms, systems of bureaucratic administration involving direct relations between state bureaucracies and managers of corporate enterprise. However, what is often vaunted as 'capitalist planning' is in fact very far from achieving this self-defined impossibility.[20] As Joachim Hirsch puts it: 'This means that the anarchy of monopoly competition reproduces itself at the level of the administrative state apparatus and creates a many-branched system of mutually independent, partly competing and contradictory activities . . . The state apparatus therefore is not the negation of competition, rather competition reproduces itself within the state apparatus itself'.[21]

It is important to consider the development of these changing forms and relationships of state and firm on a global scale. The process of concentration and centralisation of capital takes place initially on a national scale; but the large corporations which resulted from this process in the period 1865–90 were very soon seeking new markets to dominate.

The period 1890 – 1914 saw the first international expansion of monopoly capitalist firms, the first internationalisation of industrial capital.[22] However, as Mandel has emphasised, this was a process of *international concentration* and *national centralisation* of capital, which 'pitted national imperialist monopolies against each other as antagonists on the international market for commodities, raw materials and capital. Only very rarely was there any actual international fusion of capital.'[23] Attempts were made to contain the increased international competitiveness by the formation of cartels, but these proved unable ultimately to restrain the forces which impelled the European powers to the imperialist war of 1914 – 18. The inter-war period saw an even closer integration of the growth of monopolies within the national state (including its colonial and other dependencies) and again the imperialist rivalry created the underlying pressures that impelled the great powers into a new war. This led to a fundamental re-evaluation and reformulation of the international system, the main impetus for which came from the United States, where planning for the new post-war international economic order began in 1940.

The reorganised international state system after 1945 facilitated a new period of capital accumulation on a global scale, dominated by the United States (although the U.S.A. had to accept the loss of much of eastern Europe to Soviet influence and the victory of Maoist communism in China). The political and economic reconstruction of western Europe and Japan established a basis for a new and rapid capitalist accumulation which accelerated through the 1950s and 1960s. During this period capital investment and trade within and between the major industrialised countries far outstripped accumulation in the 'periphery' of Africa, Asia, and Latin America.[24] This new accumulation has been characterised by the development of new productive forces on the basis of a new concentration and international centralisation of capital: most notably, U.S. firms significantly penetrated into Europe through direct investment. Although firms in the fastest-growing capitalist states of Germany and Japan expanded largely on the basis of home-based production until the late 1960s (due essentially to the high rates of labour exploitation that were possible following the experience of fascism and war), their dependence on foreign markets meant that, as circumstances changed in the 1970s, they too began to internationalise their production. However, by the end of the 60s, the contradictions of capitalist accumulation had become acute once more, and the 70s saw the first phase of a new period of capitalist crisis and restructuring.

3. THE BLOCKAGE OF CAPITAL ACCUMULATION IN THE PERIPHERY AND THE NATIONALISATION OF FOREIGN-OWNED CAPITAL

We have stressed so far that the process of capitalist accumulation must be seen as a global process, which however does not proceed evenly around the world, but creates unevenness, disparities, complementarities. First the amassing of money capital in the various forms of looting, piracy and slavery, and other trade conducted by European merchant capital prior to Europe's industrial revolution, while it contributed to the processes of primary capital accumulation in Europe, had the reverse effect elsewhere. Not only was wealth sucked out of the looted territories, but more important, this caused a hardening and stagnation of the traditional systems of production and social relations, and reinforced or created hierarchical or despotic political forms based on the direct appropriation of surplus product. Subsequently the emergence of industrial capital based on machines and factory production, first of all in England and then elsewhere, took place as part of the creation of an international division of labour:

> By ruining handicraft production in other countries, machinery forcibly converts them into fields for the supply of its raw material. In this way, East India was compelled to produce cotton, wool hemp, jute and indigo for Great Britain. By constantly making part of the hands 'supernumary', modern industry, in all the countries where it has taken root, gives a spur to emigration and to the colonisation of foreign lands, which are thereby converted into settlements for growing the raw material of the mother country; just as Australia, for example, was converted into a colony for growing wool. A new and international division of labour, a division suited to the requirements of the chief centres of modern industry springs up, and converts one part of the globe into a chiefly agricultural field of production, for supplying the other part, which remains a chiefly industrial field.[25]

It is important therefore to consider the emergence of particular capitalist states as part of the development of the international state system as a whole, and in relation to the position of other states within it.[26] We have pointed out that the general effect of the development of the capitalist mode of production (which takes place as a concrete historical process of class struggle) is to undermine the pre-existing social structures. Since this process dissolves the social links which binds a population into a polity, social forms are recast as 'public' entities defined in terms of territory. Within this geographically defined state there must be established a class hegemony which can constitute a viable unity for the reproduction of the totality of social relations of production and appropriation. Here we see the very important role played by nationalism as an ideology, which is generated as part of the process of a struggle to establish (or maintain, or recreate) a class alliance with a viable hegemony over a given territory. With the development of the capitalist mode of production there is a constant transformation and reformulation not only of the forms of state (discussed in the previous section) but also of the entire international system and the interrelation within it of its constituent units.

Thus, in an important sense the international state system as a world-system dominated by Europe was established from the beginning of the mercantile period.[27] However it was undoubtedly transformed by the French revolution, the Napoleonic wars, and the decolonisation of much of the western hemisphere, so that in many ways 1820 may seem a more appropriate starting-date for the modern world system. Yet it was essentially during the period 1820–70 that the process of capitalist industrialisation in Europe finally established the national boundaries and international framework for this accumulation, in the form of an economic and political unity within each state, a class alliance, and an economic base, which permitted the domination of accumulation by industrial capital. Even in Europe, important states such as Italy and Germany only became defined as part of this process, while the territorial subdivision of much of the rest of the world took place during this period, as the annexation in various forms of dependent and colonial territories, culminating in the partition of Africa. In another sense, therefore, the birth of the modern world can be dated from around 1870, as an imperial system dominated by the European states and their rivalries: but from the moment of its formation this system was already being undermined by the conflicts and contradictions generated by the higher stage of development of capitalist production. Hence, yet again, a further stage of development of the international system was inaugurated after the first imperialist world war, with the dismemberment of the Ottoman and Austrian empires, the formation of nation states in east and central Europe, and the breakaway of the U.S.S.R. to establish a hitherto unique position in the world system. Yet the inter-war period was in many ways an interregnum, and the post-1945 restructuring, together with the break-up of the European colonial empires in the period 1947–65, opened up another new phase. In fact, all of these changes must be seen as transformations of the system as a whole, as well as of the position of the various units within it, as part of and in response to the unfolding contradictions of the capitalist mode of production.

An important feature of this changing global system has been the uneven pattern of capital accumulation; above all the retardation of large areas of Asia, Africa, and Latin America, which have been called the capitalist 'periphery'. In considering this question we must again bear in mind that the uneven development of capitalist accumulation is not simply an economic question: it does not concern only the patterns of investment of money capital, or the flows of trade, and the pricing of commodities. The analysis of capitalist accumulation concerns how capital exploits labour; this is a social relation, a relation of classes. Therefore, in analysing the patterns of international investment and trade, what is important is to consider how these patterns affect social relations in each different society: above all their effects on the formation and transformation of class structure and the characteristics of class struggles. The creation of a centre-periphery relationship, as a result of the process of capitalist industrialisation, is not an immutable constraint of a structural character, determined by purely economic factors, as is sometimes implied by theorists of 'dependency' or 'underdevelopment'. This type of approach is misleading where it implies that 'underdevelopment' is the product of external economic links between existing societies, resulting in a dominance of one society or state over another, embodied in the internal economy of the dependent society and its external structural relation to the centre (monoculture, export dependency, etc). While these features undoubtedly exist, they are not simply a matter of national economic policy, but are embodied in national and international class relations. To that extent there is some truth in the argument that 'The real reasons are to be found not in the process of international investment or in international division of labour but in the internal economic and social structures of these countries, and the colonial powers were partly responsible for the maintenance of these conditions.[28] However, even with the addition of this last clause, this argument is also clearly inadequate, since it fails to make it clear that the 'internal economic and social structure' of underdeveloped countries results crucially from the patterns of international trade and investment. What is needed is to relate the actual historical patterns of capital accumulation on a global scale to the specific modes of exploitation of labour and hence class relations that were produced. It is in that context that the formation of states and their changing relationships in the international system can be best understood.

Broadly, the fostering of raw materials production in peripheral countries from the latter half of the nineteenth century created a characteristic pattern in terms of their social and economic structures, although with many significant variations in each case. Since many raw materials, especially agricultural products, can be produced in quantity without any significant mechanisation and on the basis of noncapitalist methods of production, the growth in world demand for such raw materials initially led to a strengthening rather than a weakening of merchant capital, which mediates the relationship between industrial capital and noncapitalist production through the circulation of commodities. However, the nature and role of merchant capital was significantly altered by its domination at the centre by industrial capital.[29] Merchant capital was no longer the vehicle for the primary accumulation of large amounts of wealth through unequal exchange, but became dominated by the need of industrial capital for the sphere of circulation to be based on equal exchange. Thus, for instance, the revival of the Chartered Company in the form which took place in Africa in the last quarter of the nineteenth century largely failed, since they 'could not finally solve the problem of supplying long-term capital for territories in which opportunities for immediately profitable production were absent.'[30] These companies were very different from their rapacious and opulent predecessors, but became instead the classic merchant middlemen, export-import houses (with nevertheless a great deal of power). Through this mediation, capitalism transformed agricultural production throughout the 'periphery' by foster- ing the production of 'cash crops' by peasant farmers, resulting in a variety of forms of petty peasant commodity production, which became inevitably dominated by capitalist relations of production.

At the same time, many types even of agricultural production were directly transformed into capitalist production, notably through the introduction of capitalist farming by colonial settlers (as pointed out by Marx in the comment quoted above) or by plantation agriculture introduced by industrial capitalist firms. Although this type of production was in most cases capitalist in character, it did not thoroughly transform labour into wage labour, but interacted with noncapitalist modes of production (for example, by using labour seasonally on a migrant-labour basis) to produce various forms of semiproletarianised peasantry. The direct introduction of capitalist agriculture in these ways involved wide- scale expropriation of land and the forcible interference with social relations. Main task of colonial governments was to accommodate the different dominant class interests involved, and to control and concentrate such use of force. Thus, while colonial governments had no compunction in carrying through colonial wars where they proved necessary to secure changes in land rights and other social relations, in other circumstances, they could resist pressure from settler and plantation farming interests. For example, in British West Africa, the strong state apparatus of 'indirect rule' expressed an alliance of merchant capital and oligarchical or feudal rulers, based on the early success of peasant farming of crops such as palm-oil, rubber, coffee, and cocoa, as well as traditional trade. The refusal of the Colonial Office to grant long leases of land caused considerable frustration to William Lever, of the soap firm, who considered that if the 'native chiefs' refused to 'develop' their lands other people should be allowed to do so.[31] However, Lever found the administration of the Belgian Congo more amenable both in providing land and in facilitating forced labour, and was able there to establish his extensive palm-oil plantations (in 1911).

The exploitation of mineral raw materials was quicker to develop along capitalist lines, since mechanisation of mining and processing improves quantity and quality. Even here, however, capital had to take social relations as it found them, and the result was often the semiproletarisation of peasants. The concentration of capital and its centralisation in the hands of a few firms was also frequently very rapid in mining, because on the one hand of the great advantages of improved productivity through mechanisation, as well as of the need to reduce the turnover time of fixed capital, by controlling rates of production, which can be greatly affected by wild fluctuations in demand for raw materials. This process of concentration took on an international dimension, since the adventurers of all kinds who very often began the mining resorted to Europe and north America for engineering expertise and money capital, which became increasingly available after 1865 or 1870. The process of concentration in the raw materials sector also complemented that of the industrial capitalist firms of the centre, which benefited from reduced costs and planned production of vital raw materials. Conflict was caused, however, with merchant capital, which sought its profits from trade with wide profit margins, and on occasion with the small local bourgeois class which may have managed to establish itself in the initial raw material boom, but found itself squeezed by the greater power of the internationally centralised firms. Such class conflicts meant that the restructuring of the raw materials sectors had to be carried out through the state. However, the global interests of capital were not expressed fully in the local state, which was often dominated by merchant capital and its local allies, or by small local capitalists, or landowners. Where a directly colonial structure existed or was established, the conflicts could be resolved within the machinery of colonial government set up by the metropolitan power, and this broadly ensured the domination of metropolital industrial capital. Elsewhere, notably in Latin America, the transnational nature of class conflicts led to interstate conflicts and foreign intervention. The history of nitrates in the Tarapaca region of Peru and Chile provides an interesting example: the restructuring of the industry by the Peruvian government in 1875 was planned as an 'expropriation' with compensation. When the government failed to raise the necessary finance from foreign money markets, the mineowners were permitted to hand over their mines to the state in return for two-year compensation certificates. Some mines were closed, but the rest continued to be run by the former owners as 'tenants', on a system of fixed quotas and prices, supervised by the banks. Marketing was handed over to an important merchant trading house, which also had financial interests in production; but the Peruvian government's need to integrate the exploitation of nitrates with the rest of the country's economy (by maintaining high prices to reduce competition with guano, and to increase revenue needed to pay off bonds which had financed railways and public works) led to conflicts with the mining enclave, which was lost to Chile in the War of the Pacific.[32] The devaluation of mining titles due to the war was a golden opportunity for a well-placed English mining engineer with access to money capital to gain control of a large section of the industry. The subsequent attempt by President Balmaceda to integrate the nitrate industry into the Chilean economy, reorganised in order to provide a basis for industrial accumulation, in many ways presaged the conflicts of the Frei and Allende years, and failed due to a similar combination of opposition from local conservative and foreign capitalist interests.[33]

The specific patterns in which capital penetrated the peripheral regions therefore established the constellations of class relations both within those regions and binding them to the world system. The creation of an international division of labour between raw materials and manufacturing production meant that these class relations could stabilise around different levels, and rates of accumulation in the peripheral countries compared to those of the centre: hence the apparently structural retardation of accumulation in the periphery. The patterns established in the 1880s and 1890s were shaken by the depression of the 1930s, but not until the reconstruction of capitalism after 1945 was there a major inflow of capital into raw-materials production (e.g. Middle East oil). The resulting cheapening of the costs of raw materials (by increasing labour productivity both in existing fields of production and in new methods of production of 'synthetic' raw materials) played an important part in stimulating and maintaining the boom of the 50s and 60s. It also involved, with increased mechanisation, changes in the labour force, which became relatively smaller in general but more proletarianised, thus establishing a sounder base for the establishment of import-substitution, consumer-goods industries. These developments found their expression in the struggles that led to the national independence of those among the peripheral countries that had been formal colonies. At the same time, as the underlying tendency for the rate of profit to fall became increasingly manifest during the 1960s, the profit margins of the firms producing raw materials declined in relation to those of industrial firms: most notably in the oil industry prior to 1971 the crude oil price had been declining in real terms. The onset of a new global crisis for capital in the 70s led to a period of acute instability: although declining demand put a downward pressure on prices of raw materials, the need for fresh investment once again to cheapen the costs of raw materials and thus to contribute to the restoration of profit rates had the opposite effect. It was these underlying tendencies that structure the social conflicts of the present period.

4 CONCLUSION

The intention in this article has been to sketch out a broad framework within which we can view the changing relations of firm and state. As we have seen, this is not a relationship of mere opposition. Indeed, it is the very separation of the economic and the political spheres characteristic of capitalism which results in social control over production taking the form of state 'intervention' in the economy. Furthermore, whereas the central impetus of capital is to break through all bounds to its free development, its own internal contradictions create social pressures resulting in the imposition of limits which are necessary to its social reproduction, yet which will be undermined and broken through by its further development. It is in this light that we should view the changing forms of state intervention in the economy, especially the direct intervention in the operation of individual firms involved in nationalisation. State intervention necessarily raises the question of the relationship of the political to the economic, and it is in a sense the general function of the institutions and processes of the capitalist state to channel the exercise of social (i.e. class) power through forms which maintain that basic characteristic separateness. For this reason it is important to analyse the specific characteristics of state forms in their relation to the basic contradictions and historical development of capitalism. These forms are not timeless but specific to the conditions of the particular historical period to which they are a response. Thus, today's giant multinational companies, with their increasingly close corporate links to the state, may be seen as the successors to the merchant trading monopolies of the mercantile period. However, they must not be simply compared in institutional terms, but rather the relationship must be traced theoretically and historically. In this perspective, the attempt to assert a greater control through the nation state over international firms expressed a very different conjuncture of social forces from the granting of a royal foreign trade monopoly in the seventeenth or eighteenth centuries. By helping us to grasp the characteristics of the particular conjuncture this approach enables us to conceive its possibilities as well as the limits posed by the existing social forms.

NOTES

1 Galbraith, *The New Industrial State*, (Harmondsworth: Penguin, 1967) p. 90
2 U.S. Senate Subcommittee on International Trade of the Committee on Finance, *The Multinational Corporation and the World Economy*, Staff Print (26 February 1973)
3 See S. Hymer, 'The Multinational Corporation and the Law of Uneven Development' in H. Radice (ed.), *International Firms and Modern Imperialism*, (1975)
4 See John Holloway and Sol Picciotto, 'Capital, Crisis and the State', *Capital & Class* 2, (1977) pp. 76 – 101.
5 L.C.B. Gower, *Modern Company Law* (3rd ed., 1969) p. 24. Gower gives a good summary of the history of the company form in England, which is provided in more detail by Cooke, *Corporation, Trust and Company* (1950), and by Holdsworth, *History of English Law* vol VIII. A thorough analysis of the business of the trading companies is given in W.R. Scott, *The Constitution and Finance of*

English, Scottish and Irish Joint-Stock Companies to 1720, vol II (1912, reprinted 1951). A comparison of the various European forms of trading company and their relationships with the monarchies is given by E.L.J. Coornaert, 'European Economic Institutions and the New World; the Chartered Companies', in E.E. Rich and C.H. Wilson (eds.), *The Cambridge Economic History of Europe* (1967) chapter 4.

6   See Coornaert, *op. cit.*, note 5.

7   P.L. Payne, *British Entrepreneurship in the 19th Century*, chapter 3.

8   See D. Roberts, *The Victorian Origins of the Welfare State, (1960)*

9   K. Marx, *Capital*, vol I, (Moscow edition, 1965) p. 604

10 K. Marx, *Capital*, vol III, (Moscow edition 1966) p. 213

11 J. Hirsch, 'The State Apparatus and Social Reproduction: Elements of a Theory of the Bourgeois State', in Holloway and Picciotto (eds.), *The State and Capital*, (London: 1977) p. 74

12 This is analysed by Marx in chapter 5 of volume III of *Capital*.

13 Even so, the extent of concentration was less in Britain than in the United States: see P.L. Payne, 'The Emergence of the Large-Scale Company in Great Britain 1870–1914' *Economic History Review* xx (1967) p. 519

14 *Capital*, vol III, p. 436

15 The more common argument based on the notion of 'economies of scale', since it begins from the viewpoint that profit is simply a return on capital, assumes that economies of scale are essentially a technical question, and this fails to grasp the matter as a social and political process.

16 C. Wilson, *The History of Unilever* vol I (1954), p. 46

17 K. Marx, *Grundrisse* (London: 1973) p. 531

18 I take much of the general trend of this analysis from D. Läpple, *Staat und allgemeine Produktionsbedingungen* (Berlin 1973), although I disagree with him on some fundamental points.

19 F. Neumann, 'The Change in the Function of Law in Modern Society' (1937), printed in *The Democratic and the Authoritarian State* (Free Press, 1957)

20 The corporate capitalist's view of the impossibility of state planning in a 'competitive environment' is expressed by F.S. McFadzean in 'The Economic Planners Viewed from inside a Large Corporation', in Cairncross (ed.), *The Managed Economy*, (1970).

21 'Theses on the Character and Function of State Intervention in the Technological Area' (mimeo, 1976)

22 See M. Wilkins, *The Emergence of Multinational Enterprise: American Business Abroad from the Colonial Era to 1914* (Harvard, 1970)

23 *Late Capitalism* (London, 1975) p. 313–4; although, of course international centralisation need not take the form of fusion, if the number of firms competing in an industry internationally is reduced.

24 OECD, 'Analytical Report', *Gaps in Technology*, (1970) (Book IV, 'International Economic Exchanges').

25 Marx, *Capital* vol. I, p. 451

26 See Claudia von Braunmühl, 'On the Analysis of the Bourgeois Nation-State Within the World Market Context', in Holloway and Picciotto (eds.) *The State and Capital*, (1977).

27 See I. Wallerstein, *The Modern World-System*, (New York, 1974)

28 Brinley Thomas, 'The Historical Record of International Capital Movements

to 1913', reprinted in J.H. Dunning (ed.) *International Investment* (London, 1972) p. 49

29 This change seems to have been underestimated, or placed as occuring in the 1930s by Geoff Kay in his thoughtful analysis in *Development and Underdevelopment* (London, 1975)

30 S.H. Frankel, *Capital Investment in Africa*, (1938) p. 23-4.

31 C. Wilson, *History of Unilever*, (1954) vol. I, p. 166

32 Greenhill and Miller, 'The Peruvian Government and the Nitrate Trade 1873-1879', *Journal of Latin American Studies* vol. v, (1973) pp. 107-131

33 See A.G. Frank, *Capitalism and Underdevelopment in Latin America* (1967) pp. 73-85; H. Blakemore, *British Nitrates and Chilean Politics 1886-1896*, (1974)

Index

238 *Index*